A SOLID RIGHT CROSS

Biblical Boxing and Conservative
Counter Punching
Against Liberal Loons and Godless Goons

AlfonZo Rachel

A SOLID RIGHT CROSS
Biblical Boxing and Conservative Counter Punching
Against Liberal Loons and Godless Goons

www.BronzeSerpentMedia.com

TABLE OF CONTENTS

CHAPTER I
LIBERALISM; THE LEFT HOOK.

I'm going in grumpy. Just a heads-up. I'm not in a good mood as I write this chapter. I'm frustrated and disappointed. But despite some of the frustrations I share, the bottom line is, I'm still a republican. I'd like to borrow a line from Frederick Douglas. "I am a Republican, a black, dyed in the wool Republican, and I never intend to belong to any other party than the party of freedom and progress."

What Freddy D was saying was that he was already a Republican to the core before the fabric of the Republican party was even sewn together, and that his grip on it won't fade. I share that sentiment. Even though many Republicans get on my nerves, I'm still a Republican. But between you and me I feel pretty alien in the Republican party and the so-called conservative tent. I don't feel entirely unwelcome. Just more... Alien.

It's like going to church in a building that says "church"; a facility provided to accommodate folks wanting to gather to learn and abide by the Word of God. You know?... Church. However, you keep running into members wanting to talk about multi-level marketing. You're there to be lead to the Kingdom, while some are trying to lead you into their pyramid scheme, even though according to them it's not really a "pyramid scheme". They'll say, "I know it sounds like one, but this is totally different."

Like I said. I reckon I'm in the right place, but I feel alien.

A lot of Republicans have had similar feelings and have stopped referring to themselves as Republicans. They don't recognize the Republican party anymore so they split. I'm in the Republican party for what characterizes what it is to be republican, but that idea seems to be fading out of the tent and replaced by ideas of what others think it should mean to be a Republican.

I'm often tempted to drop out of the Republican party myself. It's not like the majority who are familiar with my work would really notice I was gone. That's proven. For a few years mediums like

Facebook, Youtube, Twitter, and Google have been keeping my work hidden. Do most of my Republican viewers come look for my work? No. They just thought I stopped making videos because they didn't see them in the feeds. One would think if they really valued my work even a little they might have checked my website or my page to discover that I was still publishing two videos a week. I would get people saying, "Good to see you're back and making videos again! I haven't seen a video from you in months! Where did you go?"

And I'm like, "Actually it's good to see YOU'RE back! I haven't stopped making videos. Where did YOU go?"

I don't produce videos regularly now because I no longer have enough supportive viewers. And of course, I have to consider that maybe it's because my work just sucks! But Thank God for the few who do try to help keep me on the scene.

But folks give me their reasons for why the thrill is gone. When I was recruited by PJTV some viewers said that PJTV took control of what I did, and so these viewers didn't like ZoNation as much. For the record, PJTV didn't control my content. They didn't tell me how to deliver my content. I think the only suggestion Roger L. Simon had for me was to not put my hands in my pocket so much.

PJTV Never wrote any of my scripts. They only furnished the studio and crew to record my content and published them. PJTV only had one stipulation on me, really. And that was to not talk about same-sex marriage. That stipulation itself came to an end and I had free reign to comment on whatever concerned me.

The reason why the rants seemed a little more different at PJTV was because for expediency I used a teleprompter to do my commentary. I couldn't take up studio time doing the rants I used to do. Other commentators had to come do their commentaries too. So yes, using a teleprompter taxed some of the rawness and gave me less time with how creatively I would deliver my points, but with a teleprompter it was faster to produce. When doing the rants in my own studio I could experiment more with how I delivered my points without crew distraction.

But I can't please everybody. When I was doing the "Brick-wall Rants", and just working with what I had, people complained about the poor production quality. Then when production quality improved with PJTV they said they miss the "Brick-wall rants". Now with the Zo Loft, I'm working on balancing production quality with the time I had with the Brick-wall rants without taking up studio time for other content creators, but now people say they miss ZoNation!

A lot of people who watched ZoNation don't even know I have a new series called the Zo Loft! They just think I quit. I guess it just bugs me that so many people just assumed I gave up. They didn't even check my page or website. They just wrote me off and assumed I quit. I didn't quit. Facebook, Youtube, Twitter, and Google are fading me out. God willing they won't succeed.

There's a point to why I'm saying all this. I'm not whining, folks. I'm just pointing out that I sympathize with a lot of people who have stopped referring to themselves as a Republican, and that it's tempting for me to do the same. I know how you feel and why many of you don't call yourselves republican anymore. I sympathize. I feel betrayed, abandoned, and snubbed by other right-leaners in media and a lot of my audience - just like you feel betrayed, abandoned, and snubbed by Republican representatives, But I'm not ceasing to be a Republican. Lots of people calling themselves Christian get on my nerves too. I'm not going to stop being a Christian because of them. And of course, I probably get on many of their nerves too.

I do get tempted to just cease being a Republican. It's hard to ignore the left-wing haters who have kept saying, "The Republican party doesn't care about your black a**. After they're done using you as a mouthpiece against Obama they're going to toss you and your coonery aside and forget about you." Sure does appear that they're right. But it's not like liberals aren't forcing that to happen by shadow-banning me and making my work difficult to discover. A bit more on that later. Trolls are hardly even alerted to my posts anymore because trolls increase view-count. The objective is for liberal social media operatives to keep my view-counts low. Low view-counts deter potential viewers because low view-counts imply uninteresting content. But I understand, out of sight out of mind. I don't really expect to be on my audience's mind all the time, and I understand that if they aren't reminded they will forget. McDonald's is world famous, but they still make advertisements to remind people that they're still making burgers.

For the record, I would rather be taken for granted and forgotten by the Republican Party than embraced by Democrats for becoming a hateful bigot like them while preaching their false doctrine of tolerance.

It's kinda hard to ignore the haters who say I'm just mouthpiece for the GOP who'll dump me after Obama is done, when I've seen headlines by republican news articles posted about me titled, "(WATCH!) Black Reporter Calls Michelle Obama a SPOILED B*tch,"

Don't get me wrong, folks. I really appreciate that my video was well received, but it was a cheap Click-Bait way to promote it. We're better than that, aren't we? Do republicans promote videos by other white commentators saying, "White commentator shreds white political figure!"? No. So things like this make the hater's assertions valid that GOPers use me as a mouthpiece to express their concerns with Obama, and what's worse, use my brand, my image, and my color to call Michelle Obama a B***. I never called Michelle Obama that. I do not use such language regarding women.

Is this what these Republicans feel they need to resort to for attracting readers? Race-click-baiting and misogyny? I never said what those headlines imply, but that's what's been headlined, and such right-leaners want to talk about journalistic integrity? This kind of stuff lends fuel to the haters who charge republicans of just using blacks to achieve their goals. It promotes the idea that Republicans are so stuck on the idea that black men always refer to black women as b*tches, just like in their rap music. *And since AlfonZo is black he must call women b*itches all the time too.* So they totally ignore the fact that I didn't employ such language and promoted my video as a black person who does. However, I can't totally blame the writers for this. Too many blacks doing rap do include the B-word quite gratuitously. (And they're loyal democrat voters by the way.) Again, I'm grateful that these websites shared the video. I'm Very grateful. But if the video was as good as they found it to be, then why be greedy and promote it so cheaply?

I want to stress, this isn't some *woe is the black guy guilt trip*. This is me saying, I really, really, really understand that people get frustrated with the Republican party and cease identifying as one. I really do get it. But for all the frustration I feel, it really, really, really, frustrates me that people leave the Republican Party.

Even through my disappointments, like the Republican party showing that they wouldn't see it as a loss if I wanted to be a brat and storm out of the tent and punish them by taking my cookies - many haven't seemed to want them anymore anyway. That doesn't leave me with much incentive to stay. And since there isn't someone who hates my guts (Like the aforementioned internet entities) going around and letting them know that I brought cookies, my viewers just assumed that it was me that stopped baking them, rather than recognizing that it was actually the people who hate my guts who blocked me from delivering them.

But in the words of Deneen Borelli, "Here's the Deal". I know me leaving the Republican party would satisfy Democrats even more than it would punish Republicans. People leaving the Republican party are just gratifying democrats. Democrats formed the KKK to terrorize Republicans, and to deter people from voting republican through coercion. I'm not going to do the Democrats a favor and stop being a Republican like they wanted in the first place.

I reckon a lot of content creators who call themselves conservatives have just turned their backs and are taking advantage of me being shadow-banned - especially the newer crop that's coming up. They want to be seen as the new independent thinkers that are blazing a new trail for their generation and aren't in lock-hoof with the herd. Then my name pops up. "Oh wait. You mean there was this guy called Zo who was already doing this and doing it while I was still in middle school, and he's got something about him where he could still fit in with the hipster crowd just as easy as we could without having that mangy alley-cat hipster vibe? But I don't want you to pay attention to Zo. I want you to pay attention to me. I'm the new and fresh Meeee-Lineal! I'm the new independent voice of my generation! Let the liberal internet overlords keep Zo confined to the shadows! It's my time to shine!"

But on the other hand, I consider they may see me as a Republican relic; too old-fashioned.

To them, I'm too focused on the Kingdom rather than college. Or I'm not enough of an info-junkie or not qualified enough for their political clique. I'm not confrontational, and no-nonsense enough, or not enough of a fire-breathing debater etc. I understand. That's not my disposition. I'm not a confrontational guy. I don't have the passion to debate. My passion is to illustrate.

Many conservatives think the only way to get your point across is to argue with them, and the liberal they're arguing with is somehow going to be amazed by the conservatives arguments and set aside that gargantuan ego and blasphemous arrogance of theirs, concede to them, and change their ways. Meanwhile, conservatives actually seem to be delighted when they see liberals meltdown rather than wake up. They want to see liberals get triggered. They want to see liberals meltdown when the light hits them, not wake up. That's childish.

This generation of so-called conservatarians as many like to call themselves, act like exposing the belligerence of Democrats is something new, and that it's some big revelation. It's not.

Democrats have been showing their belligerence for over a hundred years. People act like triggering is some new thing with Democrats. Democrats have actually been losing it and pulling the trigger on people for over a hundred years. I already know who the Democrats are. I've been talking about it for years. The Democrats know I know who, and how they are, and do not want me to ever gain the ability to publish illustrations about who and how they are. They know that illustrations work. That's what they've been doing for years. They can't have conservatives doing the same. No. They just want people to see conservatives as white people sitting in a chair shaking their finger in judgment at people. And conservatives help the liberals maintain this view of conservatives.

Conservatives don't really support presenting ideas in any other way except from a soapbox. They act like the mouth is the only part that matters. And if you don't have the mouth for it, throw the rest of the body away. Forget the rest of the body that can perform other functions to achieve the common goal. Nope. Just a mouth and that mouth can only be used for voicing politics. If not, conservatives will hardly support any other angle. There's some. Don't get me wrong. But they are a few albeit a blessing.

If conservatives supported conservative illustrators the way the rap industry supports rappers we'd be so much further ahead. Scouts are always bringing rap acts into the game. Now look at how much influence the rap industry has, and these people hate each other! The dominant theme of rap music is about killing each other! But amazingly they've supported their market enough to make rap one of the most influential sounds of the country. Most conservatives don't like each other. I don't think they want to kill each other, but it's a shame that we don't have the same support that even rappers who publicly fantasize about killing each other do. I get people asking me if I've heard this person or that person- over and over again, promoting other commentators on my page, and I RARELY see people asking these other commentators that they promote in my threads if they've ever heard of me. And I wouldn't want them to. 'Cause it's straight up tacky! It's like going up into somebody else's restaurant and asking the owner in FRONT of all his/her customers, "HEY HAVE YA TRIED THE BURGERS NEXT DOOR? THEY'RE AMAZING!" I wouldn't want my viewers doing that to other commentators with my brand. And I don't like it when people do it to me. I'm trying to promote my brand, and people come onto my thread promoting other people's brand. It's like they're oblivious to the fact that I'm being shadow-banned and there's a deliberate effort to bury my brand, and then folks come along and pour salt in the wound by telling people to go check out somebody else's work with no effort of reciprocity or cross-promotion. If folks are going to promote other people's content in my thread at least show that you cross-promoted. Show a mention of mutual respect for both parties and tag each party with a reciprocating post in EACH party's thread. But no. Usually, over and over again I get people leaving this in my comment threads where I'm trying to promote my work, "You guys should check out such and such." Or, "Have you seen such and such's movie? It really tells the democrat's history!" (Even though I've been doing videos on it for years.) Horrible, tacky promotion practices.

This causes conservative commentators to see each other more-so as rivals than allies. Horrible communications. The irony is that Republicans love Reagan for being the "Great Communicator", but Republicans tend to not practice that and apply that to promoting. Like I said about rappers - they hate each other. They rap about killing each other, but they promote the crap out of each other too! They've put together mixed tapes, playlists, sample compilations so you can hear various artists. How about conservatives start putting together sample reels of various conservatives making quick hard hitting points? It could be like a mixed tape of sorts. It works great for the rap game. Compilation vids of conservatives, drillin' them points might be a good jam, like video vines! And of course, wouldn't it just be the ironic kicker if somebody took this idea and ran with it and left me out of it?

Maybe conservatives in media think I'm not progressive enough. Yeah, I said it.

For example, I'll happily welcome a person whose a homosexual into the conservative tent, but I'm not gonna congratulate them for being gay. I'm not going to help them promote themselves as a person that embraces their homosexuality just because they have conservative leanings.

"But how can we influence the left if we have people like Zo getting in the way of making it look like we're intolerant to gay people."

So y'all want to influence left-leaning people with something they're already into? That's good! I've been saying that all along, but there's a right way and a wrong way to do that. I can understand influencing people by relating to them, or by sympathizing or showing familiarity with their traditions etc., but participating, or enabling them in their wrong thinking is not a good way to gain influence with people.

"I'm gonna get you off heroin... By giving you a room to shoot up in or by doing heroin with you", isn't a good strategy.

Jesus welcomed sinners to His table. He didn't enable them. Sinners came to His table because they knew they were sick and wanted to leave His table well and changed.

So I try to take these things into consideration before promoting another's content. It's definitely not because I want to keep the spotlight for myself. I've proven to not be a big spotlight seeker. I haven't constantly solicited myself to be on panels of big platforms like FOX News or their competitors. If I get invited on, great! But I haven't really actively pursued it.

But there are a lot of "conservative" commentators who are spotlight seekers and do not want others in their light. That's ok. They've found their place and they don't want it messed with. I don't blame them at all, but there are consequences. The liberals are strengthening their unity with the callous of hate, and their weapon is a slander-cannon-array that salvos racism, sexism, classism, and anti-Christianity.

Conservatives are weakened by cliquish, stuck-up egotists in media that are friendly when they want to use you as something to step on, and when they reach the level they wanted to get to they blow you off. I understand. That's just how many people are, but there are consequences.

The Republican Party is becoming more and more obscure, being conservative is vague. It's become more populated with self-focused people who want to define it to suit their ideals. The culture is melting down. Public office is becoming more and more a place where we send people to disappoint us on our forced-away dime. But hey, these folks got their spot in the limelight and they're not going to let some stupid thing like unity interfere with that.

Again y'all. I don't expect them to maintain an acquaintance with me or anybody else they've schmoozed with then blew off when they reached their goal. I'm just asking, what good is that spotlight going to be when we can't keep this republic that Benjamin Franklin warned us we could lose?

But maybe I'm an embarrassment to these people. I'm a dude with this silly idea that maybe we should be trying to use the same vehicles to deliver an antidote to the masses against the poison that the liberals have effectively delivered to the masses. I don't know, things like ROCK n' ROLL! *"We don't need silly rock n' rollers to promote conservatism. Wow look! Gene Simmons is a conservative!!!"* (I guess if you say so, he is.)

But, music has always been a powerful tool culturally and politically, but Republicans don't really capitalize on it. My band 20 lb Sledge was actually getting a lot of love, but the liberal internet overlords put the brakes on us. They could NOT allow people to find out about an all-black, Christian conservative rock band that had a sound that sounded just as raw, deep, and catchy as what liberals promote. Liberals are more and more trying to separate blacks from the Bible. Many blacks are falling for the idea that *Jesus is the god for white people. Islam is for the black man.* (Even though Jesus was a Middle Eastern Jew, and Mohamed was an Arab. My band 20 lb Sledge is too much of a threat to their narrative. Especially the afro-centric narrative. *"Blacks playing rock?! No! Rock n' Roll is white-folk's music... Even though white folks stole it from black folks!"* See how stupid and self-canceling that narrative is?

20 lb Sledge takes a Sledge to that whole narrative; Black guys just having fun playing Rock n' Roll without ever mentioning in the music that we're black guys playing Rock n' Roll. We don't even use the music to talk about color, but instead the Kingdom! Liberals tend to hate that. They believe a group of black guys should use their forum to RAGE AGAINST THE WHITE MAN! I'm not going to waste my music and energy on butt-hurting about the white man. That's gay! Calling out white-devil democrats is another story, though! Ha! Liberals cannot let a project like this surface; blacks doing things outside of what liberals expect them to conform to is unacceptable. If liberals can't control blacks doing a project like 20 lb Sledge, they won't let others see it. They don't even want to criticize 20 lb Sledge because they don't want to draw any attention to it. So they just shadow-ban it. They don't want people seeing black people actually enjoying being free from what liberals prescribe as freedom. Here's a great example. Remember that street performing pre-teen power-trio that was cranking out Heavy Metal music in Brooklyn, NY, called Unlocking the Truth? America was taken by these adorable kids slammin' out these tight Heavy Metal riffs. Part of the reason why was because they're black and doing something that

"black folks don't do"; Play Rock n' Roll. (Which is a ridiculous notion) but that is a prevailing assertion. Many blacks say, "Rock n' Roll is white folks music." Then turn around and say, "White folks stole Rock n' Roll from blacks." Unlocking the Truth put another big dent in that numb-skull narrative, and liberals swooped right in to claim them. Liberals cannot have a person like me connecting my work to the masses they want to control. My videos even connected with Unlocking the Truth. After playing their brains out shredding the street with their metal madness they became a youtube favorite which turned into appearances on tv shows, and even opening up for Metallica! I'm not a big fan of Unlocking the Truth's music, but I do dig it some, and I really appreciate their embrace of freedom! It's not a put down of Unlocking the Truth. I think they have the potential to produce some slammin' jams, and I look forward to hearing more from them! UTT didn't want to be shackled to a narrative that many still insist on imposing. They just wanna rock! There are many white teenage bands, and they're really good, and many are really bad. Unlocking the Truth is good, but they don't have a *great* sound, *yet!* However, much of America really just loved it that these kids weren't wearing their race like a chip on their shoulder and just wanna rock in America. That was what was so special. With the fast climb of their notoriety, a documentary movie was even made about them called, Breaking the Monster. One of my ZoNation videos was featured in it! It resonated with the band's lead singer and guitarist, Malcolm Brickhouse. He knew and understood that liberals wanted to swoop in and capitalize on this band's image. He knew that musically and vocally that they weren't that strong to get the attention they were getting. He just knows they are rare, and free from the idea that you have to "behave like this because you're that, and if you don't act like how we say you're supposed to act then you're not being real." He knew he was having fun with his friends playing music on the street with folks stopping by to have fun getting their bones rocked by them! Even in his early teen youth, Malcolm saw that there would be people who would want to control how they are received by the masses and would use them to help maintain their racial narrative. My videos interfered with the liberal elite's programming. Do you see the problem and the threat my videos present to liberals? My videos aren't supposed to reach kids like Unlocking the Truth! But they did! Libs can't allow that to happen! Because when my videos reach them, it really is like unlocking the truth, and libs want the truth to remain locked out! Liberals want my videos locked out!

Despite how evident it is that there is a deliberate effort to limit the reach of conservative commentators, in this case, me, I've been advised by an "expert" in social media who's employed by a well-known conservative news and opinion site that he sees no evidence of my videos being shadow-banned.

I'm not sure if he understands the implication of his assertions. I have to consider that he is an expert in his field and that he does work for one of the most respected conservative online channels. If his results are true about me not being shadow-banned, then what the democrat race-baiting haters have been saying is true. I understand out of sight out of mind. The social media operators hide my views from viewers. Keeping me out of people's sight keeps me out of people's minds, and I get forgotten. But according to this "expert's" conclusions, that's not the case, and I'm not getting shadow-banned. This means that my republican audience has chosen to toss me out like an old shoe.

For years I've been cursed by democrats as being a "boot licking, sell-out, Uncle Tom, a white-man's d**k sucking token, and a house n**ger that needs his a** whooped, and have some sense beat into him." There's also the occasional cruel things said about my wife. Along with these comments, they would tell me over and over again that, "These white republicans don't give a damn about you. They just pretend to like you because you say things about Obama that these white folks want you to say. You're nothing but a black mouthpiece for them; saying the sh*t they can't get away with saying, so they use your coon-a**. And when Obama is no longer president, and they don't need you to comment on Obama anymore, they're gonna toss your black a** to the curb and forget about you. They're not gonna mention you. They're gonna grab onto others, and it will be like you never existed." Obama is no longer president. My viewers dropped away from me gradually, then drastically, and it's the expert opinion that there is no evidence of shadow-banning. If that's the case, then it looks like what the democrat haters said is true about republicans bailing on me.

But I really think that a big reason why I lost a lot of viewers is because of my inclusion of more Biblical references. It's bad enough that libs don't want that kind of content out there, but I know a lot of political junkie conservatives and Republicans weren't interested in having the Bible included in my work. It doesn't satisfy their "sophisticated" sentiments. They just want to hear somebody bark about how stupid liberals are. Meat and heat, meat and heat. Not the real Truth and Light. For them, Politics is the main meaty entree, and The Bible is just some side dish or a garnish that's more of a nuisance on the plate. That's really very sad. It's that very reason why abortion is legal. Not leaning on the Word of God and leaving Him out is how republican supreme court Judges ruled in favor of abortion with Roe v. Wade. But I know that a big reason why I lost a lot of my audience is also due to liberals not wanting me to be part of helping the Bible become more clear for more people curious about God, and also some conservatives just not really caring about God. Oh, they'll be like, "God bless America" and stuff. But It's often the country that their affections are for. Politics and patriotism are what they're more focused on, not the One Who Blessed us with this republic. Losing sight of Who blessed us with this republic is a bad way to preserve the republic. I see them with their pro-Trump #Maga banners to let people know how much of a pro-America-first patriot they are. The Word of God preserves the republic, and I'm thankful for Trump getting the Job, but God really appears to be taken for granted.

Though I'm really bothered by this I try not to let it get me down. The reason why I'm not as angered by this as I could be is because a lot of our vets are forgotten. If I'm going to be angry about people being forgotten, I'll be angry about that rather than about myself being forgotten. And what's even worse is how God is left out. That's the soul sinking tragedy. Me being left out is nothing compared to how Republicans are leaving God out.

But I reckon I'll try to keep on trucking with my silly ideas of trying to connect the Word of God and conservatism to the culture.

It would be great if more republicans saw the importance of this. But it's like unless it's somebody running for office it's deemed silly, unimportant and unofficial. Everything has to be about running for office. Running for office. Running for office. Running for office. Running for office. Running for office. As if that's the only way to make a difference. It's like if you're not running for office you can't be taken seriously while these same people say "Government is not the answer it's the problem!"

I guess I'm silly because I see the huge population of Star Wars fans. People are so into this franchise that some try to make a religion out of it. I invented a light-saber replica. I call it a "Sci-Fi Sword" so as to not intrude on their brand. Star Wars is not the only production to feature an illuminated type sword, so the illuminated type sword is not exclusively theirs. Even in the very first pages of the Bible angels are described as having flaming swords. I'm sure Moses got that info from God and didn't rip it off from Lucas.

Well, considering how much of the culture is into Star Wars and Science Fiction, I made a Science Fiction type sword that is not on the market. Fans want to get as close to the movie experience as possible, and the one thing that has been missing with Star Wars Fans who like Light Sabers is a replica that auto-extends and auto-retracts. The only thing that's on the market now is a long glow stick that you have to screw in. A Jedi ain't got time for that! Or they have telescopic Light Saber replicas that you can flick out, but you don't get the movie experience of auto-retracting the blade. You have to push it back in manually. A Jedi will burn their hand off trying to do that with the aforementioned replicas!

But my invention auto-extends, which is a closer mimic of the movie experience and it auto-retracts, which is closer to the movie experience. That does not exist on the market. That huge market - that huge market with a huge population of Star Wars Fans to connect conservatism to. A demographic that would have to be cut into with a freakin' light saber to reach! And I made a great model of one!

But I guess it was too silly for conservatives to back. We talk about being grassroots! Well, I wanted to develop this on the grassroots level. Why? Because I wanted to help show that conservatives could supply something in the culture that fans of something culturally iconic would demand. But nope. I reckon all conservatives could see was a silly toy. Alas, no imagination. No vision. All they can seek is a politician, while they lament over what's happening to their country.

Facebook, Youtube, Google, and Twitter knows that this invention would be a threat because just like the rest of my work they shadow-banned the promo-vid for it. I

could hardly promote it. Cynical Sci-fi fans aren't going to take an interest unless they can actually see it, touch it, sniff it, and be able to take it home. They don't care about my prototype, and I understand.

Like I said. I wanted to show that conservatives were the backers who helped bring this invention to market - that we're not ignorant to these imaginative works that much of the culture finds fascinating, and that we're not these anal retentive stuffy miserable old people. I thought conservatives might see the big picture and back it with my crowd funder on the development of this invention to bring this to market. Nope. "Point me to a political candidate I can send my money to. I'll pay good money to be disappointed!" Bear in mind I know it's not just that. I know that a lot of conservatives don't support because they've been blocked off from even knowing about what I'm doing. But I've been warning conservatives about this for years. Don't be dependent on these platforms. There needs to be viable competitors on our end. The rug is going to get yanked up from under us if we're standing on their ground.

Conservatives are frustrated by how the culture sees them, slanders them, and promotes prejudice against them, but don't really want to do what it takes to change that. They just stick with their denial that they don't care about what these people think while saying they're sick of being called a racist, sexist, homophobe. These ideas about conservatives are promoted through, music, movies, tv, radio, etc. Conservatives hardly support and produce the counter-messaging with these means. So much for a counter to the Left Hook.

I produced a video called Sinisturbia. Great title, if I do say so myself! Sinisturbia is a satirical, semi-suspense anthology in the vein of the Twilight Zone and Tales From the Darkside using absurdity to illustrate the absurdity and ironies of the left-wing worldview. The title SINISTURBIA is a mix of the words SINISTER and URBAN.

SINISTER means: Evil, something indicative of evil, doing evil etc. It also means situated to the LEFT or referring to the left side.

URBAN means: Relating to a city or a town.

SINISTURBIA is the LEFTward city that liberals are trying to force us to live in.

With all the lunacy of the left, it's a dang tragedy that there aren't more shows that illustrate their absurdity. Last Man Standing is the only one I can think of. And they got bullied off the station. I reckon it would be a hoot to work with Tim Allen!

I produced a pilot. Did conservatives come through with grassroots support to make more? Not really. I'm blessed with the few who tried though. I keep hearing conservatives say "How do we get our message out there?" over and over again.

First, stop depending on a politician to do that for you. Much of The culture is not consenting to conservative governance. You have to illustrate these things to the culture. Liberals have been illustrating their worldview to the culture for years. They support the promotion of it. Conservatives, not so much. Conservatives keep saying "Freedom isn't free." But they don't want to invest in what will help preserve it. If you want to preserve the republic, you're going to have to make illustrations showing what is decaying it. You're going to have to present a hero and a villain. Have you noticed that the entertainment industry has made conservatives out to be the villain? Notice how effective it is? Malcolm X said, "If you're not careful, the newspapers will have you hating the people who are being oppressed, and loving the people who are doing the oppressing."

I'll remind you that I'm telling you this because I understand how people get so frustrated with the Republican party that they don't call themselves republican anymore. I share that frustration, but I'm still a Republican. Even though most of the "conservative friends" I have in the entertainment industry not only blew me off when I shared my video, Sinisturbia with them, they just flat out stopped talking to me. I didn't expect Sinsiturbia to be received as an Emmy Award-winning production, but I didn't think it was so bad that my "Conservative Hollywood friends" would just stop talking to me. They not only didn't respond to the vid, they just flat out stopped talking to me. I'm rather introverted as it is. I'm not a big social type. I understand lapses in communication with folks, but this was with almost everyone I sent the vid to. One after the other, after seeing Sinisturbia, they would not respond. I'd Follow up with them, and still, no response.

Things like this give me much to sympathize with regarding people feeling frustrated with Republicans and wanting to leave the Republican party. I'm still a republican.

I've heard producers who are pro-military talk about how they don't invest in the promotion of conservative slanted productions because they don't expect an interesting enough return from it. That's kind of an insult. These people admire the military so much yet it doesn't seem like they consider that when a person goes to war and risks their body, that volunteer knows that there is no return for the arm they risked if it gets blown off. There's no return for the legs they risk. There's no return for the eyes they risk or their face that got burned off. Or of course the very life they risk.

But these so-called pro-military conservatives don't want to risk capital to produce entertainment with a conservative slant because they don't think they'll get back the money they risk. Meanwhile, the military we claim to love so much is risking their lives and limbs defending a country that we're too afraid to defend at home, and the country is becoming something alien to the constitution they swore to defend. Why? Because of fear of risking money and career on supporting the production of content from a conservative angle.

I don't want to rely on a Hollywood producer. I don't want to submit my scripts to them. They wouldn't want their audience to see it anyway because they don't want to lose control over them. I want the grassroots support because I'm trying help to get conservatives to be SELF RELIANT!!! Establish our OWN PLATFORMS where we can feature OUR OWN CONTENT!

I'm not talking about cutting ourselves off. I'm talking about creating something awesome that catches the attention of others. Get them curious about the noise we're making! I'm trying to do my part to show that we "Free market conservatives" can actually use the free market to promote the defense of the free market!"

Liberals hate the free market yet they make the best use of it to promote their hatred of the free market! They're going to demand more regulations and taxes and bloated bureaucracies until the state might as well take ownership of all industries. They've mastered marketing to make that quite plausible. Why, for the love of God don't conservatives support the counter to this?

If it's not red meat politics conservatives are hardly interested. I told you. All that red meat will make you constipated. That's why the conservative movement is struggling now. You've got to add the fruit of the spirit to your diet! You've got to add some colorful veggies to that plate with savory herbs and spices. If you like bland meat and potatoes that's fine, but you have to understand, other people may need a little more flavor to be interested in conservative ideas. That doesn't mean change the principle. Change how it's conveyed.

Lots of people find fruit really boring to eat. I do too. Take that same fruit and throw it in a blender, and bam! Ya got a smoothie! Now it's a little more interesting to consume. It's still the same fruit, just delivered in a way that's less boring. It's such a simple freakin' principle. Do conservatives really supply and demand this? No! There's not much supply of it, because not enough conservatives have the creativity or interest to supply it, and there's not enough support from the demand to develop competitive productions to be supplied.

I'm so thankful to God for those few who do get it and are trying to be supportive. They are a rare blessing that contribute to my work every month. Thanks to them I'm able to keep the lights on and have a place to keep trying to deliver content like the Zo Loft. But unfortunately, because they are so rare It's only enough to support doing the Zo Loft occasionally, not regularly. And it's certainly not enough supporters to develop other productions. There have been conservatives who have tried making theatrical productions, and they were pretty impactful politically, but not as much culturally because they shortchanged themselves by succumbing to their vanity. They want to be seen as the ones who brought these revelations to people, and they want others to promote their revelations but they don't reciprocate. They won't promote others. If someone promotes one of my videos, I will most likely promote ten of theirs if their content isn't a conflict of interest for me.

Because conservative content creators have this vanity problem, it slows down the delivery of the message and it shows people that we're not really solid. Why would they want to be a part of us when we're so apart from each other? This leaves the culture wide open for the Left Hook.

I've had "conservatives" play friendly with me that are now on FOX News that have spammed the deviled-ham out of my group pages promoting their content. They did it so much that I had to change my settings because they basically turned my group page that I made for MUSIC into their page to promote their content.

I've given these people passwords to my website so they could upload their content to my website whenever they wanted. My website was a better forum to showcase their political views and what-not, so I opened the door for them to do that. Now that they have their spot on FOX News they haven't the time of day for "What's his name? Oh, Zo? I think I might have heard of him."

I follow these content creators on Twitter, but most don't follow back. Then after a while when I see that they're not interested in being associated with me I just do them a favor and unfollow them.

It's like they can't stand the idea that someone else was already out there saying similar things but in a unique way. They may think to themselves that they want other people to wake up to these truths, but it's like they don't like it that someone else was already out there waking people up. They claim to be the pro-competition people, talking about how "America needs to be free to compete!" Yet they hate having competition. I don't want competition from conservatives, I want allies. But a lot of these people act like they're too stuck-up to connect. It's not like I'm going to hound them. I'm not that social!

Again, I'm not saying these things to express being disgruntled about being faded out or excluded. I'm expressing my disappointment in the lack of unity. I mean there are a lot of people persistent with their pursuit of Hillary's heels and the scandals of the Democrats, etc., but we don't have a strong united front in promoting conservatism. If conservatives could unite in promoting the real news (and the most real news is driven by the gospel) the way liberals unite in promoting hate and fake news we'd be a lot better off.

Too many claiming to lean right keep saying they want smaller government but they're more interested in promoting politicians than promoting conservatism in the culture so as to create a culture that is more consenting of conservative governance.

We're totally dependent on liberal created platforms because we lack unity. However, if you do have more of the socially liberal leanings then yeah, ya would be doing us a favor if ya wouldn't call yourself a Republican. It's weird that people who are more liberal insist on staying in the Republican tent, and conservatives are the ones who bail. It really should be the other way around.

I don't leave the Republican Party because I don't want to give Democrats the satisfaction.

Some might say that I talk about unity but they don't see me promoting other conservatives and their content, or Christian conservative actors, and some of their pet projects. If it seems to me that a person values their acting career over the kingdom, I'm likely to not promote their work. If a Christian conservative who's an actor lends themselves to productions that are apart from God then I'm likely to not support that production. When a Christian conservative yields to their desire to express themselves in whatever way they feel would be entertaining and get them attention without caring that it doesn't represent the Kingdom then I might not be as likely to support that work. Them serving what they believe is art before considering if God would be pleased just rubs me wrong. I try to be supportive of my friends in the industry but often times I'm like, "I can't get down with that."

I know God is gracious and God forgives, and that's all the more reason to honor Him and refrain from producing things He would always have to forgive us for. If we really love Him and honor Him why produce content that He'd have to forgive? No production is perfect, but dang!

None of us are perfect, and who's to say what's over the line and what isn't? Even I have some material that some people think is un-Christian. Some "Christians" think the music I play is devil worship! And if they don't support my music, that's their prerogative. I guess I'm not as uptight as some folks though.

All of us will fall short, but it's like some don't care and have no reservations about the material they put out, and go about with the attitude of, "Only God can judge me" (That alone should scare the crap out of them.)

This doesn't mean we have to be artistic fuddy-duddies. I dig tongue in cheek humor! Impious comedy can be a riot without vulgar imagery and profane language, or whatever production; from music to dramas.

As Christian conservatives, we should be able to have the creative fortitude to honor God first rather than give in to our desire to publish media that's foul in language and vulgar in theme and imagery. Some curse words don't really bug me. Some do. And sometimes it depends on the setting where it's quite plausible that such words would be voiced. But gratuitous profanity is just cheap.

It's hard to do though! But God should be worth the effort and sacrifice. Some productions warrant some profane language; war movies, for instance. Military personnel curse a lot, and a war movie would be really awkward if a character got their arm blown off and said, "Oh golly gee willikers! That really smarts!" Also, there's really no good reason for sex scenes and nudity.

As Christian conservatives, the theme of our art doesn't always have to be about God. Just not apart from God. The book of Esther is a great example. It doesn't mention God, but it's not apart from God. The Song of Solomon makes one possible allusion to God, like in Song of Solomon 8:6

"Put me like a seal over your heart, Like a seal on your arm. For love is as strong as death, Jealousy is as severe as Sheol; Its flashes are flashes of fire, like the very flame of the Lord." NASB

("The very flame of the Lord" Could also mean "a most vehement flame." The point is these books aren't apart from God even though God's not really mentioned.

I usually don't share some other "conservative" commentator's work often because of what's in their content; cursing, n-word, b-word, Confederate sympathizers, atheists and such. Why would I promote their work? It's a conflict of interest for me. I understand this doesn't make me very popular with others but if I wanted to be popular I wouldn't put myself out there as a conservative to begin with. I reckon I'm going to be even less popular with conservatives, "Classical Liberals", Republicans, Libertarians, and even Christians with this book. Hope I'm wrong.

Out of respect for my audience, I've refrained from sharing content created by others who employ this kind of language. (Meanwhile, a lot of my own audience shares the work of the people who do use this kind of language more than they share my videos anyway!)

I guess that's why people say nice guys finish last. But the Bible says many who are last shall be first! (Matt. 19:30, Matt. 20:16, Mark 10:31, Luke 13:30)

At least I make it known why I may not share other people's work. I don't sit back and act like I don't know about other people's work, or about them. I know a lot of these stuck-up people know who I am and pretend like they don't. Don't get me wrong. I'm not saying this to boast as if they should know me. I'm pointing out the disgust I have for conceited people who want to front like they're too good to be associated with a person who's more or less in the same cause - who's been in the cause longer than they have. I'm not the only one. lot's of people feel blown off. I may have caused some conservatives to feel blown off myself. If you're among any of those and feel like I've unjustly ignored you or your work, I'm very sorry. At a point it does get a little difficult to keep up with so many people. Aside from that, again, at least I say why. I don't treat others like I'm oblivious to them.

Oh, and I know that nobody's perfect. I don't throw the baby out with the bathwater. I share work of people that I have disagreements with, but if the conflict of interest is too much for my meter I tend to back away from those works. But people are often telling me about this person or that person. Ya know what I do when they do? I check that person out! It may even result in me following them on twitter, and sharing their vid. But again, if their content includes profanity, use of the N-word, B-word, and questionable if it represents conservatism then chances are I may not share it. Or I just might think it sucks! Ha! And that may very well be why conservatives in media blow my work off! But in most cases, It's just a lot to keep up with. I'm so preoccupied with these efforts to fade me out that I become ignorant of the other content out there and forget to share their stuff. But chances are, I've heard of ya. And if I have I don't make it a point to act like I haven't.

We rebuke liberals for their lack of morality, their vulgarity, and lewdness. Shouldn't we distinguish ourselves from them? There are some that don't but want to be conservative in their productions. That's fine, but I might not be as supportive of that. I try not to promote crassness. It has to have a super good message in it if I do. I'm quite a potty mouth myself, actually. But I don't think it would be right for me to profit off of it. I'm not looking for perfection with folks. I'm just saying there are certain things that characterize liberals and things they resort to that contribute to the decline of our culture, and I have reservations about supporting the same. It's not cool to frown upon them while justifying why it's ok for us to do it, or Christians conservatives who pander to this idea that there's another entity besides God to be accountable to, like Karma, the universe, or whatever. That's wishy-washy. If you're going to call yourself a Christian then you do not entertain the idea that there is another entity to be accountable to. That is an insult to our High Priest and King who took the body shredding bullet for you. You dishonor Him with ideas of Karma, or the universe. Karma didn't give you life, and it didn't die for you so you could have eternal life. Neither did the universe. I tend to keep Christian conservatives who lend themselves to these ideas at arm's length. I try to get the word out there in a way that they might receive it because I don't want them to remain deceived. I see more of this than I'm cool with regarding Republicans. Yet for all the disappointment I'm still experiencing with the Republican Party I'd take that any day over being a Democrat. Some would say, "Why be a Republican at All? Just because you don't want to be a Democrat doesn't mean you have to be a Republican."

I'm a Republican because I understand that we enjoy a constitutional republic that's built on the law issued by God All Mighty who created us equally - and endowed us with certain inalienable rights. The rule is that those rights shall not be infringed on no matter how popular it becomes with the people to do so. I am not a Democrat because I understand this is not a democracy. I agree that it is a bad idea to make laws based on what is popular with the people. The selfishness of people wins the vote of their own destruction. Thus I am not a democrat.

Democrats hate the Republican party because the Republican party was founded to impede Democrats from instituting what Democrats feel entitled to; their ideals at the forced expense of someone else's rights. Democrats don't want people to be Republican. Democrats created the KKK to terrorize people to not be Republican. I'm not going to give them the satisfaction.

Many people claiming to be Christian get on my nerves too but that doesn't mean I'm going to stop being a Christian.

But the hook of the left is selfishness. Don't get caught by the Left Hook! The Democrats have always been the party of selfishness, and that is an easy hook to catch people with; appealing to what they feel entitled to. People feeling they were entitled to keep making other people their property voted for Democrats. They didn't care about the rights of others and made arguments to say the people they wanted to enslave didn't have constitutional rights. I hope you would agree that they were being very liberal with what the constitution says, and can also agree that those who claimed to be Christian were very liberal with what the Bible says.

I don't care if it's the year 1800 or 2000, if you are liberal with the Bible, the Constitution, and people's rights it will result in oppression. Democrats have always felt justified to do this and argued that *it was the greater good and moral*. It's all manipulation to impose their selfishness and others always end up having to pay for it.

People feeling like they have the right to other people's property vote for Democrats.

The same parasitic party that demanded the so-called right to force people to be slaves and bled them are the same parasites that demand the so-called right to bleed people's pockets today for what they feel entitled to - from education to birth control.

Democrats have always been liberal with other people's rights and always argue that it's for the greater good and moral. It's all manipulation to impose their selfishness, and others always end up having to pay for it.

People feeling like they have the so-called right to deprive an unborn kid of their right to live vote democrat - another example of being liberal with the rights of what God created and the rights He endowed us with. For liberals to legalize their selfishness they have to disqualify the personhood of the unborn. It's all manipulation to impose their selfishness and others always end up having to pay for it. In this case, the unborn pay with their lives and others are forced to pay for the pro-choicer's choice. You'd think they'd be "pro-pay for their own choice", but that's just not who Democrats are. Someone else has to be forced to pay for their choices. That's liberty to a liberal.

And I know right now some folks reading this are getting all itchy britches about me calling left-wingers, liberals. They rebuke me and say, "Stop calling them liberals, Zo! They are leftist!" I know they're leftist. They also want to be called liberals, and you're passing up the opportunity to hang them on their own deceptive hook.

A lot of those who are of the conservative persuasion insist that they themselves are the real "classical liberals", and want to "reclaim" the term liberal and be recognized as the "true liberals". This bugs me, dang it!

I hear people of the right-leaning persuasion say we need to get rid of the word conservative because it doesn't have the cool factor or something, and it repels people. Meanwhile, these weenie left-wing liberals are able to hi-jack the words "conservative", "conserve", and "conservation", and make 'em fabulous, sucker people into donating to their "conservative" efforts, and voting for reps to impose more fees, taxes, and regulations and so on for their conservation efforts. They get their chic, swanky, celebrities to host expensive get-togethers to talk about how much better they are because they care about the conservation of our resources.

But actual conservatives think that we have to ditch the word conservative because it's not seen as cool? Errrrg!

Liberalism is the term to be embarrassed by, not Conservative. You know what being conservative leads to? Prolonged enjoyment. Liberalism leads to desiccation. Liberalism is a parasitic, cross-hating, vampiric worldview that bleeds it's host dry. Yes, that means classical liberalism too.

The left-hook is liberalism. It sounds friendly, liberating, open-minded, and all that other skull-snot. In the words of Admiral Akbar, "It's a Trap". And people on the right are trying to claim classical liberalism are caught in the trap too, like a raccoon with its paw-hand in a coon-trap trying to cling to the shiny liberal object.

Do you know what people did with classical liberalism? They enslaved people! "Classical Liberalism" can be traced back to the Whigs in Great Britain. I reckon the Whigs were like cowboys, being that Whig is short for "Whiggamor" meaning Cattle Driver. Yeeee Haaaaw!!! Or since this was Great Britain they probably hollered "Tally Hooo!", or something. It's funny imagining a Brit in their accent saying, "G'on now, Git!" You tried it, didn't you? It's hard, ain't it?

Catholicism got on the Whigs nerves and the Whigs were pro-Protestant; the oppressive approach of Catholicism and a heavy-handed monarchy that was very liberal with asserting power over the folks. Or should I say asserting weakness? Because people suffer when those with power are weak to their desire to lord over people. And when the higher-ups rule with a doctrine that affords them to be liberal with other people's rights, you will have the lower folks who will think of themselves as liberals creating a movement demanding liberty from the institutions that were taking liberties with their higher position and liberties with their subjects.

Sure. We can say some of the founders were "classical liberals", but what did some of those "classical liberals" do with their "classical liberalism" when independence from the crown was won? They took the liberty to deprive others of theirs.

Being conservative with the Constitution doesn't do that. Being liberal with the Constitution does. This "classical liberal" mindset carried up to when the Democrats took the liberty to establish the Confederacy and the liberty to establish their own constitution. Why? Because they wanted a constitution that reflected their pro-slavery demands. So when people try to say the U.S. Constitution is pro-slavery, you can prove to them that their statement is as false as a set of Hollywood tranny-teataaayys. What? I can say teats! Amish people say teat, don't they? So it's ok!

The proof that the U.S. Constitution is not pro-slavery is in that fact that the Democrats made their own Constitution of the Confederate States so it would be legal for them to maintain slave markets, since the U.S. Constitution DOES NOT permit slavery, and DOES NOT contain pro-slavery clauses. Furthermore, the Confederate Constitution drawn up by Democrats specifically puts the negro in their slave sights.

The U.S. Constitution is ambiguous on race when regarding slaves and still acknowledges them as persons. The U.S. Constitution can't acknowledge a being as a person without acknowledging their rights. In the U.S. Constitution even the servant is still acknowledged as a person. Which means that person can only be a servant if they agree to be. They cannot be forced. No person can be deprived of liberty without due process. They'd have to commit an actual crime according to our laws, then be tried and proven guilty with the ratification of their peers to be deprived of liberty. Being black does not qualify as a crime punishable by enslavement in the U.S. Constitution. In the democrat established Confederate Constitution it does.

The Democrats take the liberty to abuse even "classical liberalism" and felt they were being "oppressed" by the union because the union "opposed" the Democrats who took the liberty to deprive

31

other persons of theirs. That's a nasty case of childish hypocrisy on part of Democrats.

Liberalism, even the classic kind ultimately leads to taking liberties with another person's rights.

But it's ok because it's liberalism! Conservatism in the hands of conservatives just doesn't have that hipster thing working for them.

In order for us to sustain our republic, it's going to take a conservative approach interpreting the constitution. Leftists are wooing the culture with words like "sustainability" and "conservation" and conservatives just hand it over to them.

It's sad, like a person handing over a rock that has flakes of gold in it but it couldn't be seen through the mud, and it was just handed over to someone else, and that person took that expensive rock and bashed the rock-giver over the head with the rock they just gave them. But things like using these words - That's the Left-Hook!

The Left-Hook is the most executed punch associated with a knock-out in boxing, and the left has been knocking out the right in the culture for a while.

The left even hooks people in by using conservative language and uses that hook to knock-out the right.

Let's examine some elements of this punch that contribute to its effectiveness - like the angle of it, the proximity, the velocity, the torque of the torso and so on in politics there are also contributing elements to the Left-Hook's effectiveness; racism, classism, sexism, poking other people's victim and entitlement triggers is a Left-Hook the Democrats use against the right in the culture, for the prize-fight of votes.

Many Republicans believe they've got a victory because of the election of a Republican president, a majority in the house and senate, and the election of more Republican governors and such. Meanwhile, much of the culture doesn't consent to conservative represented policy.

Political representation isn't stable or sustainable without the foundation and frame of cultural representation.

Republicans are drastically deficient in cultural representation. The culture is growing rabid while Republicans have their little political victory (and it is a victory to be thankful for! I'm not downplaying that), but too many Republicans aren't doing the real meat work it takes to sustain political representation, and that is investing in cultural representation.

This is a lot to do with why Democrats are able to be the race-baiting, bigoted, sexist, class-baiting, anti-Christian perverts they've always been while making people think it's been Republicans. Democrats knock Republicans out in the culture with the Left-Hook and hook people in with slander. This works by gaining the trust of people by causing them to not trust others.

It's unfortunate that Republicans haven't been able to come together to decimate Democrats in the culture and promote the antidote to their poison. Republicans are just getting lucky that Democrats are being exposed by their own, but that doesn't mean people are going to take to being conservatives just because Democrats are being exposed for their evil. It just means most of these people see both the representatives of both ideals as two sides of the same corrupt coin, and they'll just be suckers for the same crap with a new face, and even eventually give a pass to the old face they admonished. For example, Harvey Weinstein will probably be hosting Saturday Night Live in a few years.

Many Democrat voters can't even show enough integrity to admit to the wickedness of Democrats without trying to mitigate their actions by saying, "Yeah, but Republicans, pooty poo pooooo!" And for all the pro-defense talk of the right-wing, they have poor defenses when it comes to this.

I know I sound like a broken record, but I stay amazed at how Republicans keep saying government is not the answer, yet get all giddy over politicians like they're going to fix things and more often than not they end up with disappointing politicians who go in posing as eagles and turn out to be jive-turkeys.

Too many Republicans grossly take cultural representation for granted. They put a premium on political representation. They'll go on and on about how they don't care about what these Hollywood celebrities think, but if a celebrity says something that sounds right leaning, then all of a sudden that celebrity is fawned over by them.

Why? Because people **are** interested in what celebrities think! That's why they're celebrities! Because there is a large enough validated number of people who take an interest in what they do. I so often hear conservatives say, "Who cares what these people think?" and "We should just ignore them." Well, millions of people care about what they think, and millions of people are influenced by them! Ignoring them isn't a good idea. Since when is it a good idea to ignore a spreading infection?

I agree it's a good idea to ignore their ideals so as not to be infected by their ideals, but it's not a good idea to ignore that they are influencing people, and assume that nobody cares what they think.

People do want their values, or lack thereof, validated and endorsed by those with fame and influence, and when a celebrity doesn't share your ideals you get all sour-grapes about it and say, "Who cares what these people think?!" Remember… Millions do.

Many people care about the thoughts of people who entertain them, and want celebrities to validate their shallow world view. Shallow celebrities want a big audience and there's a lot of shallow people to appeal to - shallow people wanting their selfish entitlement victim mentality, questionable behaviors, orientations, and views, validated. Celebrity artists are happy to do that because their occupation is make believe and drama. They make believe things that are un-natural are natural, what is illegal should be legal, what belongs to someone else should be re-distributed, what satisfies their idea of equality is special treatment, and so on. It's all make-believe, backward thinking, and they make a whole bunch of drama with this, so they're quite comfortable pandering to their audience. Plus, they want to be seen as open minded, imaginative, and accepting to their audience. This is all part of the Left-Hook that the right has neglected to train its defenses for and counter with.

The right wins when the left gets cockier than they usually are and gets caught with a lucky punch. That's not a dependable strategy. The left doesn't get knocked out for the count. It keeps getting back up like Jason, or Mike Myers. The referee is bought by the left. The left has big money in their corner paying the left to hit below the belt. The arena is owned by the left. The judges are paid off by the left.

The broadcast is owned by the left. Look at all these things liberals own! T.V. Movies, Radio - they're the overlords of the internet, creating platforms that conservatives are dependent on to get their message out with. Youtube, Facebook, google, and twitter, have conservatives herded into using their platforms, and conservatives have the nerve to call liberals stupid while liberals have us trapped in their cyber box.

Too many on the right think they can duck the left hooks and avoid social issues that the left wails about in the culture, but it backfires on the right as they get caught by the right upper cut they should have used themselves instead of dodging.

Too much of the right doesn't understand that the left always brings this stuff up. The right doesn't have to bring it up, but the right should be prepared to counterpunch when the left attacks with it. The right should be prepared to counter with a righteous right cross to knock the teeth out of their argument and leave 'em with mental mush mouth, but too many on the right are too busy sticking their own foot in their own mouth.

Since too many on the right say we should avoid social issues, many on the right are not trained up and prepared to counterpunch when attacked with it. The right should be trained up with conservative counterpunches and Biblical body blows to knock the wind out of the left. This causes the body to fold and bring their head into range to be skull struck by a solid right cross!

Or I reckon a good strike to the gut to blow their head out of their mud-pipe would be doing them a favor!

Too much of the right is told to avoid social issues while the left is infecting more people with liberalism in the culture. Republicans gloat over a political victory while the culture is melting down. And a lot of so-called republicans are melting down too. Since it's not the victory they wanted they're going to childishly sabotage it all together rather than make the best of the opportunity we have to better preserve our republic. Why? Because politicians are people too. They are a product of the culture. They are representatives. They represent what people want so they can get re-elected. That often entails being more concerned with the affairs of men over the affairs of God.

Jesus really hates this by the way. He hates it when people do things according to what man thinks is right over what God knows is right. This is Satanic as far as Jesus is concerned. Jesus Called Peter Satan because of Peter's tendency to such a view. We have Republicans that are like this. We have Republican politicians that represent this. This is normal for Democrats. That's just what their platform is. But for Republicans this is deviance. It is deviant of the frame of this Judeo-Christian based constitutional republic. Establishment Republicans are deviant of what this constitutional republic is established on.

They're ideals and strategies aren't effective for the preservation of our republic, but preserves their term in office. And they hate it that it wasn't their skill or strategy that gained a Republican victory for the presidency. It was a lucky punch to them.

Not that Trump so much relied on luck. He had a strategy. He used his experience with his time he spent in the culture. The culture has been fascinated with "Reality TV Shows" Trump is quite experienced with that. He pulled the election process into his own reality TV Show, and it worked! He tapped into the culture which is what Republicans have failed to do for so long.

But many on the right aren't following through! Trump has shown that ya have to tap into the culture, and many Republican voters are still just focused on Trump to either fix things or fail, rather than really helping him succeed by also tapping into the culture. That's how he won the presidency, and that's how we'll win the country.

It's like I've often said about Reagan. Republicans adore Reagan for being "the great communicator". Well follow that example! Get more refined at communicating the conservative view! Or be more supportive of those who can create illustrations to connect with the culture.

We can still lose the country, ya know? It's a republic if we can keep it, remember?

Liberals are effectively distributing the poison of their social issues in the culture and the right is in short supply in delivering the antidote. The left is effectively spreading the infection and the right is absent with the inoculations for the viral infection of liberal indoctrination. It should be easy for conservatives to get the medicine to liberals! Liberals demand medicine! They get infected with STD's and mental/emotional disease and demand pills and ointment!

The left has their hooks in the culture and the worm on that hook that the left uses to attract people is liberalism. It's a parasitic hookworm! Upon taking this bait that deceives people into thinking that liberalism is synonymous with liberty - the parasitic hookworm of liberalism begins feeding on liberty and crapping in the host. This results in a septic and malnourished host.

Liberalism doesn't know when to stop. Liberalism will justify taking liberties with the meaning of rights and other people's rights until tyranny is established.

Liberalism will always feel oppressed and ultimately feel like it's not free if it can't define for itself what liberty is. Liberty has to fit their idea of it, even if their idea comes at the forced expense of someone else.

Liberalism starts off well-meaning but doesn't know when it's good intentions have bad results. Classical liberalism can only work for a short time like in a revolution from an already oppressive institution. But once separated from that institution, liberalism has to be restrained, because liberalism is at it's most dangerous in an environment of liberty.

Liberalism is only useful as a short revolution solution when people are ruled by an institution that believes they are the grantor of the people's rights. That institution will succumb to the weakness of being liberal with their power and ruthlessly lord over the people.

When people have gained liberty from their oppressors they have to put liberalism to rest and exercise conservatism through the filter of the Law that came through Moses that protects people from each other and government. Rely on the grace that comes through Jesus for respecting the rights of others, not just because the law says we have to but because we want to.

Being conservative with power and ruling with restraint makes for a government that protects the people's ability to thrive.

Liberalism doesn't want to be inhibited by laws. That's oppressive to liberalism. However, liberalism in government wants to be liberal with making laws. And even though liberal legislators are liberal with making laws, they don't like to be limited to or by the laws they make others live by.

Liberalism doesn't want to be inhibited by laws impeding what it feels entitled to. Thus, liberalism will demand laws that protect its so-called right to intrude upon others. That is the evolutionary course of liberalism. That's why Democrats don't like the Constitution. It limits them from being liberal with other people's liberty. Liberalism does not work in an environment of liberty.

Liberalism doesn't adhere to a moral standard. For example, liberalism does not adhere to Christianity because when the Word of God interferes with what they think they have the right to do they take the liberty of taking the Word of God in vain to say that God is ok with what they feel entitled to, or say that only God can Judge them and we can't say anything about it. Even though Jesus told us to rebuke the sinner and be on our guard against sinners. Luke 17:3 (You have to be on your guard and know sin when you see it, especially our own!)

With a liberal interpretation of scripture, liberalism renders God being OK with, Slavery, Abortion, same-sex marriage, income taxes, state-sponsored paganism (environmentalism), illegal immigration, etc.

Christianity is already a liberating doctrine. It is the ultimate treatise on the balance of liberty. It is the check and balance that tells us that a person cannot have what they think is a right at the forced expense of someone else's. It is already a doctrine of liberty. If you try to be liberal with it you will bring oppression, poverty, and murder... Oh! And AIDS. (American Independence deficiency syndrome) Independence and liberty decay when people want their selfishness instituted for others to be ruled by.

Liberalism takes liberties with God's "Thou shall nots." Those are oppressive to liberalism. So it revolts or revises the meanings to suit its desires. This leads to oppressing others and being forced to facilitate what liberalism feels entitled to.

Christian conservatism doesn't do this. Basically, Christian conservatism sticks to the script. God's script is perfect. It doesn't need some Hollywood liberal rewrite. God's script is the perfect script of liberty. Interpret it conservatively, square it by itself, stick to the script, and liberty is better preserved.

Liberalism always leads to oppression. Conservatism is only oppressive when the doctrine is oppressive. Strict adherence or conservative interpretation of oppressive doctrine is going to result in oppression. That's natural. Systems such as sharia or NAZIsm cause stigma concerning conservatism. They are considered "conservatives" or even "right wing" Why? It's because of strict religious adherence to their doctrine. That's not the fault of conservatism. Conservatism to a doctrine of oppression results in oppression. Conservatism to a doctrine of liberty results in liberty.

Conservatism in the hands of oppression preserves the power for the oppressor who takes liberties with people's rights as the people atrophy from the state feeding off of them. Conservatism in the hands of liberty preserves the power of the people and keeps in place a government to protect the people's power from each other and from the state itself.

The nature of liberalism does not result in liberty because ultimately it's only interested in its own and will demand the liberty to deprive another of theirs for what they feel entitled to.

Liberalism is the Left-Hook.

Its dazzling rays of light that many people feed on are the satanic rays of self-satisfying selfishness. For the devil masquerades as an angel of light.

Those seductive light rays of liberalism become longer rays of shadows that cover the people in darkness. The Left-Hook has landed. The lights are going out. Are we going to stay down for the count?

CHAPTER II
SOUTH PAW

Many people often say, *Both parties are just two sides of the same corrupt coin, and can't tell them apart.* I can assure you that it's largely in part of Republicans acting like Democrats. Not democrats acting like Republicans. Republican voters who consider themselves socially liberal yet fiscally conservative are fooling themselves. It's like saying, "I'm always faithful to my spouse when I'm at home." Or, "I'm a wellness conscious vegan health-nut who's very scrutinizing about what I put in my body... Care to go outside with me for a smoke?" That's what a socially liberal so-called fiscally conservative is like. It contradicts itself, and when the left side of their contradiction wins out, the people lose.

The South-Paw Stance works better for Democrats than Republicans. As mentioned in the previous chapter, some on the Right say we should get away from the term "conservative". It supposedly lacks the cool factor, so they try to claim to be a "classical liberal". Meanwhile, Leftists use the words some right-leaning people say we should avoid, while Leftists effectively promote their worldview with these words. This is part of what I call their South-Paw Stance. They use the language of the Right like a lead right hand.

They're not even putting their strong arm forward, but they are demonstrating proof that even with their weak hand and weak stance, right-sided language is effective with them even though they are left-side dominant.

The Left uses the South-Paw Stance to mirror the Right, and the Right falls for it and alters its stance, which is one of the reasons why so many can't tell the parties apart, and the Left gets away with their evil.

"And no wonder, for Satan himself masquerades as an angel of light. It is not surprising, then, if his servants also masquerade as servants of righteousness. Their end will be what their actions deserve." - 2 Corinthians 11:14-15 NIV

With this masquerading, mirroring, South-Paw Strategy the Liberal jabs with the right hand and keeps it in the face of the opponent. The socially Liberal so-called Republican types say we should avoid social issues. Meanwhile, Liberals tend to bring up those very issues the Right is supposed to champion. The lead hand will deliver rapid, sight obstructing punches that can cause the opponent to bring their guard up. This is like Liberals forcing Conservatives to bring up social issues.

Since so many Republican voters haven't been encouraged to train up in this area, they bring their guard up out of instinct and obstruct their own vision that the Democrats were already obstructing with the jabs; basically helping the liberal land punches.

But because the Republican voter and politician haven't been trained up for this, they're unaware that they've left their torso exposed. The Liberal goes to work on the body. How does it feel knowing that a limp-wristed Liberal is putting' the dukes to ya? That's why you'll see a Conservative candidate give some bumbling answer concerning social issues when liberals throw it in their face. Liberals will always bring up these issues until Conservatives train up to swat them down. Some Conservatives understand this and put the boots to liberals when they try. The training needs to be applied by more though.

Republicans don't have to bring these issues up. Liberals are going to attack with them. For too long conservatives get wobbly-kneed because they're not encouraged to train up on countering these attacks. These attacks come as accusations like racism, sexism, and classism. The Left uses reproductive issues, gender issues, orientations, identity issues, and the issues keep festering because Republicans have been told to ignore them. What Republican thinks it's a good idea to ignore your lawn and just let the weeds grow? You do know it's going to need some mowin' and yankin', right? And the more regularly ya mow the less yank. Keep it trimmed. Would you let your neighbor tell you to stay away from the weeds when they're growing in your lawn? No. You'd tell your neighbor to get their nose off your fence, and you'd whack them weeds. Maybe even burn 'em!

Speaking of fire, much of our culture is melting down due to liberals dumping fuel on these issues and keeping the fire blazing and blinding. They claim they're raising awareness and bringing these issues to light, but their light doesn't illuminate. It blinds.

"And no wonder, for Satan himself masquerades as an angel of light. It is not surprising, then, if his servants also masquerade as servants of righteousness. Their end will be what their actions deserve." - 2 Corinthians 11:14-15 NIV

Many Republicans have lost their touch at dealing with this because they've lost touch with God. In the twenty-first century we're dealing with racial tensions coming to a boil, and Republicans have been made out to be the culprits of bigotry and racism. Republicans! How did you let this happen?

Race-baiting is the biggest weapon Democrats have against Republicans, and the Republicans have yet to take that weapon out. The most effective means of obstruction the Democrats have against Republicans is race-baiting. People are going Poo-Throwing-Primate over the Trump Administration as they get more wound up on racial tension. I've been trying to tell Republicans for years, this needs to be remedied in the culture. Now we're back to the days where Democrats are killing people they associate with Republican voters and Christians. (And those days weren't that long ago either.)

Another example of the South-Paw stance in full effect is the mirroring strategy. Democrats have always been guilty of these things but they've placed the blame on Republicans and now people can't distinguish between who's the reflection or who's the culprit.

To this day, Republicans don't really support a delivery system in the culture to remedy that. They still think a politician is going to fix and save America, even while saying, "Government is not the answer." It would be great if Republicans would do a little mirroring too! How do liberals spread the infection? Through art, music, movies, TV, Radio, sports, fashion, video games. Do Conservatives support and supply these mediums to move the Conservative message? Not really. (But there's hope that may be changing for the better.) The left shows that the mirroring strategy works. Mirroring the strategy of using arts and entertainment to move the message to connect with the culture would be very helpful.

But for all the talk Conservatives do about "competition breeding excellence" they don't support or partake in competing in the arena where Liberals are abusing liberty to do the most damage.

Race baiting is promoted through music, movies, TV, radio, and sports. It's getting worse because conservatives don't support the production of creative content to counterpunch their narrative. It takes more than talk radio and talking head shows. It takes illustration! Liberals are like children! They're selfish, tantrum throwing kids with a mean case of A.D.D.! Kids often remember lessons through song. So where's the support for music? And dang it! It doesn't always have to be country! Not that I dislike country, but how about a little variety!? Patriotism sounds good in every genre!

Beat liberals at their own South-Paw Strategy without compromising your stance! Stay orthodox! When they mirror your orthodox stance with their South-Paw Stance and try to fool the people with the mirror strategy make it backfire on them!

Republicans in office meet way too much resistance with economic policy because Democrats bring up the disenfranchisement of race and white privilege, yet Democrats are the party that instituted racial disenfranchisement and white privilege in the first place! All the racism that America is still so bitter over was done by Democrats. Republicans have let the Democrats stigmatize them and make them the target of the people's scorn for it.

Obviously, the people want to be angry. The least we could do is point them to the actual people to be angry at! To do that it's going to take illustrations. They're kids, remember? Ya gotta educate them with a sing-along! The song has got to have a beat and a cadence that they can step to; it's got to have a melody they can sing along to, or all together songs they can stomp their feet to, pump their fist to, bang their head to, or shake their booty too! (No Twerking.) Keep it groovy and just shake your booty, but twerking is a boot out of the club. Twerking looks like a confused cat that can't decide whether it wants to poop or hurl a hairball.

Even in this age of racial tension there's so much music involving the N-word. How does that make any sense?! In this age of Political Correctness, people get offended and are ready to shut you down as they dig for racism in a box of cereal even. CEREAL IS RACIST NOW! Yet, make a song saying the N-word over and over again can make you a millionaire!

But cereal, y'all? Cereal? A breakfast food you eat with a spoon will set off the PC Police, but a song repeating the N-word, fantasizing and glamorizing violence against blacks gets a pass. People used to dig for prizes in a box of cereal now they dig for racism.

This is cultural insanity that has to be dealt with on a cultural level - a spiritual level, really, but baby steps for now. But why is it assumed a politician can solve this? We are governed by our consent. Do you think this crazy culture consents to being governed by Conservatives? These people are loony, not lucid, no matter how much they think they're #Woke. They're dreaming if they think they're woke thinking what they think.

They're trapped in a waking dream. It's not going to be a politician that wakes them up. It takes us using the mediums they use to break the spell on them. Support the production of music to counter theirs. Support the production of teleplays to counter theirs. Support the production of movies to counter theirs. Give them a new beat to step to freedom with, instead of the beat they're marching to now that keeps them stomping in a circle. Give them a story they can get engrossed in. It's a tragedy we don't support such media.

It's like right-leaning people think that their views are only validated by the election of a government official. We talk about how pro-free-market we are but the ones using the free market to their advantage the most are Liberals. Liberals market Liberalism. Conservatives don't market conservatism. Too often the free market to conservatives means boycott, which I agree with to a degree. If a business promotes what is unGodly and corrosive to our republic, I don't want to give them my patronage, but sometimes that's just not practical.

Lots of people who lean right call liberals stupid, yet the liberals are the ones creating the things we're stuck on!

Even Jesus tells us to make use of their resources because their resources are good for connecting with people. We just need the discernment to know the difference between using the resources for good or for evil.

"The rich man had to admire the dishonest rascal for being so shrewd. And it is true that the children of this world are more shrewd in dealing with the world around them than are the children of the light.

Here's the lesson: Use your worldly resources to benefit others and make friends. Then, when your earthly possessions are gone, they will welcome you to an eternal home." -Luke 16:8-9 NLT

Basically, the Lord is telling Christians that our marketing kinda sucks. There's a reason for that. I'll remind you that the truth is difficult to sell because it doesn't involve or stimulate the imagination. You don't create truth. Truth just is. A lie has to be created. Lies require imagination. Lying in itself is a creative process. This is why Liberals are so successful in the industry of make-believe because they live for the lie. Being creative is fun, and the truth doesn't lend itself much to the fun of being creative.

It's difficult to deliver truth. Jesus got killed for delivering the Truth and reminded the people that they killed the prophets before Him for telling the truth.

"O Jerusalem, Jerusalem, the city that kills the prophets and stones God's messengers! How often I have wanted to gather your children together as a hen protects her chicks beneath her wings, but you wouldn't let me. -Matthew 23:37 NLT

People want to imagine their own "truth". They want to be right in their own eyes or in the eyes of their peers before being righteous according to God. But Jesus Himself knew that the Truth was a hard thing to sell, so He reached some with the truth using creativity. He used stories to illustrate lessons. But when He recounted history and disclosed that He was the guy that was there when these events happened, that's when they wanted to kill Him. Telling the truth in engaging stories was a means of delivering truth. Telling the truth without a creative vehicle to deliver it tended to get a violent reaction. Being creative doesn't always work on everybody, but it more often connects with some, and that's better than none.

Lying is easy to sell because lying is a creative process. That's part of what makes it so entertaining. The truth is not imaginative, but the vehicle to deliver it with can be imaginative and creative. That's the thing too many Conservatives keep taking for granted.

Conservatives aren't really wired to be imaginative but rather wired to be practical. It's not really in the Conservative's chemical makeup. It's like there are certain elements to make up the color purple and colors that have to be left out. Looking at the spectrum, if we want purple we're going to have to leave out colors like yellow but include blue and red. To generally get a person who's wired to be a Conservative there's going to be certain attributes added to the formula and something left out or very little of it. Imagination is one of these things that's low in the formula.

Conservatives are more of the kind of people who see the republic for what it is, as opposed to the Liberal who sees it for what they want to imagine it to be: a democracy, and they want to force everybody else to live in their fantasy world of it. Conservatives are trying to fight to hold on to reality.

Living in America is supposed to be a good reality, but Democrats have always imagined another kind of America and have always tried to force us to live there. Take the Confederacy for example. Democrats imagined that blacks weren't really people and decided to make their own fairyland called the Confederacy where white privileged people could make believe blacks weren't really people and enslave them. The Abolitionist Republicans understood the reality that all men are created equal, and with Conservative interpretation of the U.S. Constitution they fought for the reality of what America is and what the American flag stands for; A republic that recognizes the God given rights of man, and those Republicans went to war with the Democrats and their fantasy that all men are not created equal and do not have God given rights. The Democrats imagined they should have a democracy so that they could vote away the rights of others despite the Supreme Law of the land.

Liberals and Democrats have a lot of imagination added to their make-up which is nice but it gets in the way of them seeing the reality of things. That's a really big problem when they don't know a good thing when they see it. America is a good thing and they don't see it. Democrats keep trying to change it. They are like their father, the Devil. Lucifer didn't know a good thing when he had it either. It doesn't get any better than being in Heaven with God. But Lucifer wanted to change it.

What makes America great is its foundation of being ruled by the law of God. America, of course, is not Heaven, because we're populated with a world of imperfect people, but we have the best foundation to be great because our rule of law is based on the law given by a perfect God.

Being Conservative with that law is the best chance to preserve liberty and for the people to thrive more. Being liberal with that law decays liberty and the people thrive less.

It's important that we don't let Democrats and their imagination of what they want America to be take over! Some conservatives are able to be creative and do have an affinity for art, there's just not much support for them. It drives me nuts when I hear Conservatives say things like they don't invest in creative media with a conservative slant because they don't foresee a return on their investment and don't see it as worth the risk.

Conservatives are afraid to take the financial risk to support such media while NFL teams are disrespecting the flag and the nation our military men and women are fighting, killing, and dying to protect. Soldiers are getting their chests opened up by IED's and conservatives here are too afraid to open their wallets. (Unless it's for a politician of course.)

Conservatives talk about supply and demand but are short on this, and the liberals dominate on it. Conservatives are just as much into instant gratification as liberals are while talking about long-term goals. Conservatives want to see immediate results, forgetting that we've been sinking in this mess for years and it may take years to get out.

Liberals are relentless and determined to drag us into their fantasy of how things should be. Conservatives talk about pulling themselves up by their bootstraps liberals do it all the time.

Liberals create, fail, create, fail, create, and fail but even their failures have an effect. They've promoted a failed worldview so much that it's become the demanded worldview of many! They keep at it until it sticks. They are stockpiled with propaganda to inundate the culture with - and indoctrinate them to be assimilated to the liberal idea.

And the conservatives have barely supported the development of a mere fireworks stand compared to the fortified ammo dump liberals have to bomb the culture with their ideology. The liberal depot includes the mirroring South-Paw strategy which takes on the applications of "The southern strategy and the party switch."

That crap actually works on people. I was telling people about the bigoted history of the democrat party before Hillary ran for president the first time. Rush Limbaugh and David Barton were telling people before that. Even Malcolm-X was warning people about the democrat party. Malcolm-X didn't like anybody! But he had an extra special disliking for Democrats, the founders of the KKK. Malcolm X was warning black folks about siding with Democrats before the so-called party switch. Why would blacks be siding with a party that was opposing civil rights?

You're not going to learn this in school because the school system is run by Democrats. Democrats don't want the people to know about this, and they have access to the kids that folks send them off to, to be influenced. Democrats use that time and trust to influence their students to be prejudiced against the Democrat's long-time enemy, the Republicans, making students believe it was really the Republicans who did all the evil the Democrats are actually guilty of.

We don't really have many Christian conservatives in the education system to get in the way of this, just like we don't have many conservatives in the arts and entertainment industry to get in the way of the creativity liberals use to influence the culture.

You can't just rely on talk-radio and news shows. There has to be more variety of delivery. Talk-radio and news shows have done an amazing job getting the message out there. If we could just go the extra mile and represent in music, TV, and Movies we could dial back a lot of lunacy in the culture. We'd still have some problems because we're imperfect, but it would be noticeably less.

Conservatives have to get a grip on the fact that the reason why they have such a hard time with the culture and with politicians losing their integrity is because public opinion has been influenced against conservatives as racists. Conservatives feel the frustration of being accused of being racist, but don't seem to feel the pain bad enough to say, *Ok, we need to counter this*. We can't avoid it. It's a social issue that the left will always bring up, and whoever says we need to avoid social issues needs to shut up.

The best way to help a Republican politician maintain their ability to rightly represent is to create illustrations to show the absurdity of race-baiting and how it's absurd that people are prejudiced against a party that was specifically founded to abolish slavery; the Republican party. The party that ended the Jim crow laws; the Republican party.

Race baiting propaganda through entertainment by the left goes virtually unchecked. Why for the Love of God aren't conservatives more supportive of taking out the left's main gun?

Under left-wing influence, liberal drones take to the streets and demand the removal of Confederate monuments. Why? Because these malcontents have been suckered into thinking they're striking back against racism. They don't realize that all they're doing is helping the Democrats hide their bigoted history.

Conservatives dropped the ball on this too. Conservatives be like, "It's about heritage and history! Don't take them down!" It doesn't make sense to keep saying, "It represents history and heritage", concerning Confederate artifacts. WHAT THE CRAP DOES THAT EVEN MEAN?! History and heritage of what?! It has to represent the history and heritage of something. It can't just be a symbol that means "heritage and history" That's extremely vague. Also, saying a symbol like the Confederate flag has nothing to do with racism is just an exercise in deep denial.

Let's look at the heritage and history of the Confederate Battle Flag, shall we? The Confederacy was represented by the Democrat party who wanted to keep slavery legal. They wanted to keep it legal so badly that they made their own Constitution of the Confederate States that included the pro-slavery language that the U.S. Constitution never had.

So don't try to tell me that the civil war had nothing to do with slavery. Even Karl Marx sent a letter to the Lincoln administration congratulating him on winning the war against slavery.

To continue. Note, the Confederate flag as Stars and Bars.

It was changed because it looked too much like the Stars and Stripes, so it became the Stainless Banner.

Why did the Democrats decide on the Stainless Banner? Because the white field represents the "Heaven ordained supremacy of the white man over the negro." However, it was changed because the Stainless Banner looked too much like a flag of surrender so it became the Blood Stained Banner.

Very typical of the Democrat party that's always changing its tune. That is definitely a heritage and history of the democrat party. And whether confused Confederate flag clinging republicans in denial want to believe that historical inspiration of William Tappan Thompson or not, they can't escape the democrat heritage and history of the Confederacy and their flag. You need only look at the hatred Democrats have for Republicans today to get an idea of the hatred Democrats had when Republicans terminated the democrat's false right to slavery.

Now you'll have those jumping in to correct me making sure that I know that the Confederate flag is not a national flag. It was the flag of Virginia or Tennessee or whatever. I get it, it's a battle flag. All the more reason why state buildings shouldn't fly it.

If it's a "Battle Flag", then that means you are saying your state is in a state of war against the very United States soil you're standing on. So I'm sorry guys, the Confederate flag is not a symbol of southern pride it's a symbol of democrat shame. If you vote Republican or conservative and you have any affection for the Confederate flag, you are seriously confused. You are waving a flag that was created by Democrats - who had murderous hatred for Republicans. You are waving the flag of a party who had total disregard for the rights of others and took liberties with their rights, the same way Democrats do today.

And don't give me some nonsense about me being brainwashed by the school system trying to make the south look bad. What? You mean the school system run by Democrats who hijacked the educational system so they could mask their own history and lay the blame on someone else? You think the democrats brainwashed me? No sir. They didn't get to me. They got to you.

I'm not the one waving around their flag. You are.

You're idolizing their monuments like Jefferson Davis and Robert E. Lee; Democrats. The reason why they want it removed is so THEY can remove the "heritage and history" of who THEY are, so they can continue to blame Republicans. They're obscuring history and making things disappear so people won't know it was the Democrats. AND YOU REPUBLICAN CONFEDERATE FLAG WAVERS ARE HELPING THEM! You're blinded by pride and it makes you unwitting accomplices of the democrat party to keep the racial strife going.

As it's said, "Pride comes before destruction."

Pride goes before destruction, a haughty spirit before a fall. - Proverbs 16:18 NIV

Because of that flag many of y'all are destroying the effort to expose the true history of the democrat party. And it keeps the culture deciding it's the Republicans who are racist. This can be fixed greatly if we can just get those few people to let go of that flag. And it's just a few, but that's all the Democrats need to make it look like it's all Republicans. That's why we're still dealing with all this race-baiting nonsense that's coming to a boil.

Do I agree with removing these artifacts? Not exactly, because this is an exercise in left-wing belligerence. They want to tear down everything and have chaos. They accuse America in general of slavery and racism just as much as they accuse confederacy. Their objective is to obscure the truth and promote denial about the democrat party – the party who continued to institute apartheid in America. They have to make it look like it was America in general. It wasn't. It was the Democrats.

Leave them to their course and they will come after the statue of Lincoln. They've set their sights on crosses, and Christ is the ultimate liberator so they hate Him the most! Jesus said they would hate us because they hated Him first.

"If the world hates you, understand that it hated Me first. - John 15:18 BSB

If you're going to defend these confederate artifacts, let me offer a suggestion. You should have insisted that it be left alone because they are of democrat heritage, and Americans should know it was the Democrats who represented the Confederacy. The Democrats took liberties with people's rights then, and they do it today. But the Democrats are trying to hide these things, like Hillary Clinton hiding emails.

Republicans and conservatives think that the Democrats have brainwashed Blacks, women, Hispanics, Jews and such, and that's pretty much correct. But the Democrats have brainwashed some Republicans and conservatives too. If you're waving around the flag of the party that wanted to kill you, and waving it with pride and affection, then you're brainwashed by Democrats too.

I get some of these people giving me some lame argument about how blacks fought in the Confederate army, like that's supposed to impress me. I guess they didn't notice that blacks are loyal to the democrat party today for you to see. They're loyal to their oppressors today for you to see. They are the biggest demographic for the abortion industry championed by Democrats today for you to see. They are loyal to the party that denied them civil rights and voting rights. What the hell makes any of you think I would be impressed by blacks being in the democrat represented confederate army?

You might have noticed that the Democrats use blacks against the Republican Party today for you to see. Well, news flash. The Democrats used blacks against Republicans during the civil war too. As it is today so it was yesterday. There were blacks that were also coerced into the Confederate army. Some injured themselves and tried to get captured by the republican represented union army. That was their ticket out of the Confederacy.

Or how about the argument that says that "Slavery was done under the Stars and Stripes too." They leave out the part of slavery being abolished under the Stars and Stripes too, while the Confederate flag was flown in battle to keep it legal. The KKK paraded the cross too as well as the Stars and Stripes. The cross has nothing to do with slavery. Jesus went to the cross to eternally liberate us. The American flag represents this republic where the rights of man are recognized as God-given. People taking these items and distorting them for their personal ideals is not the fault of the Cross or the Stars and Stripes. The CBF However, was founded to fight for the so-called right to deprive others of their God-given rights. That is the heritage of that flag, and you have people trying to distort its history to exalt that flag as a noble symbol all in the name of pride.

If you're whining over the removal of the statues of Democrats who went to war against America, you're brainwashed. You think I've been misinformed about the Confederacy. Who did you learn about the Confederacy from? Did you learn about the Confederacy from genuine confederates? Well, those genuine confederates telling you their rosy version of the Confederacy that you want to hear were Democrats. Of course, they're going to try to make their cause sound noble! If you're a Democrat and you want to believe those musings that's fine, I guess, but if you're a Republican and you're into this embellishment of confederate nobility journaled by the Democrats who created the confederacy then that's just plain sad.

It's like blacks that believe the parties switched sides. In order for them to say that, they have to concede that the Democrats were the party of bigotry in the first place, right? But that's their big argument;

The parties switched sides. So blacks unwittingly concede that the Democrats founded the Confederacy, the KKK, authored Jim crow, and imposed apartheid to keep the black man down, yet the majority of blacks believe these evil democrats when they tell them they've switched sides? And to this I also say, that's just plain sad.

I do not at all have a problem with the South. I dig the South. I dig southern folks! The war wasn't really about North and South. It's just more convenient to call it that. The war was between pro-slavery Democrats and abolitionist Republicans. But that's part of that switched up South-Paw Strategy; switching it up to make it look like Republicans have been the racist when it has always been the Democrats. Republicans may have switched off, but Republicans haven't switched sides.

Democrats insist that there was this party switch. If that were true they would have to show this exchange. They would have to show that there was an exchange of Republicans that became Democrats. Where are they? Where are all these Republicans who switched over to become democrats? Democrats can hardly even point to any Democrats who left the Democrat party to become Republicans. But in their fantasy world, all they need to prove that there was this big party switch was Strom Thurman. That's about all the proof they need that all the Dixiecrats became Republicans. This, of course, is false as I've explained in my previous book Weapon of A.S.S. Destruction (American Socialist States) that I published back in January 2012 and in videos I've been doing since 2007.

They even ignore that the Dixiecrats said, *They'd rather vote for a yellow dog than to vote for a Republican.* This is racist against yellow dogs by the way.

Intending to lean on the party switch the liberals expose more of their hypocrisy. Democrats cursed Storm Thurman who was a Democrat, (the party of Jim Crow), only after he became a Republican. It was ok for him to be a bigot while he was a Democrat, but when he abandoned his bigoted ideas and became a Republican that is when he somehow became evil.

For a Democrat, as long as you do evil as a democrat it's pretty much ok. If you change your thinking and leave the democrat party then all the evil it was ok for you to do as a Democrat will somehow become retroactively evil when you change your ideas on those evils and leave the democrat party. Weird right?

Look at Robert Byrd; Grand Kleagle and Exalted Cyclops in the KKK. The Democrats never gave him any grief. Bill Clinton did his Eulogy. Bill Clinton tried to be dismissive of Robert Byrd being in the KKK. Bill Clinton said Robert Bird just had a fleeting association with the KKK. (Having the titles of Grand Kleagle and Exalted Cyclops and a recruitment officer isn't a fleeting association by the way.)

During the eulogy for Robert Byrd, Bill Clinton said Byrd was a member of the KKK only because he was trying to get elected. Bill Clinton slipped the truth about the democrat party; *Say or do anything except the right thing to get elected,* even belong to a terrorist organization that blew up churches just because blacks were attending there. On a side note, to those who say the KKK are Christians. What kind of a Christian blows up a church? Answer. No kind. The KKK aren't Christian at all. We'll talk more about this in Chapter III

But despite that, Nobody in the Democrat Party judged Robert. His evil was invisible to the left as long as he was a Democrat. His apology for his association with the KKK would have been ignored had he reformed his views on race and become a Republican. His apology and repentance would not be accepted. He would only be seen as evil by the left.

We can further prove this with David Duke. David Duke has been a grand wizard with the KKK and was a Democrat during and after. He's been a Democrat longer than the republican he has claimed to be. But if David Duke were to have remained a democrat he would have had the same effect as Robert Byrd. His KKK Career would have been overlooked. He was just too lame even for Democrats to get their votes. He didn't adapt to the democrats pander method to control blacks.

Republicans don't want David Duke. Reagan refused to endorse David Duke when David Duke sought office posing as a Republican. But Democrats wouldn't have much to say about David Duke had he remained a Democrat. It's only because he tries to identify as a

Republican that they've got issues with him. And if Democrats can't get away with trying to overlook bigotry in their party they'll just try to delete you all together. That's why they're demanding the confederate artifacts be removed from public view so people won't find out that the Democrats are the ones who established these things in the first place.

Democrats should not have been able to associate David Duke with Republicans at all had republicans struck their flag in the cultural sand and showed zero tolerance for the Confederate flag in our tent, and also should have been more supportive with cultural representation. But conservatives put way to much stock in political representation. (While saying the government is the problem and not the answer.)

If Conservative Republicans would do things like this, People like David Duke and this so-called alt-right nonsense would have been as fleeting as a food-ghost on a gusty day.

If we supported illustrations in the culture of how absurd the liberal worldview is it would greatly minimize Liberals being able to associate capitalistic republicans with socialistic nazis. Or associating Israeli supporting Republicans with Jew-hating Nazis and DemoKKKrats. Or associating Christian Conservative Republicans who generally accept Jesus as the only, Way with Nazis that were occultists, and Democrats who believe all religions can get you to whatever afterlife you want.

We republicans don't have anything in common with NAZIs or the KKK. Democrats do.

I pray that people on the right get more supportive of the production of illustrations and media to counter this slander and show how absurd it is. We should not be where we are with all this tension, but what should we expect? All the people hear is what liberals tell them in music, TV, movies, Concerts, Sports etc. Where are we supplying the other side in mediums to engage their views with?

The Left shouldn't be able to pull these switcheroos. We should have counter-punching content that sends them stumbling right back to their corner. When they try to pull that South-Paw stance to put us in the mirror with, like the southern strategy myth and make it look like the Republicans somehow took on the bigoted stance, we should have productions out there to show how absurd that is.

We should have well-produced media that shows that the only real southern strategy that really worked was the Declaration of the Democrat president Lyndon B. Johnson who said I'll have those N-words voting democrat for the next 200 years. It's been almost 50 years to date since he's been president, and the majority of black folks still vote democrat. LBJ knew that by him being president the Democrats would get the credit for the civil rights act that the Republicans actually championed.

Liberals deny LBJ Said this. I reckon it's just a coincidence that the majority of blacks still vote democrat. No surprise. Liberals are in denial about a lot of things, and we should have media that lampoons their denial, or dramatizations of how tragic and sick their denial is!

They should be way too embarrassed to even think about believing some southern strategy nonsense with Barry Goldwater. We should have been pushing content to dispel that myth a long time ago. But people keep bringing it up because that's what's promoted in the culture with very little challenge.

They believe the southern strategy caused the mass movement of Democrats to become Republicans, while overlooking that if that were true, shouldn't Goldwater have won?

Barry Goldwater was more of a Libertarian than conservative, and a lot of people calling themselves conservatives today screw it up for the rest of us by exalting Barry Goldwater as a conservative. These Goldwater types put too much of a premium on state's rights. A state does not have the right to infringe on the rights of another person's rights protected by the supreme law of the land. But to the Goldwater types, it should be up to the states to decide how they're going to treat people and that the states should have the sovereignty to make whatever rules they want, and assume they have the moral virtue to do so while insisting that you can't legislate morality.

And that kind of state's rights zealotry has people saying stupid stuff like, "Slavery wasn't as brutal as people try to make it out to be, and that it would have just faded out in time." Anybody who says this, with all due respect... Screw you! You don't think people can be that cruel? If you could pull your head out of your smug condescending corn-hole you'd get a pretty good idea of how cruel people can be to each other today. How about shooting up little girls and boys with heroin to get them to be "willing" to get raped? Oh, and I don't see any signs of human trafficking fading out. And it's mainly the Libertarians who make this despicable argument concerning slavery that Republicans feel like they have to cozy up to. These republicans are a disgrace to the party's founding and are sell-outs. No wonder people think Republicans are racist.

Yeah, let's see anybody who thinks that slavery would have just faded out handle getting beaten bloody and broken, and them be ok with just waiting for slavery to fade out. No, I think a little taste of that would have them begging for a war to free them too.

If slavery just "fades" out, how could we have slavery today if slavery has been going on for thousands of years? Slavery doesn't just fade away, and forced slavery is brutal. If slavery fades away, slavery should have faded away long before now, since the time the Hebrews were in Egypt with a Pharaoh who brutally committed infanticide against the Hebrew children. God, Himself didn't wait for slavery to just "fade away". He went to war with Egypt and ended their enslavement of the Hebrews.

So this point about "slavery wasn't really that brutal and that it would have eventually faded out without a war" is garbage. It's a cowardly and disgusting insult to every child that is getting sold to be raped right now, but freedom will come slow for them because of this stupid idea that "it will just fade away."

Since Democrats have always wanted the state's right to deny blacks of constitutional rights the Goldwater stance attracted some of them. Goldwater's interest wasn't in making blacks second-class citizens. He was a member of the NAACP. (National Association for Advancement of Confused People.) I just give Goldwater the benefit of the doubt that he meant well despite the distorted direction of the NAACP. Plus, he was just really naive in thinking that these issues were state issues. He seems to have forgotten that there was a bunch of states that wanted to separate from the union so they could keep slavery legal or disregard black's constitutional rights. When you have a state telling the federal government to keep its nose out of their business you can be pretty certain it's because that state wants to intrude on another person's constitutional rights. An example would be pro-abortionist. They hate the idea of federal government interference because they want to be left alone to deprive another person of their rights. But wants the state involved to make others pay for their choice.

Barry Goldwater was so zealous about state's rights that he didn't consider what Democrats have done with state's rights and what they would do.

I'm pro-state's rights too, but that doesn't mean I'm pro-state's so-called right to ignore the supreme law of the land that protects the God-given rights of others. When the people of a state does that, that is when the federal government is supposed to get involved; to protect the rights of persons that a state is trying to take the liberty to deprive persons of.

Again, if the southern strategy was such a big deal, and brought over all these Democrats to become republicans we would have had a president Goldwater. Plus it wouldn't have been worth it for bigoted democrats who had belligerent hatred for Republicans to become Republicans. It's weird that Democrats can believe that Democrats could do that, but they can't believe that Muslim terrorist would pose as refugees.

We can prove that there was no big move from Democrats to Republicans so they could get bigoted policies put in. Because when those states were democrat run states those states had bigoted policies put in place to facilitate white privilege. Democrats who abandoned their bigotry became republicans, yes, that's true, and the bigoted apartheid policies of the Democrats came to an end, and those states became republican.

You can believe there was a southern strategy if you want, but the fact is if a Democrat moved to the Republican side they didn't bring their bigoted ideals with them. They abandoned them and did not want to be a democrat anymore because Democrats are the party of racism. They became Republican to be rid of their former bigoted ideals. These are the only people liberals can only be talking about who switched. Some switched for Goldwater but not most. They switched to be rid of racism, that's proven by the fact that there was enough demand represented by Republicans to end institutionalized racism and keep it that way.

Further proof is in that liberals cannot point to anything Republicans have done that even comes close to the evil policies that Democrats imposed over blacks. Nothing.

If all these democrats came into the Republican party adhering to their bigotry then how come the republican party didn't carry on with lynchings, trying to deny blacks of 2nd amendment rights, shooting blacks down, segregating blacks etc. Those things weren't taken over by the Republicans.

Yet in democrat run communities blacks get shot down all the time (by each other), Just like Democrats have always wanted. In the liberal education system, Blacks love to separate themselves into their Afrocentric groups away from white people, just like the democrats always wanted. Republicans don't want these things. Democrats do.

But the Democrats succeed with the South-Paw stance. Their constant assertion of the "southern strategy" is a strategy of South-Paw mirroring so that people will see the evil that Democrats did reflected in Republicans.

Democrats hate being told the truth about themselves. Sometimes the truth breaks through to them when they hear it. Imagine how much more effective it would be if we added showing them the truth too. Put it in well-produced teleplays, and movies, and catchy songs. That's what they've done. That's how they've done so much damage. Why don't we do the same so we can get some cultural repairs going? How about we train up to counter the south-paw strategy?

We've countered with some good punches when liberals try to use the party switch cop-out, but there has to be follow-through. Liberals quickly recover when that talking point gets knocked out of their mouth. They're quickly given a new mouth-piece and start swinging with the "ideological switch" talking point. Somehow Republicans were the liberals and the Democrats were the conservatives. To quote Frau Farbissina, "LIES!!! ALL LIES!!!

We've already gone over what liberalism leads to and how it has always been the right fit for Democrats who are liberal with how they'll view the Bible, the Constitution, liberal with their power over people, liberal with other people's rights, liberal with taxing, liberal with imposing fees, liberal with borrowing, liberal with spending, liberal with all things that lead to poverty, strife, oppression and murder.

Republicans were founded to be conservative. Conservative reading of the U.S. Constitution meant that the self-evident truth - heading our Declaration of Independence - that all men are created equal is stipulated to be protected of all, according to the U.S. Constitution. The only way to conclude that it doesn't include all people, respective to our nation, is to view it liberally.

White Privilege came about by being liberal with the constitution; fabricating ideas that aren't in the constitution to make white people more comfortable at the forced expense of another race. That is what the Democrats fought to maintain; that liberal interpretation of the Constitution and making up some phantom right. That's the legacy of Democrats. They have never been conservative! If what I'm saying doesn't fly with ya, let's see what Abraham Lincoln has to say about Democrats being called "conservatives".

> *"But you say you [Democrats] are conservative — eminently conservative — while we [Republicans] are revolutionary, destructive, or something of the sort. What is conservatism? Is it not adherence to the old and tried, against the new and untried? We stick to, contend for, the identical old policy, on the point of controversy, which was adopted by our fathers who framed the Government under which we live ; while you, with one accord, reject, and scout, and spit upon that old policy, and insist upon substituting something new. True, you disagree among yourselves as to what that substitute shall be. You have considerable variety of new propositions and plans, but you are unanimous in rejecting and denouncing the old policy of the fathers".*

pp. 402, 403 The Anectdotal Lincoln

That is from Lincoln, the patriarch of the Republican Party, nuking the stupid ideological switch myth from orbit from 150 years back. He's prophesying from 150 years ago about the same liberal crap Democrats are doing today; rejecting the constitution. The Republican Party was founded to adhere to the old policy that was founded to respect the God-given rights of all men. So no, the Republican Party was not founded on "classical liberalism", but to be conservative so as to not take liberties with The God-given rights of man. The Grand Old Party was meant to be the party of adhering to the old policy of our forefathers who agreed that we are endowed by our Creator with certain inalienable rights.

Abraham Lincoln was at the core of the founding of the Republican party. I'm gonna give him a little bit of the benefit of the doubt that he might have known what he was talking about. He knew that Democrats had no business trying to call themselves conservatives. They weren't. They were a party with perverse ideas concerning the Constitution and people's rights. Just like Democrats do today. It has never been correct to consider democrats conservative. Do NOT let liberals try to tell you that the Democrats were the conservatives back then and the Republicans were the liberals. Lincoln is flat out telling us that the Republican party was founded on conservatism to preserve those old ideas of the founding fathers; to adhere, stick to, and contend for the preservation of liberty for all! That is being radical! That is rooted and grounded! That is what Lincoln was rooted in, and the Republican Party was considered controversial for it.

Lincoln was a Whig, but even Lincoln knew that the classical liberalism that had come down from the Whigs of earlier didn't live up to its pursuit of liberty. Conservatism; adhering to the liberating Word of God, and abiding by those God-given rights acknowledged in the U.S. Constitution - That was Lincoln's *jam*. Again, when libs try to say the ideologies switched sides, you can tell them that's a bunch of donkey doo-doo.

Then you have those who try to discredit Lincoln and say he didn't care about freeing the slaves, blah, blah, blah. "LIES! ALL LIES!" Thank you, Frau. What's sad is that it's not even the Democrats who really push this. It's usually Libertarians and republican voting neo-confederates who try to stigmatize Lincoln. They're saboteurs to Republicans, and for some reason Republicans feel like we have to ally with them even though Libertarians and Neo-confederates are a lot of the reason why people think Republicans are racist.

Lincoln haters try to grab quotes from Lincoln to push this idea that he didn't care about freeing slaves, while at the same time they insist that the war didn't have anything to do with ending slavery. I see. They can find a whole bunch of quotes about Lincoln concerning slavery... But the war had nothing to do with slavery... Ok. The genius of Lincoln goes over the heads of these people. Lincoln didn't rely on his own boasting to promote the abolition of slavery. HE MANIPULATED HIS OPPONENTS INTO DOING IT FOR HIM!!!

Lincoln had already made it clear that he hated slavery with a passion. But Lincoln knew that wouldn't cut it, so Lincoln started playing dumb, contradictory and abstract, and it drove his opponents nuttier than they already were! Stephen Douglas talked about dragging it out of Lincoln! Stephen Douglas was Lincoln's puppet! Lincoln would trigger Douglas, debate after debate. Stephen Douglas would get frustrated and unwittingly make the case for Lincoln; that Lincoln's objective was to abolish slavery. Lincoln would be like, "Who, me? Abolish slavery? P'shaw! Y'all can do whatever you want in your states! You can retain the power to do it, oooooorrrrrr not to." That's some of the types of vague things Lincoln would say that would get the Democrats all twisty-britches! They would call him out on it! "But you said this, and you said that! We know that your objective is abolition!" Lincoln would say things like, "I don't intend to change anything about slavery where it already exists according to the constitution." (The constitution doesn't even mention the word slavery, by the way.) It is legal to bind a person to servitude after due process of law and the convicted has to do their term of service if they have been sentenced to it, but according to the Constitution, you cannot deprive a person of liberty without due process. Thus, Lincoln could make the claim that he had no intention to change the institutions of slavery where it already existed, as the Constitution did not give the power to do so. Lincoln was hedging on a moot assertion.

If the institutions of servitude square with the Constitution, as in bondservant or, a term of service for a criminal offense then that's the kind of slavery Lincoln wouldn't mess with, and he meant it. But he knew that's not what the Democrats were doing. They were forcing people into slavery. Lincoln knew it, and they knew Lincoln knew it, and were scared that he would lead a charge to put an end to it.

Read the Anecdotal Lincoln or the Lincoln / Douglas debates with what I've suggested. I think you'll see it too! Frederick Douglass was even worried that Lincoln was throwing the cause under the bus, but ultimately saw Lincoln as legit! Lincoln had the Democrats scared out of their skulls that he was going to put an end to slavery before he was even president. He manipulated the Democrat represented confederacy into giving priceless testimony that he was the presidential choice for those wanting slavery done with. That is a well-executed strategy for campaign ads!

So, why listen to the Lincoln haters of today who try stigmatize Lincoln as a person who didn't care about freeing the slaves? These people are screwing things up for Republicans and for race relations. You need only look at the writings of Lincoln's contemporary opponents. General McClellan for example accused Lincoln of sacrificing white lives for black freedom. McClellan was a democrat but he was also Lincoln's general and hated Lincoln for waging a war to abolish slavery. Don't take no South-Paw shots.

CHAPTER III
CAN'T HIT WHAT YOU CAN'T SEE.

You can't hit what you can't see, or in my case, you can't click what you can't see, and the liberal internet overlords make sure that it is very difficult for people to see me, as well as some other conservative content creators. It's part of their strategy. They have so much leverage on mediums for broadcast, from TV to internet, they can fade people out; make them virtually invisible. And we call liberals stupid. These people are evil geniuses. Selfishness and hate can make people very, very creative. They use that evil driven creativity to get the state into your pocket, allow more illegal immigration, force us to abide by people's gender delusions, and so on. We think our intellect is what's going to stop them. It hasn't. The word of God tells us to lean not on our own understanding, but trust in God. Proverbs 3:5 In other words, In God we trust. Remember?

Too many conservatives think it's going to be their intellect and common sense that's going to beat these liberals back. RAWNG! Liberalism is spreading. The left claims to be progressive. Let them claim that, because they're progressive like cancer. That doesn't mean we're not supposed to use intellect because The Lord told us to Love the Lord your God with all your heart, and with all your soul and with all your **mind,** and with all your strength.' Matthew 12:30. So we're supposed to become stronger in the intellect God gives us.

It's more than just intellect. It takes being able to deliver it. Do you think Donald Trump won by displaying amazing feats of intellectual arguments? I'm not saying he's not capable of it. I'm just saying he relied on an effective vehicle to resonate with the people that got him the votes. (And no it wasn't the Russians. That's being proven to be Hillary.)

It's so weird that Republicans clearly understand that no matter how awesome a weapon can be it doesn't mean squat if you can't deliver it. But they just don't seem to make that connection when it comes to the culture and the importance of being able to deliver the conservative idea.

The intellect of conservatives gets in the way of liberalism to a nominal degree, yes, and our intellect should be applied of course! The problem is the pride in the intellect, as opposed to the gratitude to the One who gives it. On top of that if conservatives would support and nurture some God-given creativity to go along with that God-given intellect we would be radiant!

We would be the radiation therapy to help beat back the progressive cancer of liberalism! But too often we trust in our intellect more than God. We pay lip service to our belief in God, but we pride ourselves in our intellect more than giving credit to the All Mighty who armed us with it so we can protect what He's blessed us with.

It's sad that the proverbial call to Trust in God is printed on the articles that would be circulated the most to keep us mindful of it, is somehow overlooked; our currency. We exchange these notes every day that say, "In God we trust.", but still it's people pridefully trusting more in their intellect than giving thanks to God for it, and not trusting in His counsel on how to aim that arrow, swing that sword of truth, and fire those Gospel loaded guns to defend what He's blessed us with from the legion of liars who are trying to rip this republic apart.

As I mentioned earlier, most conservatives aren't typically wired to be artistic or imaginative or creative per say. It's not part of the conservative formula that constitutes their disposition. Reality, practicality, and logic are at the core of the conservative personality matrix. But there are some exceptions - those who are a bit of both; practical yet artistic, logical, yet imaginative. Support these people!!! These people are your cultural infiltrators! Yes, I'm one of those people! Yes. I admit, when I say support, I am including myself!

There are others that I do know of, but they're so greedy for the spotlight that they can't stand the idea of working with other conservatives. I've seen it. Others have seen it too. They want to be seen as the pioneers who are blazing the trail. They don't like to involve other conservatives because they don't want anyone stealing their thunder. Unfortunately, there is so much backbiting egotistical rivalry with conservatives in media, it's disgusting. Conservatives in media practically compete with each other as much as they do with liberals. It's shameful how much conservatives in media cut each other down and blow each other off. And practically each one of them thinks they're the high priest or priestess of conservatism, and if I say that, I have to include myself. I don't think I am, but I may be perceived as having that attitude, and if I do, I'm sorry. I do not mean to be some self-exalting conservative. I pray for the Lord's correction if that be true.

Most conservatives in media can't stand each other. They think very little of each other while expecting each other to walk on water, and if they did walk on water they would hate them for that too. To their credit, if you're lucky, they will like you up front! Show any iniquity though, and you're an idiot to them.

I've seen conservatives only be nice enough, long enough to another conservative to get to where they wanted to get to. When they've gotten there they act like they never knew you or barely give you the time of day. Or they can be very cliquish and if the higher-ups on that social ladder don't approve of someone and you want to stay in the good graces of that clique you will have to disassociate yourself with that person you used to be acquainted with.

But this plays into the liberal's strategy of invisibility. Conservatives practically help liberals make us invisible. Conservatives hardly promote each other to help get the message in front of people. Conservatives act like every conservative has to walk on water and drown each other in the water walking test, while at the same time will go gaga over a celebrity who steps away from the liberal herd a little bit and give them all the promotion they want.

To a degree, I encourage this because it's good that conservatives show that we are welcoming and that we are happy to see people "get it!" We should be open armed and let artists know that they will still have a population who will appreciate them when the leftists curse them for stepping out of the herd.

A lot of artists are too scared to go against leftist groupthink because they feel like they won't have anywhere to go or that nobody will have their back. The fear is legit. Pretty much all my so-called friends went ghost.

I see a lot of conservatives say things like "If the liberals want to spark a civil war, Bring It On!" Meanwhile, a lot of these "conservatives" are too afraid to share conservative content because some liberal might troll them or a friend might de-friend them on Facebook. I have too often had conservatives tell me that they don't share my videos because they don't want the reaction it gets from rabid liberals. If we had Republicans in the 1860's like we have today we would have lost the civil war.

Conservatives in Hollywood? There's some I suppose. But to the right of center types in Hollywood they just get together in their speakeasy and lament about the political climate, but hardly pull their resources together to fight back in the industry to help counter the corrosive content cranked out by commie leftists. No. They're too afraid to be outed. They don't want to miss the opportunity to get cast or contracted with some leftist's production. They don't want to post my videos because they don't want to be outed. I've received emails on this.

Again this is why artists don't come out. Because they have a legitimate fear that nobody is going to have their six. I'm a bit of that proof. Conservatives getting together in some secret circle ain't gonna cut it. Why? Because it was a secret circle that even the people who were in it couldn't keep their mouth zipped about. Their ego got in the way and they couldn't help but talk outside of the group about this group they weren't supposed to talk about. They came in saying, "I love America, here's my script! Yaayy! The *I love America* password worked! Point me to the first celebrity I can schmooze with."

Out of ignorance, I even mentioned this group publicly because I didn't understand that it was supposed to be secret. I didn't even understand why I was even asked to be in it. Just grateful. I didn't have industry credentials. I'm not SAG or AFTRA etc. I was just a dude making YouTube vids. If the group was such a big secret why would it involve me? So it didn't register with me that it was supposed to be a "secret" or even exclusive if it included me. So on my website where I include some reviews and testimonies concerning my work I included the group as an organization that had recognized my work. It was up there briefly until I got a notification asking me to take it down because the group isn't supposed to be publicized. Understanding that, I respectfully took it down immediately. Meanwhile, I'd see people on FOX news talking about it. Maybe they thought it was ridiculous for it to be a secret group, or maybe they wanted to be the first to say they knew something about it, or wanted to show that they were in the know about this group. Like I said. Ego. Or maybe some were like me and it just didn't register that it was supposed to be on the DL.

I love the reason why the group was founded. But I'm saddened that it became more of a group of some pseudo-secret group of "Conservatives" that really don't pull their resources together to combat the left in the culture. They just have a bunch of get-togethers and complain. But the group was still not supposed to be public, and it was supposed to be an uplifting fellowship. Friends strengthening each other and a byproduct of those friendships should have bloomed into projects! Unfortunately, some people couldn't respect that and had to brag out loud that they were in it. Why? Because too many were in it for themselves, not to fellowship, not to help preserve our republic, but to satisfy their need to need to groan and to say they're in a group populated with people in the entertainment industry. Am I wrong? How many projects have you heard of that are promoting a right angle? Not a lot. Guess I shouldn't wonder why I don't have a lot of friends!

Many of the people who were in it weren't even conservative. They were liberals that hated taxes. Or just had more of an adolescent attitude of "I don't need the government telling me what to do" and based on that they were issued a conservative card. But they could be, Pro-abortion, pro-gay marriage, pro-legalization of drugs, reject God in our constitution, and still get the conservative pass, because after all, "We should be a big tent."

A tent made up of the aforementioned fragile frame of ideals will collapse. It may be a big tent but it's not a conservative tent by any means and that defeats the whole purpose.

Don't get me wrong! I loved the idea of the group! I think it was much needed, and I'm grateful for it! I just don't like what happened, and more than that I don't like what didn't happen. It's tragic that more projects didn't come from it out of creative fellowship, and that there wasn't more supportive fellowship.

To the credit of some, there are those who did attempt to pull talent together and do productions, but not with genuine support from the rest. (That could get them outed.)

Things like this help the Liberal media overlords with their strategy of invisibility. You can't promote what you can't see.

I make videos calling out Democrats for what they are, but they, of course, want to keep them invisible to people so they won't catch on. Like this commentary I published a while back:

Democrats do not want you to see this because it shines a light on who they are like an ugly girl in the club dependent on it being dark, and dudes being too drunk to care. This goes to the strategy of invisibility. There's the strategy of Democrats making their opponents invisible so their message can't connect with the culture, and there's the strategy of the Democrats being invisible so the culture doesn't know that the Democrats are the culprits driving what keeps the culture so bitter.

One cloak of invisibility for the Democrats is masquerading as Christians. (Reflect on 2 Corinthians 11:14-15)

They like to create some sugar-coated version of Jesus that justifies, accepts, or encourages their desires to sin against others. They fool the people into thinking that they are righteous according to Jesus. Here's the problem; they try to use Jesus as a righteous person that they can use as an authority figure to validate what they think is right, then turn around and say that Christianity is just as bad as any other religion because organizations like the KKK are Christian. See how contradicting they are?

Democrats make themselves invisible by hiding behind a cloak of counterfeit Christianity, and for added measure, they add a cloak of political correctness by saying Christianity is just as evil as any other religion, that way they look fair, politically correct, and not judgmental, which is the blinding effect of PC pandering.

I want to address this silly idea that the KKK is a Christian fraternity for the Democrats who try to use that angle to stigmatize the right. The KKK are confused not Christian.

First, let's examine the confusion of the new KKK and the confusion of those who think they're right-wingers. American right-wingers are capitalists. The new KKK includes the swastika in their insignia. The NAZI's were socialist. This contradicts skinheads and KKK as right-wing capitalists. Also, NAZI's aren't Christian and neither are the KKK, because they have a special kind of hatred for Jewish people, and ya can't be a Christian and hate Jewish people when the Very Lord and King of our salvation is Jewish. So no. Nazis and the KKK are not Christian.

Also, examine the ranks of the KKK. Grand wizard. What kind of a Christian organization bestows the title of a warlock to their executives? A wizard or warlock relies upon powers not given to him by God. A warlock is submitted to demons, not God. What does a wizard have to do with God? Wizards challenged Moses and Aaron. Being a wizard ain't Godly. What are they Grand Wizards at, anyway? Spelling? Solving a Rubik's Cube? Are they pinball wizards? For what reason do these KKKooks call themselves a wizard? It ain't for no biblical reason.

The Democrats created the KKK and give their highest official the title of Grand Wizard, which is synonymous with a warlock, and warlock means "Oath Breaker".

But many democrat voters don't see the promises that the Democrats keep breaking on them do they? No. Because Democrats keep them busy by blaming Republicans, Republicans who democrat voters never elected to do anything in their community in the first place.

The highest order of business for the democrat party is to break their oath with you. They Sucker you with their promises, disappear with the power you gave them, and oppress you behind the cloak of pandering. Do ya see the connection?

People fall for the promises that the Democrats make to keep them as loyal voter stock.

For what biblical Christian reason would you call yourself a Grand Dragon? The dragon in the Bible is the devil. All this suits the Democrats who created the KKK just fine, as they are the party of deception. They are the party of slander. They are the party of violence and terror tactics. That hasn't changed. This is one of the reasons why Democrats keep trying to push the propaganda that the NRA is a terrorist group; to distract people from recognizing the Democrats as the actual party of terrorism.

Quick note: BLM and ANTIFa are just the new incarnations of the belligerent tactics to press the policies of the Democrat Party. They have not changed.

Continuing with the KKK. What kind of a Christian organization needs the title of Exalted Cyclops? What kind of a Christian organization needs the title of Grand Titan, and a Council of Centaurs and Hydras? None, because these aren't Christians at all. They're a bunch of pagans.

People have been trying to stigmatize Christians for the KKK when Christianity has nothing to do with the KKK. Their Fraternity is structured on paganism, and just makes references to Biblical scripture. And big deal if they refer to the Bible or have meetings in churches. The Devil makes references to Biblical scripture too. It doesn't make Him a Christian. Also, the Devil attends church more than most "Christians". The Devil was in the garden of God. You don't think he can hold meetings in church too?

Democrats hold meetings in church, while being the very party that didn't want God in their platform. They took God out. Then there was a motion to put God back in, and it was rejected. Why was God taken out in the first place? And the only reason why Democrats would want to put God back into the language of their platform is so they could take the Lord's name in vain to invoke Him as the authority that justifies the evil policies they want instituted.

Are you not seeing them follow in the same pattern as their patriarch's namesake, Satan, the Accuser?

The Democrats point their finger and accuse others of the very evil they themselves do. Which takes the focus off of them and makes their evil deeds invisible. Many don't see the policies of the Democrats, and how they have broken the family, and how they have waged genocide on the black population. Much of the people don't see what the Democrats do.

They don't see how the neighborhoods the Democrats control have the highest crime rates, the highest suicide rates, the highest addiction rates, etc. Many don't see that they control these areas because they fall for them accusing someone else, which makes them invisible.

The low info voters, as I've heard them called, don't see it that Democrats run the cities with the most unemployment. They don't see it that they're the ones where blacks have the highest incarceration rates. For those of you who swear on the prison industrial complex, look to the Democrats who fought to keep slavery legal in the first place, You don't see what the Democrats are doing who created the KKK.

And again they don't want you to see these commentaries I've been making where I've said this for years.

Liberal voter drones don't see these things. They're in denial about these things, which all makes their evil invisible to themselves. This is why folks don't see that there is a reason why the democrat created KKK calls themselves the Invisible Empire. Can't hit what you can't see. There are still so many angry people out there. They don't know who to be angry at.

The Democrats are like a cartoon character that dives into some vanishing cream to become invisible and torments another character while making the tormented character think it was someone else.

Democrats hide commentaries I make about them pointing this out. They don't want people to know why they're the invisible empire. This is crucial. This is how Democrats have been able to get away with what they've been able to get away with for so long. They use methods of pandering, slander, race-baiting, class-baiting, sexism, political correctness, etc. to make themselves invisible, leaving people to believe that the ones who are to blame are the ones they can see. Republicans.

The invisible empire of the Democrats can count on conservatives helping them to stay invisible because too often people on the right angle of the media are too egotistical to promote each other. They want other conservatives to be as invisible as the Democrats do so they can be seen as the unique brave lone warrior, or group with their own clique so they can corner the market as the conservative voice in media. That competitiveness would be fine if it were any other product or service, but our republic is at stake. Conservatives can't afford to be pawns for the invisibility strategy of the Democrats; Democrats who make themselves invisible so people can't see them do evil, and the Democrats who make their opponents invisible so people can't get their message.

Some say, *Zo You're just sour because you're being shunned and you don't belong to a clique.* Nope. I'm not a cliquish kinda guy. I do admit that I feel brushed off, taken for granted and forgotten, and made invisible. I get kinds sick of people sending me videos of people saying things that I was saying years ago. I'm like, y'all send me these people's videos, but do you send them my videos? I hardly ever see anybody tag me in a video they sent to a person who made a video that they sent to me. I've subscribed to their channels followed them on youtube, shared their vids, mentioned them in my vids. Do they do the same? No.

I've even met some of these people in person, and even when I approached them to say hello, they blew me off. This isn't me boo-hooing about them not wanting to be acquainted with me. What troubles me is the question of how can we preserve these United States when we're not in a united state? The Democrats use that to make us invisible. As cutthroat as Democrats are, they are united in hate, while conservatives are divided by rivalry. I'm not seen as a compatriot by many but instead competition. I'm not among those that they see as a benefit for them to connect with. I'm more of a liability in the promotion of their brand than an asset, because I would subtract from their image of being the new thinkers appointed to awaken others to this new "#WalkAway" way of thinking. I #WalkedAway long before it was cool, like many others in CL Bryant's movie, Runaway Slave, for example.

Admittedly I don't share a lot of people's vids. Not because I worry about another conservative getting my light or anything, but because I don't want to promote these content creators relying on language that the left does. People already say they can't see the difference between the left and the right. Why would we use the same language as them? If there's cursing and what-not in your commentary, I'm not as likely to share it. Your point should be strong enough on its own. Cursing isn't "strong language", it's weak really. When God wanted to add strength to His language He didn't say, *Let there be F**KING Light!!!* Speaking the universe into existence is STRONG LANGUAGE! And He didn't have to drop the F-Bomb to do it. He dropped the Troof-Bomb!

Out of respect for my audience, I try to keep it PG-13, Even though a lot of conservatives share other commentator's vids that throw out the language filter. But I'm slow to share videos that have bad language. Also, If I detect confederate sympathies from a commentator, It will keep me from sharing their work. To those who think I'm *miseducated* about the Confederacy, you just remember - you learned what you think you know and what you think is right about the Confederacy from other Democrats. You go ahead and believe the Confederacy wasn't about racism. You can obviously see the Democrats are racist today and obsessed with making everything about race today, but you can't fathom that the Democrats were obsessed with race in the 1800's? OK.

Wow, Democrats with that invisibility. It works on conservatives too. Can't hit what you can't see, and some conservatives are so blind with southern pride that they can't see that they are pawns for the party that created the Confederacy. And those sentiments work excellently to turn public opinion against Republicans. Democrats effectively wiped their confederate stank on Republicans. They kill, and then drop the smoking gun in the Republicans lap and say, *See? It was republicans. See? They hate blacks, and they used a gun. We should take guns away from people, and put up more laws that actually get more blacks killed. And when blacks kill each other in the communities that we democrats run we can then say, See? Republicans don't care about black people!*

Republicans don't really support the production of counter-propaganda to this. This helps the Democrats remain as the invisible empire. Republicans make great memes though!

Isn't it amazing how Democrats are invisible when it comes to feminists? Feminists don't see their evil. They are also convinced that the Democrats have changed. In their delusion, they are no longer the party that stood in the way of suffrage. The party that didn't trust women with the right to vote are now seen by feminists as the party to trust. Wow. Why? Because all the Democrats had to do was tell women that they trusted them with the choice to kill their unborn kid. That's all it took, and then the evil of the Democrats became invisible to the feminist.

The sad Irony is that Republicans are the ones who made abortion legal in the United States. This is what happens when Republicans are deviant from the Judeo-Christian constitutional foundation of the Republican platform. This is what happens when Republicans think like Democrats and disqualify a human being's personhood.

Democrats like Margaret Sanger founded the most effective genocidal facility for the genocidal campaign against blacks. Democrats champion abortion. But feminists don't see this as evil because they're seduced by the propaganda that tells them they are empowered when they can be judge over the life and death of an unborn kid. Yeah, they are so hardcore and empowered to bully a fetus to death! But their selfishness makes them blind to their own evil, and blind to the invisible empire.

And again, it's embarrassing that Republicans are the ones who helped make this selfish act legal. Roe vs. Wade was made legal with the opinion of Chief Justice Warren E. Burger, Judge Harry Blackmun, and Judge Potter Stewart. Judge William Rehnquist was the only dissenting Supreme Court justice republican concerning abortion. The other Republicans lost sight of God given rights written into our constitution, and interpreted the law like Democrats. They were liberal with interpreting it instead of conservative and the result was a decision that was antithetical to the constitution and disregards the equal rights of the human creature.

At least many of the Republicans are trying to repent from this evil decision, and the best way to do this is to lean not on our own understanding but to trust in God. In God we trust. Remember that. Those Supreme Court justices forgot or ignored that. They leaned on their own understanding and it resulted in them viewing the constitution liberally. Had they relied on God and reflected on what His Word says, they would have seen that the rights of the created would be infringed upon without due process, and would have said no to abortion.

Let that be a lesson to Republicans; do not leave God out of the mix. You get death. We should have learned that with Adam and Eve. They left God out of the mix. It resulted in death. It's like you with your kids. I'm sure you would encourage them to have you accompany them as they're growing up because if you're not in the mix, their activities could more likely result in injury or death. And even when you can't be there, they should reflect on what you've tried to show them about right and wrong.

Republicans will become just as bad as Democrats if they rely on their own understanding of right and wrong. Trust in God and His instructions. That is the really wise thing to do. That shows more evidence of good intellect. You know you don't like prideful people. Pride is foolish, which means pride in one's intellect is foolish. Humility and gratitude are valued and wise. Humility and gratitude toward the Lord for the blessings of intellect is wise. That is the light that's needed to blaze against the invisible empire; expose them and break others free of them. But right now people can't hit what they can't see. They're angry and swinging at what they can see. If they're angry and want to swing, don't you think it's a good idea to point them to who they should actually be swinging at?

It takes more than just great debating. You have to lay the groundwork of illustrating to the culture why their representative is wrong. This helps to start breaking down their wall of denial. However, when you or our candidates beats their candidate's positions, just intellectually, they just get defensive, and fortify their wall even more against letting truth in.

Trump didn't win because he featured himself as some great cerebral debater. I'm not saying he couldn't. I'm just saying that's not what he relied on. He won because he knew how to tap into the culture. He's a proven success with reality TV shows. Reality TV shows are a hit with the culture. Trump brought the whole election process into his own reality TV show, and it worked. That's what I've been trying to tell y'all. Tap into the culture. Compete in entertainment media. That's big part of how liberals have accomplished all the damage they've done. Support creative counter-content. Expose the invisible empire. Expose the real enemy and their objective to target the embittered masses; the embittered masses that the Democrats keep influencing to taking their anger out on the Republicans, when it's been the Democrats all along who have been doing the things that these people are so angry about; programming them to be victims that feel like they're owed.

These multitudes are democrat drones that are fired up to carry on the longtime grudge the Democrats have always had for Republicans, and they're going to fire up these drones until there is another war. We might want to support the creation of entertaining and thought-provoking productions that they might want to sit down and watch rather than getting up and starting trouble and rethink their views. Get them to laugh. Get them to like some of our characters that have the conservative angle. Get them drawn into our stories. Get their attention with these things! Get them fascinated and marinating on these things so they're not preoccupied with ripping apart our republic!

Support the effort to produce entertainment that breaks the spell the liberals have had them under. Snatch off that hood and robe of invisibility the DemoKKKrats have been cloaked in so the DemoKKKrats can say, *And we would have gotten away with it too if it hadn't been for you meddling radical Republicans!*

But people usually want to make their own mistakes and will curse authority when authority interferes with them making their own mistakes, and then when authority does allow them to make their own mistakes and the mistake-maker gets hurt, they blame authority for allowing it to happen and call the authority evil, and then demand the authority to pay for the mistakes they wanted to be free to make in the first place. That's liberalism.

CHAPTER IV
KNOCK YOURSELF OUT

When I see wealthy football players who are paid loooong money to do what they love - then go about kneeling during the national anthem, I fantasize about holding up an American flag while mounted on a gassy horse. I'd trot that horse past their frowny unpatriotic faces while the horse tooted Yankee Doodle. Or considering their crappy attitude we'll call it Stanky Doodle.

It cracks me up to see people living their dreams in America while whining about oppression, and my heart breaks for the people who listen to them. They don't happen to notice that these wealthy people - from actors, to professors, to athletes, didn't pursue their dreams and step into their career in another country. They're making it here.

I still see people quoting George Carlin, like he said something really deep when he said, "They call it the American dream because you have to be asleep to believe it." People eat that crap up and totally overlook the fact that he was right there in front of them living his dream that he was free to pursue in the U.S.A.; doing what he loved, making millions doing it, and his work enjoyed by millions. It drives me nuts when I see people in America living their dreams, filling their pockets by telling others they can't live theirs in America. People pay these hucksters to tell them they're victims. They pay them to promote prejudice, ridicule, and curse against people who are living their dreams and curse the idea that you could live yours.

I think one of the biggest betrayals of America is when people use their freedom to curse a country that protects their right to pursue happiness but instead, they use their freedom to curse the country. That's betrayal and cowardice. Blacks in America have it bad when it comes to the previous statement, and there is no excuse for that now. Black folks did have a very real reason to be bitter because oppression was a very real institution. We've been beyond that for a while now though.

However, now the majority of black folks vote for the party and institution of oppression. Afro-centrics in America get smoke snortin' angry about my observations on this and shout, "You ain't never got anything good to say about black folks!" Which is a truckload of untrue doo-doo! Because when I do commend people who are black, their response is, "Yeah, but those are black folks who are trying to be white and seeking the white man's approval."

Do you notice, by their statements, the ones who belittle blacks are them? When a black person is commended for good character, good work ethic, and being an all-around model citizen, they're charged with trying to be white, as if these attributes are exclusive to white people and unnatural to black people. Nah, that's not insulting. (Eye roll.) I've understood this since elementary school and have addressed it in my vids for years.

But here's the sick contradiction; if trying to be an educated, successful, good model citizen is trying to be white, then how can they keep promoting the idea that white people are evil while saying blacks who are trying to be good model citizens are trying to be white? Is being white good or evil? Make up y'alls mind! Psssst. FYI. Good or evil isn't determined by skin color.

Now, in terms *of seeking the white man's approval*, that would be afro-cenrtics, again. These afro-centric voters vote for these white Democrats because they want their approval. They want them to approve social assistance, minimum wage increases, healthcare, education funding, legalized drugs, money for abortion, special accommodations, etc. None of these things have proven to make a better community, but they want these things approved of by some white democrat politician, while accusing Republicans who are black of wanting the white man's approval.

The afro-centric continuously votes for their oppression by repeatedly voting in Democrats and then blames Republicans for the lack of prosperity in their communities when they never voted for Republicans in their communities to have any effect in their communities in the first place, but somehow their problems are the Republican's fault. Their own thoughts betray them.

"What have Republicans done for black folks?" is still an ongoing question as they ignore the answer which is, Republicans abolished slavery, and reinstated civil rights and voting rights that were denied to blacks by Democrats, Desegregated schools and the military ya know? Stuff like that. And actually did it. They didn't just sign a piece of paper to pacify blacks. Republicans actually did it.

I marvel at how bitter afro-centrics who vote Democrat can still be, asking, "What is the republican party going to do for the black community?" If black folks have it so fabulous with the Democrats who they vote for over and over again, why would they need to even ask what are Republicans going to do for them? They should want for nothing. Democrats provided it all and the black community should be the happiest most taken care of race of people on the planet. But they're not, and they vote for their misery over and over again just like the democrat LBJ said they would when he said "I'll have those n**gers voting democrat for the next 200 years." Here they are fifty years later and afro-centrics are still voting for Democrats and blaming Republicans for somehow depriving them of their pursuit of happiness.

Malcolm-X spoke against the self-betrayal of the black community. He said that "If you vote democrat you're a political chump and a traitor to your race." The majority of black folks still vote for Democrats. Malcom-X was shot to death by black men, yet the majority of blacks fall for this idea that it's white folks in general that are out there killing black folks. For the record, the white people that they should be worried about are Democrats. The party of people who jailed MLK, and who shot MLK. Democrat voting blacks literally let Democrats get away with murder and what's worse they reward them with loyal votes just because Democrats gave them a block of cheese and a check, but somehow I'm the sellout?

But consider this concerning the majority of blacks who voted Democrat. They want states like Alabama to return to being a democrat run state. Alabama like the other southern states was a democrat state far longer than they were Republican states.

All the institutionalized bigotry that black folks particularly southern black folks are so angry about to this very day is when Democrats ran the southern states.

You would think that black folks who are obsessed with dwelling and butt- hurtin' over racism would never vote for a Democrat. How is it that black folks refuse to let go of their anger over racism but totally overlook the democrat party that institutionalized it? The party that facilitated white privilege for the white democrat voters they represented.

The majority of blacks believe that racist democrats became republicans and then in some weird alternate reality put an end to segregation in the south and institutionalized racism? How the fruit-loop does that make sense? When Democrats ran the south you had apartheid. When Republicans won the south apartheid was defeated. And what did blacks do when Republicans removed the democrat boot from their neck? They fell for the democrat lie that there was a switch and believed that Republicans hate black people. Rather than enjoying the civil rights republicans stood up for, for them, they chose to cling to their anger and blindly listen to the accusations of their oppressors.

Many blacks voting for Democrats to rule over them doesn't surprise me. And it's sad that these blacks receive what I say as hatred, as they respond to me with the racial epithets that would impress the KKK. They're all cut from the democrat cloth.

But y'all, I want to reflect on Exodus. The sons of Israel were crying out to God because of the oppression they were being subjected to. God heard them. Moses and Aaron were commissioned to go to Pharaoh to petition their release. This ticked Pharaoh off, and he was already meaner than a two-headed cobra. So he ramped up the oppression even more so.

It's like blacks crying out because of oppression. Republicans came in and said to the Democrats, "Let them go." Democrats got so mad at Republicans for abolishing slavery that they created the KKK. The terrorism by the Democrats was getting really bad.

Blacks were being faced with the burning hatred of Democrats. They could clearly see their oppressor. Or at least they should have been able to.

Pharaoh was pouring out his burning hatred for the Israelites. They could see their oppressor.

The Democrats wanted to hate blacks and wanted to oppress them. Pharaoh wanted to hate the Israelites and wanted to oppress them.

That was his chosen desire. Yes folks. There are people who actually want to hate. Looking at what pharaoh wanted, God gave Pharaoh over to his desire. He hardened pharaoh's heart even more than it was. Why would God do that? Why would God make this person more oppressive? Because God wanted the Israelites to be absolutely certain they wanted to be free, and who they would want to be freed from. Do we not ask, *Hey, black folks! Are you sure you want to be free? Because y'all sure do seem to like to vote to be on the plantation of the party that fought for the so-called right to enslave you.*

The point is this. Freedom wasn't the desire. The desire was just for the suffering to stop. That's not the same as not being slaves per say. God allowed the oppression to increase so that the Israelites could be sure of what they wanted. And what was revealed was that the Israelites just like many American blacks - they didn't want freedom. They just wanted the suffering to stop. What they wanted was to be issued comfort, not freedom. Despite the result of liberation, Israelites accused Moses, and American blacks accuse the Republicans of leading them to destruction. Freedom gets rough and warrants risk. The Israelites wanted security. They felt secure as slaves. They preferred that than the challenge of freedom. This is why you will still hear many blacks saying, "What are Republicans gonna do for black folks?" Because freedom wasn't what blacks of this mind-set desired. Being taken care of is what's desired. It's the same syndrome the Jews had in Exodus. It wasn't freedom they really wanted. They just wanted an institution of fairness and dependency. In other words, *We're happy to be your slaves and serve you rather than God, if you make slavery comfortable for us.* God Himself is the only One who can send the Comforter. Not the state. You cannot be dependent on anyone without allowing them to control you and take from you. It ultimately leads to tyranny. God is the only One Who can provide for us without taking from us or taking from others to make another comfortable.

Now after God had allowed Pharaoh to oppress the Israelites long enough to really be extra motivated to leave the rule of Pharaoh and the oppressive state of Egypt, what did the Israelites do when they got a gritty taste of freedom? They cried out to go back to Egypt and be slaves under the rule of Pharaoh.

The majority of Blacks have cried out to go back under the rule of the Democrat party.

Moses was leading them to liberty from their actual oppressors, and they complained and accused Moses of wanting to lead them to destruction.

Republicans lead the way for blacks to have liberty from the actual oppression of the Democrat party and many blacks complain and accuse Republicans of wanting to lead them to destruction.

They cried out to be put back into the matrix.

Remember y'all. The matrix was still slavery. It just changed how it enslaved people to make it more pleasant to keep better control over the slaves.

So when black folks be like, "The democrat party has changed." I'm like, Yeah, they changed how they've enslaved you. The Democrats have their hooks deep into the black community. They do not want to let blacks go. They feel entitled to have control over blacks. And the majority of blacks enable them to. Let me offer this to anybody who thinks the Democrat party has changed. Here's a statement by John Wilkes Booth; the Democrat who assassinated Abraham Lincoln.

"This country was formed for the white, not for the black man. And, looking upon African slavery from the same standpoint held by the noble framers of our Constitution, I, for one, have ever considered it one of the greatest blessings (both for themselves and us) that God ever bestowed upon a favored nation. Witness heretofore our wealth and power ; witness their elevation and enlightenment above their race elsewhere. I have lived among it most of my life, and have seen less harsh treatment from master to man than I have beheld in the North from father to son. Yet, heaven

knows, no one would be willing to do more for the negro race than I, could I but see a way to still better their condition.
But Lincoln's policy is only preparing the way for their total annihilation. The South are not, nor have they been, fighting for the continuance of slavery."

This is John Wilkes Booth letting you know right off the bat the Democrats have been the party of white privilege. In JWB's mind, blacks should be beholden to Democrats and credit the Democrats for the betterment of their lives. In JWB's mind, blacks are better off being slaves under Democrats than any place else in the world. Like a typical Democrat, JWB tries to justify slavery in the South by accusing the North of doing it. JWB seems to have forgotten that there were Democrats in the North too.

He seems to have forgotten that slaves weren't trying to leave the North to go South. The Underground Railroad went North not South.

It's like People from south of the border accusing America of oppression, yet they're not leaving America to go south of the border, they want those who are south of the border to come here. Why? Because south of the border is where the oppression is, not here. Yet we're accused of oppression. JWB is a model Democrat, assuming to know what's best for black folks. He tries to mitigate his evil by saying someone else is doing it, and just like Democrats do today he charges Republicans with trying to destroy black folks! Democrats are still the same!!! They cause blacks to distrust whom you accuse so they'll trust you to destroy them instead! It's been that way since the Garden of Eden! Satan accuses God of wanting to keep them down, so they trusted Satan to keep them down instead. Are Democrats not like their father the devil!? Democrats be like, *Republicans just want to keep black folks down, now make an appointment to kill that black child you're pregnant with.* JWB, just like a democrat, is confused about love. I'm sure that JWB thought "Love Wins" too when he shot Abraham Lincoln.

I know, I know. *I just hate my own people and I hate myself because I'm black,* even though I try to warn black folks (all people really) that the black community has been the primary target of population control via abortion. I'm the guy shouting, "Stop participating in the genocidal campaign waged against you!" But somehow that means I hate my own people, meanwhile the blacks who support putting a defenseless child to death get the black stamp of approval. (For the record, MY people are those who are in Christ and those who put Christ before any color.)

I say, "Black folks, don't allow the state to replace the husband. Black men, how do you go around talking about 'how much you love your black sistahs', but you don't marry them, and you ditch them and the kid you knocked them up with? And for all that black pride, that kid is either doomed to grow up without a father or doomed to be aborted." That looks like hatred for a race. But I'm the guy who hates his race because I say. "Stop doing that." If I hated black folks I would encourage them to keep doing it!!!

I see black single mothers talking about how they don't need a man and how they're a strong independent black woman, (as they depend on their state-sponsored EBT and WIC programs.) I see white women dependent on these things too, but I've never heard a white woman say, "I'm strong white woman" for it.

Don't you see that the democrat party is not only trying to make the black husband obsolete and replace him with the state, the democrat party is trying to replace manhood altogether? The democrat party celebrates men who forfeit their manhood! *Fathers, forfeit fatherhood! Give your child to the state. Fathers are not needed. Men, come out of the closet and embrace your homosexuality! Go even further, and deny your manhood and identify as a woman! Women! Be equal to men, and show your strength by being attracted to other women!* All this results in effeminate male figures, and that's what Democrats want; emasculated males, and disarmed through more and more gun control propaganda laws. Emasculated men can't put up that good of a fight when the State moves to become a dictatorship. White Democrats have engineered this. But somehow white people in general, especially Republicans, are seen as the culprits.

Knuckleheads like Kaepernick has all this blame for white people, meanwhile, the very first person to do Kaepernick dirty was his father, who was black and walked out on him and his mother. He was taken care of by white people, but somehow white people are evil, and afro-centrics never do anything wrong.

These are self-betrayals that keep the majority of the black community in the state of discontent. Afro-centrics accuse me of focusing on their faults and I have no solutions. Wrong. Afro-centrics are so insecure that they only register criticism and look for excuses to ignore or reject solutions. This is because they're addicted to misery, false fulfillment, and the pseudo satisfaction they get from blaming white people - mainly republicans. That's what they want to use their freedom to do; curse white people indefinitely. To which I say, you can be angry or you can be free. You can't really be both.

My solution to them is stop voting democrat. Stop being a pawn to a party that has thrived on racism. Stop crying for diversity when you yourself bundle into inner cities where almost everybody around you is black, and then when white people do come in to add diversity to your city you cry gentrification.

Stop fueling an industry that promotes violence and that calls black people the N-word more than the KKK every had time to, and demeans women. No black person living today or within even the past thirty years has ever heard white people call them the N-word more than they've been called it by another black person, or in their music that fantasizes and glorifies violence against another black person. They play it as loud as they can in their cars to let other black folks know how much they hate their guts, and that they're all just a bunch of n**gas.

This, of course, gives shallow white people the cue that it's ok to call black people the N-word and join in on the "Slay the N**gah Sing-along!" And notice that these violent lyrics still use "ah" at the end of the n-word? Too many blacks fool themselves into thinking the word is a term of endearment, yet will use that same word in bloodthirsty hatred for another black person as they gun them down. The n-word is a hateful word, whether it ends in "ah" or "er". Period. The point of the word was to press the idea that blacks were less than human. Here it is black folks say it to each other all the time. It's no coincidence that blacks commit so much violent crime against each other and would kill another black person as easy as they would kill a dog.

Why not? They condition each other with the idea that they're less than human all the time. Fooling themselves into thinking *they're just being "real black"* and expressing one love with their fellow blacks by calling each other the n-word, yet not noticing that when they get mad at each other they call each other the N-word, and when they pull their gun and shoot down another black person they're going to call each other the n-word and it doesn't matter one dang bit that it ends with "ah", or "er" the hate is still all there. I reckon they make the KKK proud - maybe even jealous. Heck, blacks commit more violent crime against blacks than the KKK has. Blacks were enslaving and selling other blacks long before white folks were, and are still at it today.

Afro-centrics believe that white people today have benefitted off of the legacy of slavery. But If people benefitted off of the legacy of slavery Africa would have the richest population of people on Earth.

Booker T. Washington warned of blacks who would sell out and make their money off of the grievances of other blacks and made sure they'd stay angry, burning with blame and victimhood, and always make them think they're still oppressed. (Paraphrased)

Much of the black community has put a premium on qualifying as "authentically black", and authentically black folk have to identify as victims. That's what's authentic, really "woke", and empowered, I guess. The more you embrace being a bitter victim the more empowered you are! *That's black power!...* So flipping sad.

You have to believe that blacks can't possibly be racist and that only whites can be supremacists because white people are the only ones with the power to be racists. This is truly the afro-centric so-called rationale on this. But this so-called rationale is their own admission to so-called white supremacy, because if they say that white people are the ones with the power to be racists, then that would be them claiming that white people have supremacy. DUUUUHHHH!

I have to stress to afro-centrics that I am not at all against the black community. I'm against what too many in the black community think, and how it keeps them down. Helllooooo! I am against what keeps you down!

Wanting reparations keeps you down! Afro-centrics vote for the party that denied them reparations in the first place. Republicans drew up and approved Special Field Order 15 (40 Acres and a mule)

This was approved under Republican president, Abraham Lincoln. Lincoln was assassinated by the Democrat John Wilkes Butt-hole Booth, then the Democrat President, Johnson, took office and revoked the order for 40 Acres and a mule.

Democrats have been hiding that little truth from black folks with the distraction of gub'ment cheese, a can of stiff peanut butter, and a bi-weekly check while pumping a program of prejudice against Republicans. Too many blacks vote for the very party that owes them while demanding America, in general, satisfy their reparation demands. Some do this while getting more money for doing nothing than some people get for working. Proof that reparations aren't the answer.

This thought process is cultivated. It's not like we have to be taught to be victims, or covetous, and blameful, etc. We already know how to do that. But it's reinforced from childhood to voting age. Blacks are force-fed the misery that happened generations before them. They're force-fed the poisonous idea that they have to be down with the struggle. It's like being forced to take heroin until your addicted. They're made to be addicted to the idea that if you aren't bitter and brewing with blame then you aren't authentically black, and being black has to come before anything else. That is the prime directive. Blackness takes precedence over all.

You have to be black before being:
An American,
Educated,
A business owner,
An employee,
A man,
A woman,
A husband,
A wife,

A father,
A mother,
A child of God.

There is nothing you can be before being black. There is nothing more important than being black. This is at the core of what is keeping the majority of the black community in the state of discontent they are in. And Democrats have harbored this.

I'll use my father as a prime example of the prejudice that Democrats promote and their hateful hypocrisy. I don't disclose these things out of spite for my father. I've forgiven him a loooong time ago. He just happens to be a prime example of what a Democrat is, and that's what I'm showing. Democrats are slanderous, projecting, judgmental hypocrites. My father, as a democrat, exemplifies this. Though I hold no ill will towards my father there is something that I do take quite personally, as the following will show.

It's bad enough that my father is a bigot, but my wife is white, and that doesn't hold him back one bit from expressing his hatred for white people. He would contact me out of the blue to try to make me feel guilty (as Democrats always do) about how we don't have a "father-son relationship and how I'm his only offspring, and we should be tight!" Basically, I owe him a relationship he didn't earn, and he can't even receive the relationship gracefully when grace is given. But that's Democrats. They just feel they're owed and entitled to things they didn't earn. They don't own up to their evil. They blame others for their evil and remain evil even when you try to be gracious to them.

Despite his claims of how much he "values me", he hates the people who have been the kindest and supportive towards me, and those people have been Republicans. You would think he would be grateful to Republicans for being as receptive to his only son whom he claims to value so much, but no. He shows no graciousness at all. His response to their kindness is, "You white folks (Republicans) just like to be entertained by black folks."

The poisonous propaganda that my father helps to fuel is getting people killed. Democrats throughout history resort to violence and murder. Democrats have always promoted violence against groups.

Their target today is Christian conservatives. I know some white Christian conservatives feel like they're the target. If you're among those, I'm quite disappointed in you. You think Democrats just hate you? Do I need to bust out with my hate mail again, and remind ya of how they're trying to snuff me out? They hate Christian conservatives of any shade. There just happens to be more white Christian conservatives for them to hate. On a side note, the reason why it's specifically Christian conservatives they hate so much and not liberal "Christians" is because liberal Christians aren't really followers of Christ. They have created an idol they call Jesus and their "Jesus" conforms to their ideals of acceptance and entitlement. We Christian conservatives are as imperfect as anybody, but we tend to acknowledge Jesus for Who His Word says He is, not for what we fantasize Him to be. Do we follow His Word to the letter? No. We fail, just like anyone else, but we still understand that we have a responsibility to not serve sin whereas the liberal "Christian" believes that Jesus accepts their willful sinning, and what's worse, the liberal so-called Christian doesn't understand what qualifies as sin.

Example: The liberal Christian doesn't understand that taxing income is a sin. Not only is it a sin it is a sin that is made law. It is theft under the guise of good intentions. It still violates the commandment to not steal. It is a policy driven by covetousness despite the commandment to not covet. It puts the state before God as the state deprives people of their first fruits before they can make an offering to God. Taxing income is a violation of our right to property. It is a sin. The liberal so-called Christian does not understand this and takes the Lord's name in vain to justify policy that gives the state the power to steal from earners.

Democrats have always been about racism. They are obsessed with it. They have a racist and murderous history. They are the party of slander and violence. They are still the same. All these acts of politically motivated violence and destruction are virtually all perpetrated by left wingers. Democrats push for this. My father, being the democrat that he is, is all about this propaganda to hate white people and Republicans.

Democrats claim to be all about love and togetherness, and my father who is a Democrat to the core claims to be all about love and togetherness, yet on Valentine's day, of all days, he comes on to my Facebook page attacking white people and implicates me, (his only son whom he claims to value so much) as an "Uncle Tom House N**ga". That's just how he is. That's just how Democrats are.

My father, the democrat, had the nerve to act surprised when I told him about the bigoted epithets and fantasies of violence liberal trolls would send me, as I tried to reason with him about the party that he is loyal to. He has also fallen for the party switch thing, even though Malcolm x was rebuking blacks for supporting democrats before the so-called "party and ideological switch." What was black folk's excuse for siding with the enemy then?

So even though my father tried to publicly shame me as an "Uncle Tom House N**ga", I didn't take that personally. What made it personal for me is that he came in attacking white people in a thread I posted where I admonished a painting by Kehinde Wiley, (The afro-centric homosexual that did the Barack and Michelle Obama portraits.)

His notable works include paintings of black women holding up severed heads of white women. He clearly says, "It's sort of a play on the 'kill whitey' thing", but even with him making that declaration, the liberals bolster their denial by trying to give it the noble thrust of saying "the Painting is based on the Bible." It's bad enough that liberals ignore his statement about "killing whitey" but they also ignore that the scriptures concerning Judith and Holophernes isn't Biblical, it's Apocryphal. Some try to validate it more by calling it Deutero-canonical. Yeah, whatever. Apocryphal. This means dubious and not trustworthy.

Liberals tried to give me that song and dance that the painting wasn't about racism, (Even though Wiley, the painter himself said, "It's sort of a play on the 'kill whitey' thing") and what's even worse; I even had some sucker so-called "republicans" attacking me over it. My favorite kind of "republicans." The Hollywood kind. The kind that hide in the closet about their views and whine in their speakeasies, but consider themselves brave for making their political statements public when they can contort to make themselves look objective and above the fray. I reckon attacking me is a good way to do that. Maybe some liberal Hollywood producer will see that and be impressed.

But these self-righteous suckers insist that the painting isn't about racism. It's just a rendering based on an episode from the book of Judith. These are the same kind of people who think that the rapper, Common, was really just talking about burning a bush like in the account of Moses. "He was just making a Biblical reference." No. He used that reference to suggest burning George W. Bush. But just like people are in denial about Wiley's racist and bigoted painting and try to justify it by saying, "It's a 'Biblical' reference." (These people don't even care about the Bible by the way.) And even though Wiley says "It's sort of a play on the 'kill whitey' thing", they ignore that. Just Like they try to justify Common, as they say, "He was just making a Biblical reference." Read the lyrics, y'all. Common personifies the "bush" himself.

"Burn a Bush cos for peace <u>he</u> no push no button
Killing over oil and grease
No weapons of destruction
How can we follow a leader when this a corrupt one?"

If you're one of those who refuse to see that He's talking about judging George W. Bush by fire, then… I guess I would just have to say that much denial is impressive.

The painting by Wiley is racist. It promotes the image of superiority, with a black woman having defeated a white woman. The image itself isn't racist just because it is a woman who has killed a woman. The color doesn't matter, but Wiley's intentions are bigoted and racist, being that he declared, "It's sort of a play on the 'kill whitey' thing."

The pursuit of dominance over another race is racist. That was his intention. That makes the painting bigoted and racist. The image is also sexist and is in contradiction with the women's solidarity thing. Holofernes was a dude. The beheaded figure in Wiley's paintings doesn't appear to be a dude. It looks like Wiley discriminates against women so much that not only does he prefer to have sex with men instead of women against our biological order, he would rather paint a woman killing another woman, instead of painting the conquered man if the painting is really based on the book of Judith. But liberals are the champions for women. Ok.

Instead of my father seeing the racist and sexist hate propaganda of this painting and denouncing it, he instead takes to the thread attacking white people, expressing his hate for Republicans, and insists that Trump voting republicans are racists and liars etc. Now here is why I take this very, very, very personally.

He is describing my wife.

When he makes these slanderous statements, that is an attack on my wife. I'll remind you. Democrats are belligerent, tantrum throwing, violent people. They commit mass murder. The propaganda that my father the democrat contributes to and helps to promote is putting people like my wife in the crosshairs. To my father, the democrat, it would be fair play if my wife were gunned down for being white and a Republican. She deserves to get blown away in a bombing. The race baiting hate and slander that my father, the democrat, is a part of promoting could render someone like my wife a casualty, which would suit my father, the democrat, just fine. He has already told me if I ever wanted to marry a white woman I would not have his blessing, and that he doesn't like anything white. Needless to say, we didn't hear from him for our wedding. He's tried to be tolerant and hospitable towards my wife, but the true colors come out.

I didn't marry my wife because she's white. I married her because she rocks! What a friend the Lord has sent to me!!! What quality character this woman has! This woman has shown my democrat father's only son, whom he claims to value so much, more God-sent love, support, and joy than I deserve. But to my father that just equals a racist that just likes to be entertained by her black house n**ga husband. Her family, made up of mostly Republicans, came from across the country to be at the wedding to witness my wife's parents give away their precious white daughter to a house n**ga as my father, the democrat, implicates me as. Right under my father's nose has been republicans being supportive and receptive of the very thing he claims to value so much, yet his response is hate.

What my father, the democrat, really valued was Obama. Ohhhh, how my father, the democrat, would cry about anything critical said about Obama! To him *everything was racist and violent, and no president has ever been treated as bad* as his precious Obama! (Even though other presidents have been assassinated.) But that's Democrats for ya.

My father, the democrat (Remember y'all. I'm using him as the model democrat) Boo-Hoo'd about the so-called racist treatment of Obama, meanwhile, there really wasn't any. There have been plants, and there have been staged incidents, and there have been people who have tried to come to tea party events expressing questionable sentiments and they were called out and told that those ideas were not welcome.

My father, the Democrat was so hurt and offended by the so-called hateful treatment of Obama, but it didn't faze him one bit, when it came to the hateful treatment democrats showed me; his only son, whom he claims to value so much. It didn't faze him at all about the bigoted hate-mails and comments. It doesn't bother him at all that liberals have shadow-banned me and have ruined my livelihood, and I'm having to start from scratch. God willing He'll bless me to build my brand, and career anew. Not only has he been indifferent, but has even tried to come off as oblivious to the hate the Democrats show me, which is B.S. One, it doesn't change his loyalty to the Democrats, and two, while he claims to be oblivious by the Democrats treatment of me, he publicly sends me the same kind of hateful messaging democrats send me. Let that sink in. Again, this isn't me calling out my father; I'm exhibiting the level of hatred and hypocrisy Democrats have. Their selfish disposition is so deep that they will put that before anything and anyone else. This behavior is overflowing with Democrats, and my father, the democrat, is the poster child.

My father, the democrat, crashes my page, charging Republicans of being sexists who voted for a man who "Grabs women by the p**sy." This was something that Trump said. And though I do not approve of the language, it was a verbal statement, not an act. But while my father, the Democrat, tries to posture himself as a champion for women, as Democrats do, and tries to judge Trump over a statement about grabbing - my father, the democrat, actually DID grab a woman so fiercely that he broke her neck. That woman is my mother. She survived the assault. I was four years old, having to help her dress, and maintain her "halo" to support her neck through her recovery.

This democrat so-called champion for women would punch my mother in the face while calling her a b*tch. Guess he really loves his black queens, right? People of the left-wing persuasion express sentiments like this in their music to this very day, but they're the champions for women, right? My father, the democrat, isn't a champion for women. He's an abuser of women. Democrats are the most objectifying and woman exploiting people in America there are. The only time my father would contact me was when it was time for me to meet the new woman he had hooked up with to tyrannize, yet he's trying to judge Trump?

My father, the democrat, is hypocritically trying to judge Trump as a sexist because of a statement, albeit-tasteless, about grabbing a woman by the p**sy? Y'all I've heard my father, the democrat, and his masonic buddies yuck it up before they go into their "meeting of secrets". WHOA-HOOOOOO! Do they ever have some doozies about what they would do with a woman's p**sy!!! Lil' Wayne himself wouldn't be able to keep up with these guys! I don't want to hear some lame excuse about Trump being the president and having to set an example. That's such a weak cop-out. Well, hey. My father the democrat is a past worshipful master mason. Doesn't he have a responsibility as a leader figure to set a better example?

Here's more on the hypocrisy, selfishness, and shallowness of Democrats.

As my father, the Democrat, was attacking my viewers, Trump, and me, I responded by calling him out on his hypocrisy. I asked him how can he pass himself off as a champion of women and qualify himself to judge other men as sexist, considering his history of abusing women?

My father, the democrat, in true Democrat form said, "You don't know what went on between your mother and me"

Let's break that down.

Right off the bat, he justified his abuse. I guess I should just let him explain it to me. That way I will find myself being like, "Oh heck yeah, dad! Beating the crap out of your women is totally understandable. You and you alone get a pass! Nobody has a better excuse than you! Forgive my ignorance for not understanding! It's all so clear to me now! Heck, if I would have known better, I would have helped you beat up my mom too!"

My father, the democrat, and selfish hypocrite, thinks he's the only man who had a woman problem and that it was too unique for anybody else to understand, therefore he is in an exceptional category to abuse women. See what I mean by selfish?

Now, let me place myself in the formula. Despite my father, the democrat, asserting that I don't understand what went on with him and my mom, I've actually been in a few relationships myself. He's so self-focused and self-justifying that he didn't consider that his only son, whom he claims to value, has gone through the mental and emotional anguish of being in the brain boiling, heart hammering exercise of being in a relationship with women that were not right for me, and women I was not right for. Yes! I've been there, myself! Shouting matches that would get the police called to our home! High-speed car chases. Holding a knife in my hand, tempted to drain all the blood from my body, because my own blood felt like it was poisoning me. I was in relationships that made my blood feel sour and rancid. Yeah, I think I can understand what goes on between couples. It's beyond insulting that my father, the democrat, would think that I wouldn't.

But that's Democrats; Selfish, and think their abuses are justifiable. They think their suffering is unique. Like blacks acting like they're the only ones who have ever been enslaved. Indeed I am quite familiar with the emotional, mental, physical, and spiritual toll that can come about in a relationship. But despite all these things that make a person feel like they're turning inside out, I have NEVER tried to resolve it by beating a woman into understanding why I think she's wrong. My father accuses me of not understanding. The only thing I don't understand is the weakness to not restrain oneself from beating a woman. By the grip of the Lord, may we never understand.

My father, the Democrat didn't like this episode of his past being brought up. Others have weighed in to reprimand me for publicizing this past event.

But wait… Don't democrats judge us for the past all the time? They call themselves forward-thinking progressives while guilt-tripping people about the past all the time! Democrats keep people angry about the past all the time and they're the ones who instituted what people are so angry about in the first place!!!

As far as me making this public - Not only do Democrats try to publicly shame people, they slanderously shame people. They publish things that aren't substantiated and try to ruin people's lives with it while being the actual guilty party of what they accuse. For example: accusing Trump of Russian collusion when more and more it's being revealed that it was the Clintons, Obama, and their comrades.

They're trying to attack Trump for being a monster over women when it turns out that over and over again it's these left-wing elitists that are the biggest exploiters of women. I've been saying that for years. But of course, the democrat overlords don't want the people that they want to keep control over to hear my observations. My father told me It was a dirty move to call him out on how he treated my mother and how I didn't understand. Typical Democrat; *he's the real victim.* He comes in being rude to everybody, and when he gets called out for his hypocrisy, he becomes the victim. He subjects women to abuse, yet he's the victim. Typical Democrat.

Democrats posture themselves as the champions for the LGBT. My father the democrat teased his younger brother for having "sugar in his britches", and would implicate me as being in the same "queer" boat as my uncle. Larry was my favorite uncle. Sure, I knew he was gay. I didn't agree with the orientation, but my sisters and I didn't love him any less. My sisters and I grew up estranged, but we had fun together when Uncle Larry would visit. He wasn't overt with effeminate behavior. He was fun and so comical without trying to exhibit a behavior that pointed to his homosexuality. We just detected it. He did have flamboyant antics that were more like the absurdity of Bugs Bunny dressing up like a woman to make a mockery of Elmer Fudd.

My uncle Larry died from A.I.D.S.

Despite Democrats being so "pro-education" My father, the democrat, never asked me about my homework. Instead of asking me if I was getting my homework done he would ask me if I was getting any p**sy. I was like twelve by the way. Getting some p**sy was very important to him. As he would put it, "I don't want to be raising a little fa*got." (Even though he didn't have much to do with raising me at all.) He didn't want me to end up in the same boat as my uncle Larry, as he put it.

Despite Democrats being so "pro-education" my father, the democrat, offered me drugs before offering to help me do my homework. And as we know, Democrats have been the biggest proponents of legalizing marijuana. They'll be blaming Americans for not spending enough money on education, as more kids will be coming into school too high on more available marijuana to process an actual education, but will be in prime stoned drone-mode to let their imaginations get stimulated with the mind- trip of utopia that the legions of liberals continue to indoctrinate them with.

My father, the democrat, accuses me of turning my back on my family and my people. Nothing says turning your back on your family like divorce. I didn't do that. He did. I don't hold these things against him, I assure you. It's the hypocrisy I take issue with. It's the narrative that he is part of promoting which is rendering violence in America. And considering the race-baiting nature of it, and the animosity that it is building towards Christian conservative Republicans (especially the hate towards the aforementioned who are white) that ups the instance of someone like my wife being a casualty of left-wing belligerence. This is what I presently charge my father, the democrat, with. His hostility towards white, Christian conservative, Republicans can't be expressed without including my wife. He's brainwashed into bigotry by the MSM, meanwhile, in the real world, right under his nose, Republicans are the total opposite of what he wants to believe. The truth is as obvious to him as the wife of his only son, whom he claims to value, and the blessings of her ultra-conservative family. But He rejects it.

I'm not guilty of turning my back on my family. I turn my back on what they believe. One of the reasons why I am not a Democrat is because I see how much pain racism has caused my family. Racism has wounded them deeply. They do not understand that out of respect for my family I vigorously reject Democrats, because Democrats are the party that instituted what my family is so bitter over. But my father, the Democrat thinks I'm crazy. Jesus' folks thought He was crazy too. Jesus warned us that people are gonna trip on us just like they tripped on Him.

Then Jesus went home, and once again a crowd gathered, so that He and His disciples could not even eat. When His family heard about this, they went out to take custody of Him, saying, "He is out of His mind." And the scribes who had come down from Jerusalem were saying, "He is possessed by Beelzebul," and, "By the prince of the demons He drives out demons."... Mark 3:20-22 BSB

My father, the democrat, just thinks I'm this crazy person and the crowds that listen to me are just white folks who like to be entertained by an uncle tom house n**ga, and that my ability doesn't come from a place of good but from evil.

It is indeed sad to see families divided like this, but Jesus warned us that He Himself ordains this. My father, the democrat, displays his arrogance concerning God, just as left-wingers tend to do, and even more disappointingly as some Republicans do too, but this is quite typical of Democrats; defining God on their own terms. They'll claim to believe in God, but it's a god of their own shaping. Jesus Himself will divide families like this. Jesus will divide you from even your family if there is a family influence that would lead you to Hell with them. Jesus will drive the sword between you and that person, even if that party is father and son. My father, the democrat, does not acknowledge Jesus for Who He is.

But whoever denies Me before men, I will also deny him before My Father in heaven. Do not assume that I have come to bring peace to the earth; I have not come to bring peace, but a sword. For I have come to turn 'A man against his father, a daughter against her mother, a daughter-in-law against her mother-in-law.... - Matt-10:33-35 BSB

My father the democrat accuses me of turning my back on my [black] people. For the record, my people are those of any color who are in Christ for Who He says He is. Color, country or party affiliation doesn't make anyone "my people." If you are a servant of Christ, then you are my people. But concerning my democrat father's charge of turning my back on my [black] people, the truth is, turning your back on your people happens when you support Democrats. I'll reiterate Malcolm X's statement. "If you put your support behind [Democrats] you are a political chump and a traitor to your race. The white liberal panders to the black race and use them to gain more power to have more control." Voting Democrat IS turning your back on your people. I'm not the guilty party here. The ones guilty of turning their backs on black people are blacks who vote democrat, like my father.

I'd listen to my father, the Democrat, judge other blacks walking down the street as a bunch of "low life n**gas". Meanwhile, he's a "pillar of positivity" for his people. But one of the biggest qualifiers of being black is to be overly critical of other blacks, and then curse white people for not praising black people enough.

God commands us to honor our father and mother. I hope I am doing that. Many who misunderstand that command are sentencing themselves to Hell by their own misunderstanding of it. Honoring your father and mother doesn't mean you can't disagree with or be critical of your parents (respectfully of course), what it means is that no matter how messed up your parents are, live your life in a manner that makes people think you must have had the best parents in the world! My audience has often expressed very kind and honoring assumptions regarding my parents. They have viewed my parents as exemplary! I try to live in a way that brings honor to my parents and inspire folks to have respect for my father before even knowing anything about him. That is honoring the father and mother.

The truth is my father didn't have much to do with my upbringing. My mother has been super high-strung with abuse all her life. Her parents were abusive and despised her because she was the darkest of all her siblings. My mom doesn't even have that dark of a complexion, but she was too dark for her own parents and they treated her the worst for it. Remember. In "black culture" it is the black thing to do to hate the darkest. They'll go on, and on, and on, about how pro-black they are, and how proud of their blackness they are, but watch what happens when they get angry at each other. They will curse the other for being black and will target how dark they are as the ugliest thing about them, and that aspect of their being is what they'll attack the hardest while hatefully calling them the n-word.

My mother decided that when she had children she would treat her darkest child the best. That child was me. This, of course, caused great sibling rivalry. This was destructive because I was favored based on color, and my sisters were despised based on color. My mother was scarred by her treatment by not only racist whites in the south (democrats), she was also traumatized by the treatment from her own family for her being too dark. That haunted her into her parenthood.

Though her intentions were to make up for how she was treated for being dark, it rendered her conflicted with how she would be. Though she wanted to treat me better for being the darkest, her animosity for me being black would come out and fuel her anger. "You little black this, and that, etc." And of course being that I reminded her of my father, didn't help much either! But this behavior was beaten into my mother all her life. By the grace of God, I saw this behavior and understood it even as a child. I saw it in my family and I saw it in black culture and knew that I didn't want to be a part of it. I also knew that it would cause me to be alienated and ostracized. But one thing my mom is not, is lacking in generosity.

But that's a big part of the black culture that claims to "love each other so much". When they get angry at each other, they preface their grievance for the other person by attacking them for being black. Let's say a black guy scratched another black guy's car. The response isn't, "Dude! You scratched my car!" Or even, "Hey, a**hole, you scratched my car!" It's more like, "N**gah! I know your black a** didn't just scratch my car!" This means that not only is this person guilty of the offense of scratching the car, they're guilty of the offense of being black.

Many in the black community want to be respected for being black, like respecting them for being black is a birthright they're entitled to. But they vote for the party that oppressed blacks for being black and these white Democrats asserted the idea that it was their white birthright to rule over blacks.

Blacks are conditioned to this day to think America is the center of slavery. Like, when you think America, think slavery. Never mind that black Africans were already slave trading other black Africans long before Europeans became new customers. Nations in Africa and then Muslims sold other blacks and then the slave trade rendered black slaves in Cuba, Haiti, South America, etc. but somehow America is the only guilty party of slavery in the history of mankind.

Somehow the American flag is the symbol of oppression, and the constitution of the United States is a document that somehow entitles whites to enslave blacks. It's funny when afro-centrics boast about being the original Egyptians that built the pyramids, and already had electricity and stuff. (talk about cultural appropriation) Afro-centrics want to make these claims about their intelligence and strength, yet somehow weren't smart, strong, and fast enough to keep white people from snatching them up for slavery. Ok. Ohhhhh, but the white devil plays dirty, right? He's a cheater, right? That's no excuse. If the afro-centrics who think they're descendants of genius and powerful kings and queens then they should have been strong, smart, and fast enough to stay ahead of the cheaters.

The declaration of independence states that "ALL men are created equal and that we're endowed by our Creator with certain inalienable rights." It is the supreme law of that land that those laws are to not be infringed upon. Our U.S. Constitution is the document that says these God-given rights are to be protected in this republic. The American flag is a symbol representing the acknowledgment that the rights of all men are God-given. They are not issued by the state, and these rights cannot be deprived of any person unless that person has been given due process for violating someone else's rights. That is a flag worth pledging allegiance to. That is a God-given constitution worth defending.

It is not the flag or the Constitution's fault that people ignored what these items stood for and twisted their meaning for their own selfish desires. There is no reason to curse the flag or the U.S. Constitution for the corruption of others.

Too many blacks have been conditioned to believe that the U.S. Constitution is a pro-slavery document. I can disprove that it is pro-slavery very easily. If the U.S. Constitution was a pro-slavery document, why did the Democrat represented Confederacy take the liberty to draw up their own Constitution of the Confederate States? Because the U.S. Constitution doesn't render language in it that makes forced slavery legal. The Constitution of the Confederate states wrote in clear language which satisfied the pro-slavery population. Too many blacks have been led to blame the wrong Constitution and the wrong party.

The Democrat authored Confederate Constitution was the pro-slavery constitution, and the democrat party has always been the party of racism.

Their very platform is all about them being entitled to the fruits of someone else's labor. That's just who they are.

I'm not saying Republicans are saints. I'm saying that the foundation of what it is to be republican is to understand that we live in a constitutional republic where it is fundamental to acknowledge that all men are created equal, and we're ruled by a fixed set of laws that come from God, not by what's popular to man at any given time.

When laws are determined by men like in a democracy, you will end up with a majority rule that demands to deprive a group of their rights for the comforts of another group.

I'll give ya an example. Liberals claim to love democracy so much, yet Israel is a democracy, and the liberals accuse Israel of apartheid all the time. Liberals even hate it when there is a democracy. And Israel, unfortunately, has chosen to disregard the personhood of kids in the womb. It's really sad that this is one of the things Israel decided to do with their democracy. They've got people trying to wipe them off the face of the Earth, and the Israelis are helping them by killing off their own pre-born kids. If Israel answered to Mosaic law they would adhere to following the commandment to not murder. But in a democracy, the popular vote is what's right according to what feels right to the people not according to what is right according to God. They have put what they think is right before the law given through Moses.

There is a way which seems right to a man, But its end is the way of death.- Proverbs 14:12 NASB

In this constitutional republic - built on a Judeo-Christian foundation - the supreme law of the land rules that no matter how much of a majority demand there is for slavery or any institution that deprives a person of their God-given rights without due process, it cannot be made legal.

Black so-called leaders influencing blacks to believe the U.S. Constitution is pro-slavery would have been a pro-slavery minded person's dream! *Heck yeah, that negro is making the argument for us that the Constitution is pro-slavery! See? Even these negroes agree that slavery is legal! Thanks, boy! Now get back out in them fields!*

See how foolish it is to insist the U.S. Constitution is a pro-slavery document when it isn't? It's also not wise to allow oneself to be influenced by race-baiters - especially by race-baiters who are wealthy, telling folks that they're victims. They are the ones who get richer while the poor get poorer. They make money off of the poor's perpetual misery.

It's unfortunate that many afro-centrics will reject this and say that the only reason why these white folks like me is because I just say what republican white folks want to hear. This makes no sense. If republican whites really hated me for being black there wouldn't be anything I could say to change that. Unless... They would be judging me by my character like MLK Dreamed of.

What's even worse is that all these liberal Democrat voting whites pander to blacks because so many blacks say all the things white Democrats want to hear from them. And Democrat whites love to hear blacks call each other the N-word. They put lots of money behind that. How come it's ok for blacks to say all those things Democrat whites want to hear? Democrat whites like blacks who reject Christ and embrace Islam or atheism. Democrat whites like to hear blacks say abortion should be legal on demand at someone else's expense. Democrat whites like to hear blacks promote class warfare etc. Democrat whites like blacks who say what they want to hear.

People are indoctrinated to accuse the wrong people because the education system is run by the democrat party, and they mask their history and put it on others. That's why they want confederate artifacts removed. Because they don't want people to find out that they are attached to the democrat party, so they have ignorant belligerent drones who are too poisoned to register the truth, pursuing the artifact removals.

The big question is, "How do we fix this?" The answer, stop saying "government is not the answer" while fawning over a politician to fix it. The answer is with the Lord. Republicans act so broke when it comes to supporting God-given creative means to connect our values to the culture, yet always seem to have money to promote a politician while saying "government is not the answer."

The biggest medium of influence used to corrupt minds is entertainment media. Conservatives still haven't learned the power and value of this. Start demanding the supply of entertaining counter-content to compete with the liberal narrative. Stop depending on liberal owned platforms. Support the creation of our own and make it good enough to catch the attention of those shackled to brain chains. They may realize they have the key, and head towards the light the Lord has given us to share.

I get it conservatives, you're smart. But what good are your smarts to people who only want to see you as evil and people who call evil good and good evil? Your smarts are only perceived as evil by people influenced through culture and media. I keep saying it over and over again; you have to support the production of counter-influence that's entertaining enough to keep their attention long enough to convey the message. And not just support anybody calling themselves a conservative and saying a few conservative ideals while still behaving not much different than a liberal. You don't want people sending you mixed messages. Why support sending them out?

I'm not saying we should be a bunch of prudes with butts slammed shut tighter than a bear trap. But I'd hope we can be distinguished from liberals with our presentations. We see the damage liberals have promoted with their way. Let's not repeat the same but rather carry ourselves differently in our creative efforts.

These multitudes in the black community especially have already been exposed to too much mind rot as it is. Conservatives tend to not grasp the importance of this. They understand the importance of reaching the black community, they just don't understand the value in how to do it. It's important to reach them because they are the ones who are most used by the left to press the leftist ideology. Do you remember how important it was to Democrats to keep control over blacks in the 1800's? So much so that they'd rather have a war than consider them people and not see them as property.

Democrats have that same grip on blacks today. And will resort to practically anything to keep that hold on them. Democrats are morbidly and desperately dependent on blacks and have made the black community dependent on them. The democrat party is finished if they lose the black vote. Why? It's not because of the population of blacks. it's because of the guilt they can lay on the rest of the population with blacks. Even though Democrats are the perpetrators, keep in mind, Democrats are masters of framing others for democrat crimes. They will make others feel guilty for black suffering. It works like a bloody charm. Want higher taxes? Use blacks. Democrats say, "Republicans don't care about black folks. They just want them poor and stupid," and "They're gonna put y'all back in chains."

It was Democrats in the first place that kept it illegal for blacks to be educated, and they certainly couldn't be educated in white schools. Republican president Eisenhower sent in a national guard to make sure that black kids could go to school without being harassed by democrat voters who didn't want blacks to attend their school. But

Democrats boast to the public that they're the champions for blacks being educated. No. They want blacks in their classrooms now so they can indoctrinate and control them. They need them to get people to vote out of guilt, and motivated by self-righteousness to show that they are a "better person" for willingly wearing the scarlet letters of WG for White Guilt. See? Democrats are still about supremacy. They're the "better people."

Want Gay marriage legalized? Use blacks. According to liberals, It's only fair that homosexuals should be able to marry each other since there was a time when it was illegal for blacks and whites to be married. I go more in detail on this in my audiobook Weapon of A.S.S. Destruction (American Socialist States) on how blacks and whites being married has nothing to do with - and is incomparable to the misnomer of gay marriage.

However, the point that I'm making here is that the black plight (that Democrats wanted to keep blacks subjected to), is used by Democrats to gain sympathy votes for the LGBT Cause. Which means; gaining their votes and the votes of those who think they're better people for thinking love wins when you're open minded to rebel against nature.

It's funny. Liberals claim to love nature so much while rejecting it. It's also funny that the LGBT Community used blacks and voted for Democrats to get a marriage license. Yet it was Democrats who denied marriage licenses to black and white couples to enforce the anti-miscegenation laws they imposed.

Want Sanctuary cities for illegal immigrants? Use blacks. Throw out hot-button words like Jim Crow. Oh no! Do we want to do to the immigrants what was done to blacks? Do we deny them the right to vote and education? Again. This is incomparable. Blacks didn't migrate here on their own. They were enslaved already by other blacks who traded them in Africa. This has been going on long before America was even thought about. White people became new customers and bought black slaves from other blacks. Thus blacks did not migrate to America. Blacks were migrated to America.

Illegal immigrants migrate here by their own will, leaving their country and enter ours illegally. That alone makes slave migration and willful illegal immigration incomparable. It had been determined that blacks have constitutional rights. Democrats did not accept this. But now Democrats try to use what they denied blacks in the first place to say Republicans are denying the same things to immigrants that were denied to blacks.

I'll remind you, anybody born here to people who are legally Americans are born here with certain constitutional rights. If you ignore our law and come into this country illegally then you are not at all in the same situation as blacks. Blacks did not commit a crime by being black. Their rights were denied them without due process. There was no crime committed to sentence blacks with. But if you enter our country illegally that is a crime. And when you commit a crime you can legally be denied or deprived of things. If you break our law and enter illegally you can be denied the things that you feel entitled to; things these people should have been able to get in their wonderful country, but couldn't, yet somehow we're the evil ones. As I've mentioned before, we're accused of being bigoted, arrogant, swindling, and greedy etc., but these people want to live here. I guess their country wasn't the place where it was really like that. They must have just gotten so sick of how wondrous their country was and just wanted to sneak into a country of racist, imperialistic rapists who abuse black people and do foreigners the same. Yeah, that's got to be it.

Want more gun control? Use blacks. Accuse the NRA of being a racist organization. Forget that the NRA was helping blacks protect their lives with bettering their marksmanship against the KKK who were still sore about black folks having constitutional rights and all. Meanwhile, the Democrats are putting millions of black kids in the womb to death. But the NRA is somehow racist, while the infanticidal campaign facility of Planned Parenthood who's largest demographic are black visitors - as they set up shop mostly in black populated areas, somehow isn't racist. Ok.

Express no outrage about blacks being the largest committers of violent crimes against other blacks, make excuses for them, and somehow make it gun's and white people's fault. Make the police out to be the bigoted boogie man who loves to go around shooting black people while insisting that the people should not be allowed to have guns... Only law enforcement should have guns?... The ones they say are a bunch of bigots who like to go around shooting black people are the ones should have guns? Like you, I have seen the eye spinning irony of this. HOW FOR THE LOVE OF GOD WHY ARE WE NOT ILLUSTRATING THIS ABSURDITY???!!!

Anyway folks, it is true that there have been abusive bigoted cops that have harassed blacks. They were democrats by the way. Liberals like to use footage of blacks getting abused by police officers using fire hoses, releasing dogs and what not on blacks. These things happened in Democrat run states, with Democrat governors, Democrat mayors, and democrat sheriffs like Sheriff Bull Connor, who was also in the KKK. These are the abusers liberals like to point to, but they leave out that they were Democrats. The places where you hear about police brutality today are in cities run by Democrats.

They put in policies that exacerbate the problem of children growing up without fathers as they want to be the nanny-state to replace the father. Which makes the nanny-state the tranny-state as it assumes to replace the father while wanting people dependent on the nanny-state boob. And trying to get milk from bogus boobs is very unfulfilling, and the black community wonders why it feels so unfulfilled. That milk doesn't really come from the government. It's stolen from others, and it leaves those whom it was stolen from less able to hire others.

People grow up in the inner city, insecure, confused, and angry. They want justice for how rotten their life is, and are willing to take it out on anybody around them to satisfy their idea that they are owed for their misery. They will rob and kill each other in these democrat run areas that Democrats have fashioned. So yes, you will see cops on edge. They're dealing with people who will shoot each other over nothing. So yes, they tend to be more strict with them for the cop's own safety. Are there cops out there with a power trip? Yes. I've run into them myself. One example was a female police officer who drew her gun on me and taunted me, saying "Yeah. You don't like having a gun drawn on you do you." Why she said that, I don't know. I've had a police officer spit in my path and look me right in the eye like he was itching for me to react. Both in democrat run areas by the way.

I know there are police officers out there that have a chip on their shoulder. But I've enjoyed encountering more police officers who represent their sworn duty with honor, treated citizens with respect, and not act like bullies with a badge. But Democrats want to push the idea that blacks are targets for cops and are targeted by the prison industrial complex while overlooking that these blacks are getting locked up in democrat controlled areas. The point is, Democrats have to make blacks look like victims. Victims who have to be dependent on Democrats to be in their corner while keeping them oblivious to the fact that Democrats are the very ones cornering them. With blacks under their control, they use them to play on people's guilt so people will side with them on infringing on our second amendment rights.

Do you see the insidious work of Democrats and how they use blacks to do the devastation that they're doing? Do you not see the importance of getting in the way of the democrat influence and grip the Democrats have on blacks? This will always be an ongoing struggle. Democrats will ALWAYS try to own blacks. This will go on until Jesus steps in personally to put an end to it. In the meantime, we still have a responsibility to not just lay down and let the deception take over.

When Republicans stepped up to directly get in the way of Democrats intruding on the rights of blacks, and blacks were able to enjoy their rights, there was prosperity, but the Democrats jumped right back in and before you know it blacks lost their rights again. This back and forth went on from the 1860's to the 1960's. Republicans stepped up to directly get in the way of democrats intruding on the rights of blacks, and blacks were able to enjoy their rights and there was prosperity. But the Democrats jumped right back in only this time what the Democrats have done was even worse. The Democrats aren't trying to force blacks to not have rights, (unless it's a pre-born kid.) The Democrats are instead making blacks believe that someone else is denying them rights. And the perpetrators are made out to be the Republican Party. And while blacks are distracted with cursing the Republican party for something they didn't do, Democrats work on tightening the shackles on blacks; controlling their population with abortion. Keeping them in public school where they can indoctrinate them and control them to use them as voter attraction tools.

Democrats will fight tooth and nail to keep them in public school as opposed to letting them go to private schools where they'd be free from the democrat's indoctrination. You can't even homeschool your kids without Democrats wanting to be involved. Like here in California, where we have CAVA "California Virtual Academy." It's not home-school its "virtual public school". Which just means the indoctrination goes right to your home. It's not just the teacher indoctrinating the students; they're using the parents to do it right in their own home. And why not? Those parents received the same indoctrination. Democrats are obsessed with controlling people, especially blacks. Blacks are who they depend on the most to push their agenda. "You're not a bigot, are you? Because if you don't support our policies you hate black people." See how that works?

That's all it takes! Don't you think we have to destroy this absurd narrative? To do that it's going to take illustrations of their absurdity.

Like I said, this is ongoing. Democrats want to control blacks. Republicans intervene to break them away from Democrat control. Blacks prosper, and Democrats come back in pushing to reclaim blacks. They are obsessed with blacks. Republicans, it's that time again to deny Democrats of what they think is their prize. This isn't about treating blacks like we're special and having to go out of your way to help black because we can't help ourselves. Much of the black community is being conditioned by Democrats right when they start learning how to read. It used to be that Democrats didn't allow blacks to read to keep them enslaved. Now the Democrats want blacks to know how to read what democrats write for them, so they can keep them enslaved mentally.

They are the ones creating most of the entertainment and content that blacks see, which is a deep drilling instrument that gets in deep enough to make a lasting imprint. And though it's not difficult to deposit these shallow ideas so deeply, the ground somehow becomes very difficult to drill through to extract them.

Democrats will always try to find a way to control blacks. That alone should tell you that something makes blacks really important to Democrats. It takes ongoing vigilance to keep interfering with that influence. We have to stay in the way of Democrats influencing blacks to knock themselves out, because if we don't, we knock ourselves out too as Democrats will just use blacks to convince people that Republicans just want the right to have guns so they can go around shooting black people thus keeping the country divided with racial tension, and tension causes meltdown. This isn't about coddling blacks and always having to take care of blacks. That's not what we need. The point is that Democrats are obsessed with blacks, and are always trying to use blacks to achieve the evil ideas of Democrats. It's not about always making blacks a special project. It's about interfering with Democrats succeeding at using them. It's like with Israel. There are people obsessed with eliminating them and controlling their territory. It isn't about coddling Israel. American blacks and Israelis don't need to be coddled, but for some reason, it's really important to the Godless to control us. That's what has to be interfered with. In America the more Democrats have control over blacks, the more damage they can do. We are the most valuable and effective commodity for Democrats to do that. They will always try to seduce or coerce blacks to keep blacks as their voter stock and use their plight to attract others. Support the productions of illustrations to exhibit this and it will make it more difficult for Democrats to sneak into the black community's mind, and then be used by Democrats to screw up other people's minds.

CHAPTER V
YOU FIGHT LIKE A GIRL

There's nothing wrong with fighting like a girl... If you're a girl. However, a man fighting like a girl, or shall we say fighting against reality, society and biology, and most importantly against God with the idea that they're a woman despite actually being a man, then that's not a good way to fight like a girl.

A woman who will fight for her marriage and the children that she and her husband have is a woman you do not want to mess with. To fight like a girl in that sense is of high nobility and a formidable one to try to trifle with.

However, a woman who assumes to fight like a girl because she thinks it's empowering to deprive a kid in the womb of their God-given rights, or fighting for people to accept delusions about gender, or throwing tantrums about equality while demanding special treatment, then this is a disgrace to what it is to fight like a girl, and only the terribly weak are afraid of such people.

I'm not afraid of bullies who demand the so-called right to rip kids apart in the womb. The women of the suffragist movement were respectable. Women who are taking the rights suffragists fought for just to demand the so-called right to deprive other people of theirs, are repugnant.

They demand equality for all, but somehow they don't extend that equality to the kid in the womb. Despite all that feminine pride, they'll still even murder a little girl. But, I guess, in their so-called reasoning, the girl in the womb didn't decide if she really wants to be a girl. So it's fair game.

These are not new issues. The Bible has been warning us about these things in the Old Testament. Gender confusion was an issue back then. It was such an issue that God said it had to be dealt with it in the most stringent fashion.

Why? Why would God demand to have men killed for having sex with other men?

Doesn't God know that mankind would hold that against Him and accuse Him of being a bigoted murderous tyrant? Ok, so if God were to say homosexuality is ok, then people would still curse God for double the instances of marriages breaking up because now there's twice as many people to commit adultery with. If some dude, or woman, thinks they want to explore their curiosity, go ahead. Double the adultery; Double the possibility of divorce, and a broken home for kids. People would curse God for that, too, when their suffering results from their own selfish desires.

Look at people today, going further off the deep end due to feminism. Feminists, Liberals, and atheists get all twisty britches over Bible verses like 1 Timothy 2:12, which says:

"I do not permit a woman to teach or to assume authority over a man; she must be quiet." Many women, in general, wince over that verse - even some conservative women. My wife struggled with it. Then, the Lord gave us peace concerning that verse. He offered me this, to tell my wife: "Be quiet! Gimme some booty and a sandwich." "I'M KIDDING!!!" But, seriously...

The reason why the Lord allowed this opinion to be included as canonical isn't because of chauvinism, or lack of respect for a woman's opinion, or position of leadership. The problem is when a woman teaches and exercises authority as a woman with something to prove as a woman. When pride is at the core of her motivation to teach or assume authority, this is when she needs to be quiet. A woman looking to glorify herself as a woman before doing things for the glory of God is satanic. It's pride. The first sin. This was a problem back then, and it is a problem now.

Feminism is a diseased influence. These women are teaching and abusing authority, and their influence yields men trying to emulate women. The results are wicked. These women want men to behave more like women, and then they wonder why and are frustrated that men aren't stepping up and being men. They're confused and wicked worldview of feminism yields women despising men while they try to behave like men, and then get angry when men treat them like men because all along it's special treatment they really wanted in the first place. Treat a feminist with respect and they tend to see it as an insulting attempt to make them conform to a social construct. Treat them equal and they're still unhappy because equality isn't their goal. Entitlement is.

Entitlement, however, never satisfies. That can be seen in men feeling entitled to be recognized as a woman, and they find that they still don't feel fulfilled. When men submit to feminist influences they end up confused, and it negatively affects society. Society accelerates in decay. Progressive decay. Liberals ask, "How are these people being 'what they want' and loving 'who they want' going to affect you?! All the while, their declared objective is to affect change for people to have to abide by. They're determined to affect culture and politics with their perversion while hoodwinking people into thinking their desires aren't going to affect anybody. It's no big deal. Meanwhile, all they've been doing is making a big deal about it, and demanding people be affected by it, and if you're not affected by it to their pseudo-satisfaction, they'll have you sued. But feminists' wanting to influence people doesn't affect anyone, so they'd have you believe. Prideful women teaching and exercising authority over a man does harm.

A woman teaching a man, or having a position of authority, isn't a problem. A woman poisoned with pride and a feminist mindset teaching and excising authority over a man is. If her motivation is to bring God glory, that is good. Glory to herself is bad. This goes for men too. A man trying to prove something, for the glory of himself, is bad. Pride screws things up.

God wasn't being harsh in His judgment of homosexuality; He was being merciful in instituting such a law to spare us the problems it causes. Homosexuality is a notorious disease spreader. When the Bible spoke of these men, they were uncircumcised. An uncircumcised penis is more prone to infection. So, if a man takes that thing and puts it into another man's orifice that was designed to be the primary portal of eliminating waste from the body, then you're inviting problems, and will spread problems. These people are selfish and are hung up on pleasure. So much so, that the consequences don't concern them. Instant gratification does. They will justify their desires and continue doing what they do, disregarding the risk they present to someone else. This spreads disease and wipes out populations. This is why God says to have them killed. I would not want to kill a person for being gay. I also would not want to see a population get diseased due to the unclean lifestyle of homosexuality.

Fortunately, although God's truth on homosexuality hasn't changed, how He will deal with it has. We do not put homosexuals to death. God's word tells us:

"Or do you not know that the unrighteous will not inherit the kingdom of God? Do not be deceived: neither the sexually immoral, nor idolaters, nor adulterers, nor men who practice homosexuality, nor thieves, nor the greedy, nor drunkards, nor verbal abusers, nor swindlers, will inherit the kingdom of God." - 1st Corinthians 6:9-10 ESV

So for the homosexuals that so selfishly think we or the Bible is just picking on them, they are mistaken.

God didn't just have homosexuals put to death. Straight people were put to death too. A man who had straight sex with a woman was put to death if he raped her.

"But if out in the country a man happens to meet a young woman pledged to be married and rapes her, only the man who has done this shall die." -Deuteronomy 22:25-26 NIV

See? A man having heterosexual sex outside of God's ordinance is punishable by death.

When a man has sex outside of God's ordinance it is punishable. Homosexuality is outside of God's ordinance. It is punishable. A man forcing himself on a woman is punishable. A man committing adultery with another man or woman is punishable.

Why does it seem that homosexuality gets the harshest punishment? Because homosexuality is the greater offender of nature. It's a greater contributor to cultural breakdown, while at the same time a symptom of breakdown. Rape is wrong, detestable, and deserving of harsh punishment. It violates another person's rights. It violates the commandment to not covet. It violates the commandment to not steal.

It violates the commandment to honor your father and mother. Rape totally brings dishonor, but it is still male and female, (if it is rape where the rapist is a male and the victim is female), so it hasn't violated the law of nature. It disgustingly violates: physically, mentally, emotionally, morally, and spiritually. But it did not break the natural rule.

When you mess with the rules of nature, such as with homosexuality, you are messing with the laws that God put in place to facilitate His creation of life. Without life, there is no morality, physicality, mentality, emotionality, morality, or spirituality to abuse or enjoy anyway.

Naturality (yeah, I said it), has to be abided by too. When you go against the rules of nature, you are going against the very thing God set up to facilitate life for us to even have populations, civilizations, cultures, and what not. This is why homosexuality is a practice that God does not dig at all. And notice, the commandant is to honor your father and mother, not your father and father or your mother and mother.

But as I said earlier, Jesus changed how homosexuality is dealt with. He didn't change the sin status of it. Those who insist on engaging in homosexuality will receive the same sentence as straight people who commit adultery, the same sentence as straight people who fornicate, the same as all people who are drunks (I'm quite sure that includes druggies), and verbal abusers too. So also, if you're verbally abusive to your spouse, your kids, employees, employers, co-workers, parents, or if you sit around all day trolling people - promoting bigotry and slander online, then you will receive the same fate as homosexuals, no matter how straight you are.

If you are a greedy, swindling thief, then you and all of the aforementioned will not inherit the Kingdom of God. See, Homosexuals? It's not just your behavior, but your behavior is included in what will deny your being able to inherit the Kingdom of God. So, dude. Be a dude. Resist the temptation to be effeminate. It's one thing to be a little flamboyant, which is ok, but flamboyant should not become flaming. It's one thing to dress up like a woman for a gag,

119

but dressing up like a woman because that's how you see yourself, and how you want others to see you, is a problem.

These people refuse to keep it to themselves. They insist that what they do is their own business and others should butt out of it, but just like they give way to delusions of thinking they're the opposite sex, they delude themselves into thinking they just want people to mind their own business, yet these people are demanding to make it everybody's business. This happens when the influence of feminism becomes more authoritative in the culture. This is who the Bible is telling to sit down and shut up.

To the effeminate male: When your delusions of being a woman start assuming authority over your thinking, then you have allowed this bossy, feminine phantom to lead you to go against the law of nature authored by God. This is the woman the Bible is telling to sit down and shut up. This breeds confusion in the culture. A culture breaks down when there is an increase of men giving way to feminism and women gaining more influence with it.

Along with this delusion is them thinking it's progressive. It's only progressive in that it's getting worse as a mental and emotional disease. I must add that effeminate and homosexual behavior is not the only cause of societal breakdown. It just helps out a lot. It's both contributor and result. We are plagued by a lack of husbands. Not fathers, but husbands. We'll explore that more in a bit. But, for a long time, people have been raised by single mothers telling their kids that *she has to be both the mommy and the daddy.* I hear women, to this day, boasting in their single-motherhood, talking about how they've been both the mommy and the daddy.

Well, look how that's turning out. On top of that, we have a liberal culture that promotes the idea that a woman doesn't need a man. She's applauded for raising her kids on her own. She's strong and independent! Even though Liberals demand people should be taxed more for that single mother to be dependent on WIC, EBT, and such tax-funded programs. It's cruel to promote the idea that a woman is strong to raise children on her own. It should be discouraged as much as possible. It is not meant for a parent to do it alone. A strong woman is a woman that her husband will give his life for. Her sweetness draws him willingly. He's not stuck with her like an odor he can't he wash off from her being spoiled. I'm not ignorant to the fact that there are abusive men, and the women may have to get the kids away from them. However, I'm just holding to the assertion of feminist who are supposed to be strong, invincible, roaring women. How is a mere man going to cause these p**sy-hat wearing pole scratchers to flee with the children when they've got p**sy-power? I'm not being facetious about spousal abuse. Putting a spouse and children in danger or any kind of trauma is detestable.

The bitterness of a woman is not her strength but her weakness. The sweetness of a wife is her strength. She is given by the Lord to crown her husband as king. A man cannot be king until the Lord gives him a wife to serve.

Do not mistake sweetness for weakness. The sweetness of a woman is the strongest magnet. It's like the sweet kinetic poetry of a ballerina. Her movements are mesmerizing with elegance and fluidity. She may move with the softness of a breeze, but you would not want her to kick you in the face.

It takes a lot of muscle strength, not muscle size, but muscle tone, to execute such graceful motion and sustain such poise. It takes power to move that sweetly! A woman with the attitude of not needing a man and that she's a queen on her own is selfish. A man who says the same respectively, is the same. A woman cannot be queen until the Lord leads her to a man to crown as her husband and king.

His strength is in using his dominion to serve, not to be domineering. Men and women who resist their royal design to serve each other as king and queen do so out of pride that makes them not want to be humble before each other and before God. Both, men and women, claiming to not need one another is a prideful cover-up of their insecurities. They're superficial, and on the surface they think or try to show that they're too good for anybody, but underneath the surface is someone who can't see why anybody would want them. They can hardly stand to be alone with themselves.

So, to spare themselves the pain of rejection in someone finding out just how miserable they are to be with, they just guard themselves with the declaration that they don't need another. But, more and more, that's what's promoted in the culture; the so-called, empowerment of women. That is often promoted as the so-called empowerment of a woman not needing a man to raise a kid with, and a woman not needing a man to decide to kill the kid in the womb. Feminism wants things like this to be standards for women. This is authoritative to feminists.

This isn't just the fault of feminism trying to take over. This is also the fault of males not being the men God created them to be. A man of God will be a husband to his wife. A woman of God will be a wife to her husband. They will take what God designed to be the best chance for their children to grow up with a minimized possibility of being insecure because they were brought up with parents who found security with God, Who made them secure with each other. We can see this lack of security has given birth to people growing up more and more insecure. These husbands and wives who left God out of the mix didn't minimize the possibility of their children growing up confused.

As we can see, more and more people are growing confused as God's design of husbands and wives are in shorter supply. But these dynamics feed each other. There's a lack of husbands and wives because of insecure confused people, and there's insecure and confused people because of the lack of husbands and wives raising up more secure people. Both of them occur when God is left out. That is the core that all these problems stem from.

It's so sad to see spouses who have so much, yet they are so flippin' miserable because they don't have God. They're way too insecure to be that vulnerable to God, which makes them insecure with their spouse, and they make each other miserable. They don't realize that lowering your guard before God raises your security.

Now some may be thinking, I'm only targeting men as being the only ones with the problem of being affected by feminism and them succumbing to the delusion that they identify as a female. *How is it feminism when a woman identifies as a male, or non-binary, or gender neutral, or whatever unstable ideas concerning human biology they have?*

None of that matters, because you can still be pretty darn sure that every one of these confused females are feminists. She could be the most male wanna be, mullet wearing, pressed-down-boob-bra-sporting, armpit hair having lesbian on the block. She's still most likely a feminist. See? A man falling for the delusion that he's a woman has fallen to the spell of feminism. A woman who has fallen for the delusion that she's a man still tends to be a feminist. She will still embrace feminism. She will feel like she's entitled and empowered as a woman to identify as a... Wait for it... MAN! How's that for irony and a self-defeating pursuit!?

But homosexuals and gender-confused people feel like it's not fair that they alone can't pursue their sexual and gender interest. These people are so selfish. Didn't we just read the Word of God that says none of us can pursue the aforementioned sins and inherit the Kingdom of God?

You think heterosexuals don't want to pursue sexual interests? If a straight person wants to fornicate they don't inherit the kingdom either. A straight person who is married has to resist temptation too. A heterosexual has to resist burning desires and urges too. Not just homosexuals.

On top of that, everybody has to resist the urge to steal, covet other people's stuff, slander, and murder. From one degree to another, these things can be very difficult for some people to resist. We aren't always successful resisting them at all. So yes, homosexuals, you have to resist temptations just like the rest of us. There's no excuse or special circumstance for you. Do you want to be treated equally? Here you go. You have to resist sexual immorality just like the rest of us. Fornication is sexually immoral for heterosexuals, and fornication is sexually immoral for homosexuals.

Heterosexuals can enjoy the most super fantastic sex all they want within their marriage. Homosexuals cannot because nature does not recognize it. You cannot marry poles to poles and holes to holes. It physically does not work, and our physiology doesn't lend to the mutual exchange of pleasure in homosexual practice. Homosexuals may be having a blast having sex, but they're lying to themselves if they think they're married. I go more in-depth on this in my

Audiobook Weapon of A.S.S. Destruction (American Socialist States.)

I understand that homosexuality is pleasurable to them, and since it's pleasurable to them they don't see it as wrong. But just because something feels good, or right, doesn't mean that it is. Scratching chickenpox may feel right, but it is definitely the wrong thing to do.

A lot of homosexuals consider themselves very health conscious while ignoring that their so-called orientation is unhealthy. They can see when a person's diet is harming them, but the person who's eating what they enjoy is just satisfying their desire. It tastes good and feels good to indulge in their diet that is most likely going to result in diabetes. Doing what feels good is often not good for you. God understands the desire to have sex. He created sex, but He also created it to be enjoyed between a husband and wife. Homosexuals want to have sex. That's very understandable, but they want to have sex outside of the design of sex. This is symptomatic of mental, emotional and spiritual illness.

Homosexuality tends to surface in people's behavior when their mental, emotional, and spiritual state has been compromised. When people get drunk they're not in their right mind, and tend to lower their inhibitions, and may engage in homosexual activity. It happens a lot. Ask a person who's tried gay sex. They'll be like, "Yeah we were drinking, and…"

A person who has been abused has been compromised mentally, emotionally, physically, and spiritually to one degree or another. Homosexual tendencies tend to surface. Notice, I said surface. Why? Because, I don't care how straight you are, homosexuality is a bug that's in all of us because the hearts of all of us are wicked. Each one of us has the potential to act out homosexual behavior just as much as we have the potential to steal, murder, commit adultery, or slander.

Many of us don't commit murder because it doesn't interest us, and we know it's wrong, but that doesn't even come close to meaning that it's not possible for any of us to do. Many commit abortion or support it because they don't see it as wrong. To continue, something happens to where you're mentally, emotionally, physically spiritually compromised, and you may find yourself feeling justified to murder.

People fantasize about murder. You want to murder somebody who cut you off on the road. There's a murderer in all of us. Some are weaker to it than most.

There's a thief in all of us. Some people resort to it when life throws a curve at them so hard that they may really struggle to recover from it and find themselves stealing to try to survive what came against them. They might have been decent people, but life just might have 'went upside their head' with a devastating blow.

Then you have people who steal for the thrill, or to satisfy their idea that they're entitled, owed, or to just satisfy their greed. These people don't need much prompting to steal. But these people are mentally, emotionally, physically, and spiritually compromised as it is. You know that, because we tend to view people who feel entitled to things as having something wrong with them. And entitlement minded people <u>are wrong</u>, because their mentality leads to them feeling justified in taking things that belong to someone else. How do people get like that? A lot of times it comes from them being told over and over that they're owed. They want justice, and it feels empowering to them to demand or take what they feel entitled to as recompense for what they feel was taken from them. There's a thief in all of us. Some are just weaker to the urge of it than others, for whatever reason.

There's a slanderer in all of us. There's an adulterer in all of us. And yes, there are homosexual tendencies in all of us. It does not mean you're gay, or even a little gay. It just means you're a sinner, and everybody has a sin they're weaker to than other sins to some degree. It doesn't mean that a person is left powerless to whatever sin they are weakest to. It just means they may struggle with certain sins more than others. Sin is a package that we've all been infected with. We all inherited the same contents in that sin package. The contents of that package contain the same sins, but they surface in people in different degrees.

A person who commits a crime has been mentally, emotionally, physically spiritually compromised. Even if they haven't had a hard life, and they've got a good education, they've come from a loving family, they've never known what it's like to be hungry, etc., but still

125

feel the urge to steal. Are there cases of this? Yes. Are these people mentally, emotionally, physically, and spiritually compromised? Hell yes!

Because considering the good life they came from, they'd have to have some screws loose if they still feel the need to steal from someone else. Sure, it's just a little harmless fun. Who cares, Right? For all they have, taking what belongs to someone else is fun for them?

The point is, major prompting, or minor promoting, steal little, or steal big, it still means that all of us could be a thief. Even if you despise theft! Thieves hate thieves too! You could still be a thief!

Now when that thief is put in prison for doing things out of being mentally, emotionally, physically, and spiritually compromised, they're going to be even further mentally, emotionally, physically, and spiritually compromised because they are going to be in another state that is unnatural to us; not free.

It's not natural for us to not be free. When we are locked up and not free, we are mentally, emotionally, physically, and spiritually compromised. Freedom is among the most important states God gave for us to be in. The first commandment includes this statement,

"I am the Lord your God who brought you out of Egypt."

The word Egypt itself means oppression. That statement doesn't sound like a law, does it? But it absolutely is a law. Why? Because the Highest truth there is - is that God IS. And He is that God who liberates from oppression. This means God has it written in the law that we are supposed to be free. It is the law that we are free. If you break the law, you will be punished by being deprived of what man desires the most, and usually what man abuses the most; freedom.

People abuse freedom. Why? Because, they're mentally, emotionally, physically, and spiritually compromised. You ain't right if you're abusing freedom. Especially when you're in denial of when you're doing it, and can only see it as an intrusion on your freedom when people resist you intruding on theirs or other's. If you intrude on the freedoms of other's, yours will be taken away. When a person is rightfully punished with being placed in the unnatural state of no freedom, they are even further mentally, emotionally, physically, and spiritually compromised. But they forfeited they're right to be in the natural state of freedom by intruding on another person's rights. And this is when homosexual behavior tends to really surface. It's not just because they're only locked up with the same sex. It's because they're mentally, emotionally, physically, and spiritually compromised.

If a person needs sexual release, one would think that masturbation would be the remedy for that. Nope. Masturbation seems to lose its appeal compared to having sex, even with a member of the same gender, because not being free is not the right state to be in. And people ended up in this 'not right state' because they succumbed to their desires that were of the 'wrong state.' Put those together and homosexuality is likely to surface when a person is affected by being in the unnatural state of not being free.

That's not me saying that a person should not be imprisoned for their crimes. It means they've allowed their desires to put them in a state that's going to be even more difficult for them to right their state. Now they're having gay sex. But this further makes my point of what I said in my previous book, Weapon of A.S.S. Destruction. (American Socialist States) The primary function of sex is to procreate. Yes, sex is basically the most pleasurable experience humans can have, and sex is far more often engaged in for pleasure than for procreation. But, considering that the marriage of the male seed to the female egg is the only way we get here, that means that the primary function of sex is to procreate.

The primary function of sex can be proven even with homosexuality. For instance, many people who are attracted to the same sex struggle with it. They know it's wrong to feel desirous of the same sex. If they're feeling the urge to have gay sex yet feeling conflicted about it then why not just self-stimulate; just release the urge and be free from the inner conflict? As mentioned before, the need for sexual release should be easy to resolve by just "rubbing one out" with a "selfie", but that won't do. Sexual release isn't the real motivation... Mating is.

When a person is mentally, emotionally, physically, and spiritually compromised, promiscuity and homosexuality often become stronger tendencies. Sometimes people in these states may shut down sexually. But I'm talking about the surfacing of homosexual behavior due to being mentally, emotionally, physically, and spiritually compromised. Why can't a rapist just be content with masturbation? Why can't a homosexual be content with masturbation? Why can't a pedophile be content with masturbation? Because these people are mentally, emotionally, physically, and spiritually compromised.

But, they are also proof that the primary function of sex is to procreate. We are not asexual creatures. We know instinctually that there has to be another party involved in our sexual activity. That is paramount. This is why masturbation will not suffice. A person who rapes is not driven by sexual release, but has blindly submitted to their urge to mate. However, since they are mentally, emotionally, physically, and spiritually compromised, their mating instinct is corrupted, and the corruption manifests as a sense of entitlement. This results in the rapist subjecting another to their corrupted filter of the instinctual drive for their compulsion to mate. Homosexuality is the same in that the mating instinct is unchecked. A lot of times a person with homosexual tendencies knows something is wrong about it, but they are driven by their instinct to mate, not by sexual release. Our reproductive design knows there has to be another party involved for us to perpetuate our species. Masturbation does not fulfill the reproduction routine. There has to be a partner. But the reproductive programming has been corrupted. The person has been mentally, emotionally, physically, and spiritually compromised. It results in a glitch in the reproductive routine that renders questionable mating practices and the pursuit of unsuitable mating partners. Consider, for instance: incest, pederasty, bestiality, and homosexuality.

Homosexuals don't like homosexuality to be put in the same boat as bestiality, yet homosexuals are the ones who try to make the case that homosexuality is natural because beasts do it. Beasts also have incest, they don't age discriminate (we'd call that statutory rape). Beasts eat their own poo, eat their own young etc. But homosexuals don't want their orientation to be compared to bestiality while saying their orientation is natural because beasts do it. Ok.

But . . . again, my point is, homosexuals and liberals try to say that pleasure is the primary function of sex. They say that because if they concede that procreation is the primary function of sex, then that would be them having to sign the reality-check that their orientation is unnatural, and that they are mentally, emotionally, physically, and spiritually compromised.

If pleasure is the primary function of sex, then nobody should frown on people comparing homosexuality to bestiality, incest, pederasty, or rape because all of these things would be done out of the pursuit of pleasure. But, the truth is, people do these things because they're driven by an instinct to mate that is filtered through a person who's mentally, emotionally, physically, and spiritually compromised.

Which of these do you think a halfway well-adjusted person would do for sexual gratification?

Masturbate oooorrrrrr:

A. Rape,

B. Molest,

C. Have sex with their relative,

D. Have sex with another species?

E. Put his penis where another man poops from.

I think the person who just sticks with the *selfie* would win the contest of being seen as being closer to being, even halfway, in a better frame of mind than the others mentioned. Especially if we're abiding by the liberal humanist model that the primary function of sex is for pleasure. If a person is masturbating and thinking they're involved in procreating, then I'd say, "Yeah, that person has gone mental." But, like I said, if sexual pleasure was the primary function, people would be satisfied with masturbation, but it's not. Mating is the primary function, and these people are driven by a corrupted instinct to mate.

But strangely enough, people would rather engage in detestable acts, engaging with, or subjecting others to their sexual immorality. Why can't they just keep it to themselves and rely on themselves to gratify themselves sexually, rather than involving other people to satisfy their urges in a way that is immoral? Because our reproductive directive dictates that there is supposed to be joining. And being mentally, emotionally, physically, and spiritually compromised corrupts that directive. This results in the desire to act on the driving instinct to mate, having a corrupted discretion about who, or what, to mate with.

But these people don't do it in their mind to procreate, they do it for pleasure, and according to homosexuals, that is their prime directive, and if that's the case then homosexuals should not mind being lumped-in with what other people do for pleasure. They don't understand that pleasure is part of the motivation to mate in the first place. It's tied in with our instinct to mate.

Like I said, many homosexuals know that being gay is wrong, but they are driven by the need to mate, not just by the need of the pleasure of sexual release. You can masturbate and achieve that. But it doesn't satisfy the mating instinct. Those who act on their corrupted mating instincts also feel unfulfilled. This is why depression is so prominent with homosexuals. They even have to call themselves "gay" to convince themselves that they're happy when they're really not.

I'm not saying masturbation is the solution, because we couldn't survive as a species if people just engaged in selfies for pleasure. Often, people suffering from depression, and whatnot, engage in masturbation a lot. This contributes more to their depression as they rub away their self-esteem. And being that it doesn't fulfill the companionship aspect necessary for mating, they feel even more incomplete. (I'm not saying masturbation is wrong, but it can be abused.)

Some would ask, "What about straight couples that can't have children? Do they feel incomplete?" Naturally they will, and many are affected by that feeling to one degree or another.

But a heterosexual, mutually consenting couple is at least standing on the natural foundation that is supposed to yield the natural biological result of procreation. Their engagement might not render it, but they are still engaged in the act that concurs with natural law and moral law.

Homosexuals may not prefer heterosexual sex, but no homosexual can say that married heterosexuality is wrong. A man and a woman having sex in the agreed covenant of marriage is not wrong. It does not violate moral law. It does not violate natural law. If they cannot have children, that has nothing to do with them doing something immoral or unnatural. They may feel a sense of incompleteness, but their broken heart is at least mendable on a solid foundation of what's natural and moral.

Homosexuality and transgenderism are not natural, or moral. They subject themselves to lots of incompleteness, and it doesn't mend well because their emptiness is based on an unnatural and immoral foundation as it is.

It's an exercise in selfishness that makes one weaker when exercise is supposed to make one stronger. These people, and those who encourage them, are not strong in their acceptance of it, they are weak in their submission to it.

All this is the influence of feminism. A man assuming to be a woman has submitted to the internal urge to behave as a woman. His maleness has been dominated by femininity. And feminism wants to dominate over males. They don't want equality, they want dominion. And a man who is homosexual, and or transgender, has given dominion to feminism. He has allowed it to assume authority over him.

A woman assuming to be a man will still consider herself a feminist. She's a contradiction, of course. She's pro-woman... but wants to destroy her female self... Why?... Because she likes women... Yeah... It's that screwed up.

These people are deceived into believing that they are of the "live and let live" mindset. This is one of those areas of why I'm so at odds with the Libertarian view.

(Not so much Christian conservatives with the 'small l' libertarian streak, however.) The "small l" libertarians are those who still understand that liberty is given by God and is preserved by adhering to God's statutes, not their own ideas of what they think liberty means. They don't put their own assumptions of liberty before God's safeguards of liberty. The downside is, that even with the 'small l' libertarians, they tend to give way to never being satisfied with how much the government should be limited. Kind of like how a liberal is not satisfied with how much control the state should have.)

The Libertarian view, however, if left to unchecked desires and ideals of limited government, would lead to anarchy, and then the demand for a regime to solve it, which will result in tyranny. Liberalism on the other hand certainly leads to totalitarianism. So, even though I am more comfortable with the Christian conservative with the "small l" libertarian streak, I am cautious of their inclinations from being so adamant about limiting government to appease their thirst for liberty. This to me is idolatry. The idol, in this case, is liberty, and if one is not careful, liberty can be more valuable to them than the Giver of liberty Himself. Even "Small l" libertarians seem to take for granted that not everybody exercises the kind of Godly responsibility necessary to handle a society like this, and it will backfire and explode with laws; laws that will institute chaos.

But the outright Libertarian view is just as much an enemy to liberty and the republic, as a Left-Wing Liberal. They both say, "live and let live"', but their worldview really doesn't allow that.

The Libertarian believes the same thing a Left-Wing Liberal does. The difference is that the Libertarian thinks that the individual will assume all responsibility over whatever they want to take liberties with, whereas the Left-Winger believes society should bear the responsibility of what people want to take liberties with. Both are delusional, caustic to liberty, and prove contradictory to the "live and let live" philosophy.

Libertarians and Left-Wing Liberals are both pro-choice. Libertarians just believe that the chooser should bear the responsibility of their choice. Left-Wing Liberals believe society should bear the responsibility of an individual's choice. Libertarians don't understand that if a person feels entitled to deprive the human creation of their God-given right to life, they will also feel entitled to deprive others of their right to property to facilitate their choice. This, of course, means bigger government, the very opposite thing Libertarians claim to want.

This is in total contradiction to the "live and let live" idiom. Because, if they really believed in the "live and let live" idiom, they would simply let the kid in the womb live. There would be no question. I don't care if they claim to be anti-abortion, yet believe it's still ultimately the mother's choice. That is still absolutely contradictory to the "live and let live" premise <u>because a party in this is not allowed to live</u>. The kid in the womb is put to death without due process. Is this what feminists pride themselves in by fighting like a girl? Feeling empowered by beating a defenseless unborn kid to death?

Is this the Libertarian and Left-Wing Liberal view of liberty and "live and let live"? I'm afraid their ideal is a mockery of liberty. They both say it should be an issue decided in the states. They're both wrong again. You are not even supposed to waste the people's money, or the courts time, trying to make a ruling against the rights of man codified in the supreme law of the land. The right to life, liberty and the pursuit of happiness are God-given, certain, and inalienable. I'm all for state's rights and sovereignty, but you can't abuse that and assume to take the liberty to deprive other people of theirs. That is hardly "live and let live'.' It is the destructive effect of feminism that thinks this is empowering.

Libertarians, like Left-Wing Liberals, also think 'live and let live' means people should be allowed to identify as whatever gender they choose, and marry the same sex if they choose. But I think even Libertarians hit a wall when it comes to transgenderism, and see the problem of people having to conform to the so-called political correctness of it. Libertarians hate conformity, thus they don't want to have to conform to appeasing the pro-transgender culture and the sanctions they're instituting.

Transgenderism is not 'live and let live'. It is another straight-up contradiction. How can transgenderism be 'live and let live' when your objective is to kill off your biological gender in a delusional effort to be reborn as the other gender you think you are? That is not 'live and let live'.

Transgenderism, gender fluidity, etc., is the devil trying to distort what God created in His image.

God purposely made this clear in the beginning, and it's a factor of biology that should be obvious and natural to us. But He stated this anyway,

So God created mankind in his own image, in the image of God he created them; male and female he created them. - Genesis 1:27 NIV

God warned Adam to not eat that fruit because this would invite death in, and what comes with death are all the distortions against what God has decreed. Like God saying, God created men and women. God knew that people would try to distort this truth, rebel against Him and the laws of biology He authored, try to further interfere with the image, and corrupt the code He created us in.

In their selfishness they think 'live and let live' means you have to join in their delusion and see them as they're deluded into seeing themselves. That's forcing others to kill off a reality to appease a fantasy. That's not 'live and let live'. These people do not respect our right to live in 'Real-ville'.

They sue us for not abandoning reality to be prisoners of their fantasy. It is the destructive effect of feminism that thinks this is empowering.

Libertarians, like Left Wing Liberals, also think 'live and let live' means same-sex marriage should be legal. This is not 'live and let live'. It is not 'live and let live' when you force other people to have to forfeit their First Amendment right to free religious exercise. The statutes of the Judeo-Christian faith say that homosexuality is a sin. God authored the law of nature, and nature does not condone homosexuality. But proponents of same-sex marriage want us to disobey the law of nature and be subject to their law. This is not 'live and let live'. This is an assault on the liberty we are supposed to be guaranteed in this republic that has rules guarding our rights.

What Libertarians are doing is emboldening a democracy. We are not meant to be a democracy. But what Libertarians are helping Liberals do is embolden the idea that if people pull enough of a population together to make a bunch of noise for their selfish ideals, then the rule of law of the republic can be trampled to transform us into a democracy.

Considering how obsessed Democrats are with transforming things around to fit their delusions, like party switches, ideological switches, climate changing, race switches, and gender switches, then it's logical to conclude that their objective is to transform our republic to a democracy. That's what they have always wanted. They have always hated the rule of law of this republic. They have always wanted to have the popular vote to do whatever it is they feel entitled to at the forced expense of someone else. Considering their persistence in wanting to transform things to fit their delusions, including promoting the idea of party switches, ideological switches (which I guess makes them trans-political), trans-race, trans-gender etc., I reckon a fitting name for them would just be the Tranny-Crats instead of Democrats.

If Democrats can make you believe the delusion that a man can switch to a woman and vice versa, then they can make you believe the lie that the parties switched sides too.

Homosexuals, wanting to be married, force people to endorse their lifestyle. For the record, if people want to be gay that is their choice, and nobody should harass them for their orientation, or show them any less respect as a person. (I'm not going to lie to them either about the eternal consequence.) But the balance to that is that they do not have the right to force us to endorse it. Making same-sex marriage legal has forced the republic to endorse their lifestyle. It was never supposed to be anybody else business. That's what they would preach. "Stay out of their bedrooms!" Yet, these hypocrites have totally pushed their private life on the public. It is the destructive effect of feminism that thinks this is empowering.

The satanic tool feminism is at the root that says, *gay people were born the way they are and can't help it.* Really? Where's the empowerment in that? So they're helpless victims from within? How can they be empowered from within if they're victimized from within?

See how it doesn't work? But this is the manipulation of feminism; men who are gay are born that way, and can't help it. They are helpless. Helpless to what? Being feminine? It pleases feminists that a man is too weak to fight against his internal feminine take over. He has been conquered, emasculated, and his junk has been claimed as a trophy for feminism. They are able to do this because the gay male is under the spell of believing he is brave.

Women who are gay are a contradiction exemplified. They tow the feminist line while being an insult to feminism as well as to their sexual orientation. They don't want a man inside of them or be dominated by a male, yet they're gay because they're dominated by the male specter inside of them anyway. The blind pride of feminism missed that one. But they still tow the line for feminism despite being internally male-dominated.

There's no excuse for them. Considering these people's obsession with empowerment, if they really wanted to show that they're empowered, they would show their strength in resisting what's unnatural. But these backward people would rather waste time resisting reality. They truly are rebels without a clue.

I won't really argue with how people are born. That doesn't matter. It's still a choice to go with it or not. If these people are as smart as they think they are, then they should see that they're ignoring biology and nature. If these people are as empowered as they think they are, they would resist their urges that contradict their biology.

But these people would rather the multitudes see it their way and abide by what they want. This compromises us as a republic and mutates us into a democracy.

The Libertarian view helps encourage this. It's a view that is an enemy of liberty by its overzealousness for liberty. Libertarians are unwitting allies of feminism. They hate the political correctness that comes with the effects of feminism, yet encourage the ideals that come from feminism because they think it's just going to stay within the confines of it, just being their individual choice and business to do so. They just don't get it that these people will expect others to be subject to their choice.

Feminism seeks to stigmatize the Bible so people won't want to read it and get truly liberated. They try to promote prejudice against the Bible as "anti-woman" with cherry-picked verses Like Deuteronomy 22:21 NIV which states,

"...she shall be brought to the door of her father's house and there the men of her town shall stone her to death. She has done an outrageous thing in Israel by being promiscuous while still in her father's house. You must purge the evil from among you."

Anti-Christians use scriptures like this to slander the Bible and promote the idea that the Bible demands the stoning of a woman for simply not being a virgin. Therefore the Bible promotes hostility towards women. There's that blinding effect of when pride and insecurity cross to blur their vision. They don't even see that men are put to death too.

"But Onan knew that the child would not be his; so whenever he slept with his brother's wife, he spilled his semen on the ground to keep from providing offspring for his brother. What he did was wicked in the LORD's sight; so the LORD put him to death also. Genesis 38:9-10 NASB

There! Ya happy!? Men get put to death too!

Women are not singled out in the Bible for the death penalty. Both can be put to death for violating God's ordinance concerning sex that interferes with life and peace among the people.

God instructing that a girl is to be stoned for not being a virgin is a lie. She's not being stoned for not being a virgin. She's being stoned for being a deceiver. Deceptions result in murder.

How do you feel about being betrayed? The betrayal that hurts the most comes from someone you love, and whom you thought loved you.

If a woman lies about her virginity, after the groom has come to love her, and on top of that his family has invested in the establishment for their marriage, then it's going to hurt real bad when they find out that she was lying.

This brings painful disappointment to the groom's family, and they are going to want satisfaction from the bride's family. The bride was living with her family while fornicating. If you're going to fornicate at least do it when you're independent. Not while living off your folks. People tend to not like their kids being sexually active before marriage. People come to accept it but they don't prefer it.

Halfway well-adjusted people don't proudly go around saying, *My kids' having sex*! (Even though we have screwed up parents who are proud of their kid's "choice", and with how accepting they are of their kids having gay sex, and gender fluid, and sexually explorative activities).

But for the most part, still, most people are not going to be proud of their kids having sex before marriage. Often they'd rather not even talk about it to avoid confronting the shame element.

But that's the operative word; Shame. And that's what a lying promiscuous daughter brought. This invited bigger problems. The anger over things like this flares up into clan wars. People kill over sexual indiscretions. People do that today, no matter what "spiritual beliefs" they have, or not. The domino effect of this can ignite a bloodbath, as families, hurt by deception, results in rage that blurs the line between justice and vengeance.

To discourage this from happening, the deceptive daughter is brought to her father's doorstep and stoned to death, in place of the mass death that would have resulted when the clans went to war over her deception. Families have gone to war over less.

It's not the Bible saying, "Oh, she's a slut. Stone her." It's the Bible saying "She's a selfish deceiver who betrayed multiple houses, and she would risk people fighting to the death because she couldn't wait to have sex until being wed to her husband." People might say, "What's the big deal? It's only sex" Ok. If sex is no big deal then she could have waited, right? What's the rush if it's no big deal?

Feminists reject the Bible because their cross-wiring of pride and insecurity only allows them to register a corrupt reception of verses like Exodus 22:18 NLT that says

"You must not allow a witch to live."

Oh, no! The Bible is singling out broom-riding women to be hostile against!

But wait. Leviticus 20:27 says,

'Now a man or a woman who is a medium or a spiritist shall surely be put to death. They shall be stoned with stones, their blood-guiltiness is upon them.'"

Why does God put the death penalty on witches and sorcerers? Right here:

…"There shall not be found among you anyone who makes his son or his daughter pass through the fire, one who uses divination, one who practices witchcraft, or one who interprets omens, or a sorcerer, or one who casts a spell, or a medium, or a spiritist, or one who calls up the dead. For whoever does these things is detestable to the LORD; and because of these detestable things the LORD your God will drive them out before you.... -Deuteronomy 18:10-12 NASB

God does not accept human sacrifice, and really, really frowns on child sacrifice. This is why God says to not have any other gods before Him because people will sacrifice human life to appease their god. Whether their god be money, convenience, their reputation, their career, etc.

The only thing that came close to a human sacrifice for God was Himself, personified as His son.

The abortion facility has become the biggest sacrificial alter there is. Kids are still passed through the fire, so to speak, as they are injected with a sodium that burns them from the inside. The same lethal injection they give to prisoners on death row, by the way.

To truly seek God means finding peace in Truth, and desiring His Justice. Any power a Christian has is, basically, to pray for the daily bread - to be fortified to do what God blessed us to do. You cannot bring God glory by harming the innocent for your own objective or gain.

Mockers accuse God of murder. These are the same people who say "If God is so good and powerful, why doesn't He get rid of all the wicked people?" News flash. He has, and then the mockers judge Him for it and call Him a murderer.

The only reason to pursue witchcraft and sorcery is for power. Period. Even if you want to call the power "Knowledge".

The premise of following Jesus is to give Him glory and recognize that He is the power, and we are to be obedient to Him and seek His strength to persevere and endure against the stealers of peace. We're not always very good at it, but that is the order.

The witch and sorcerer beg the spirits to give them power to command. The more power they want the more they're willing to deprive from another for sacrifice, even if they are the most well-meaning witch or sorcerer. They will think they are justified to make abominable sacrifices to receive the power to do what they're deceived into thinking is good.

Think Lord of the Rings. The potential to do such good, but knowing that they would be deceived into doing great evil while thinking they were doing good. The temptation of the ring's power intensified on the beholder, and the temptation of power was disguised as justification in convincing themselves that they would do great good with the power.

Another easy example would be Hitler. He thought he was doing a great good. The democrat Margaret Sanger thought the extermination of the Negro population was good. In their weakness for power they'll justify doing evil because they think they need the power to carry out their version of justice, which means sacrificing children isn't evil to them. This is why God has them put to death.

Liberals who pride themselves in the medical and holistic sciences preach that prevention is the best cure. God's sanctions are exactly that; preventative, and Liberals hate Him for it. Even Liberals who claim to be "Christians" hate God, because they don't love God for who He is. They're idolizing an idea of what they want God to be.

Mockers also single out verses like this: Deuteronomy 25:11-12

"If two men, a man and his countryman, are struggling together, and the wife of one comes near to deliver her husband from the hand of the one who is striking him, and puts out her hand and seizes his genitals, then you shall cut off her hand; you shall not show pity. Deuteronomy 25:11-12 NASB

They take this as the Bible being hostile to women. God does not want interference with the bloodline of His chosen. In a fight, with all the chaos and adrenaline, a woman might seize the opponent's testicles and crush them, compromising his posterity. They don't know by whom the Messiah may come through. God chose them to treat each other as if any one of them could be the forbearer of the Messiah. God made us in His image, and they were chosen to be the demonstrators of that message to us.

A woman who snatched up a fist-full of man-grape would not get her hand cut off for defending herself, whether she was attacked by a foreigner or by her countryman. She has the right to defend herself by any means necessary. The man has transgressed against her, and if she has to put the Jew-Jitsu grip on his jewels, so be it. He was a disgrace for trying to get his rape-on anyway.

But if two fellow countrymen are fighting with one another, and a wife jumps in and makes a gonad-grab, then God has a problem with that. God doesn't want fellow countrymen fighting with each other, but it's not detestable like rape. The men can work it out without playing nut-cracker. But if a wife intervenes to grasp the testicles of her opponent, then the fight won't end there, and it will invite a bigger fight.

The husband of the intervening wife will be humiliated as, *The man whose wife had to intervene on his behalf by seizing his opponent's genitals because the intervening wife's husband wasn't man enough to fight his own battle.* He will have to defend his manhood, which will have been just as bruised in pride as his opponent's manhood was bruised in body.

There would have to be a reckoning for that. The score would still have to be settled. The stakes of manhood will have been raised, and, chances are, others are going to want to get involved. The 'crap talkin' has been ramped up. The taunting and heckling of a sissy-man who needs his wife, "the jewel thief", to come rescue him. All that heckling can lead to a bigger fight than what was before, a bigger fight that heightens the possibility of murder.

So considering these things, God will deal harshly with a woman who grabs the testicles of her husband's opponent.

Liberals should understand this because they love to heckle people. They bully people until they snap and start shooting people, then blame guns. They cowardly troll people online because they know if people knew who these anonymous people were they'd track them down, take the device they trolled with and shove it up hiney-town.

People in those times didn't have a computer to hide behind. They would mock up front, and the fight would really be on. Actual fisticuffs. No keyboard karate.

It's funny how Liberals try to come off as the champions against bullying and harassment, yet, they do the most on-line heckling, harassment, and bullying.

Feminists see the Bible as a threat to their "liberty" for verses like this:

...28"If a man finds a girl who is a virgin, who is not engaged, and seizes her and lies with her and they are discovered, 29then the man who lay with her shall give to the girl's father fifty shekels of silver, and she shall become his wife because he has violated her; he cannot divorce her all his days. Deuteronomy 22:29 NASB

You'll get no argument from me about rape being detestable. It is a most despicable outcome of violating the commandment to not covet, and a detestable violation of the commandment to not steal. A virgin who is not within earshot of anyone who can hear her call for help has foolishly put herself at risk. There are feminists like that today. They put themselves in compromising positions, wearing clothing that implicates them as welcoming to the prospects of fornication, and then get angry when they're treated like the sex-objects they present themselves as.

They foolishly believe that a male should not view them as a sexual prospect. She just wants to *look* slutty, but you better not assume that she is slutty. And even if she is promiscuous, you'd either better not say that she is, or you'd better respect her for it. Yeah. It's that backward.

Even a feminist would see it as foolish to leave your doors unlocked and unattended when people know there's valuables in your home. People will steal your stuff. It's foolish to believe someone won't. It doesn't mean the owner wanted their place to get broken into, but it's still foolish for them to present the invitation.

It's foolish to not chain up a really nice bike. If it looks good and looks available, someone will steal it. It doesn't mean the owner wanted their bike stolen, but it was foolish to present the invitation. Should people steal? NO! Period! Even if it LOOKS like somebody wants you to come and get it! DON'T DO IT! Unless there's a sign on it that says, "FREE! PLEASE REMOVE" Like a couch on the owner's curb or something.

But, we agree that it's foolish to leave things without some kind of protection against being stolen because people steal! So why don't feminists understand that, in the Bible, a virgin walking around alone outside of the earshot of others has put herself in a position to have her body stolen? Should the male steal her body? NO! But people steal anyway, don't they? Her intention may not have been to have sex, but she put herself in the position to be stolen. There's no witnesses to hear her call for help.

Virginity was a highly valued gift for spouses to give to each other. An unwed post-virgin wasn't as desirable for marriage. That may rub people the wrong way, but if we really love our spouses, and are not taken by pride and selfishness, I'll bet we'd wish we would have saved ourselves for our spouse, and given them that unique gift that no-one else could have.

People steal out of weakness. So it's foolish to think that some weak male wouldn't steal a girl's virginity if the opportunity presented itself. A virgin out alone, too far to be heard, made herself an opportunity for a weak male.

If he rapes her in this instance, he must pay her father fifty shekels of silver and take her as his wife. Why? Because he has made her less desirable by stealing her virginity. She has less of a chance of being married.

What good would it do to kill him? She's still going to be an unwed, post-virgin. The man who raped the woman probably didn't have money to begin with, and now owes fifty shekels of silver to the father. That's a good hunk of coin. If the rapist cannot pay then he will be made a bond slave. He's got to pay off that debt.

Israelites weren't supposed to be enslaving each other, but they weren't supposed to be raping each other either. The rapist forfeited his rights by violating the girl's. He has to pay off that violation. And he is also in debt to the girl for the rest of his life.

The feminist only sees that the girl has to marry the rapist. No. The rapist has to answer to the father who makes him a slave to his daughter for life. The father doesn't have to make his daughter marry the rapist. But the rapist is now in debt to her for the rest of his life. Since it is less likely that she can get married, and since the women weren't the money makers the rapist becomes the recourse who has to make sure that the girl will not become destitute. If by chance the girl finds a man who wants to marry her even if she's not a virgin then so be it. The rapist cannot be divorced from his bond. He will die a slave of that family. Lucky for him the ancient Hebrews forbade castration. They could have made him a eunuch slave. And I wouldn't blame them.

So you see, Feminists? It's not the girl who loses her liberty. The rapist does. He is chained to a debt to the girl for life for what he took from her. But, if the virgin was betrothed, then a rapist would be put to death.

I can totally understand why women want to be independent; having careers, making their own money and such. I don't blame them, and I encourage it! It's scary and even infuriating to think that you'd have to be dependent on a man to survive. And between lots of men out there acting like bed hopping chauvinistic pigs, to males who want to be women, how secure can a woman feel with a man? I understand women wanting to establish security for themselves, but true security is in God.

Based on the way many men behave I don't blame women one bit for concluding they don't need a man. Although, they're deceived. It's man's BS they don't need. But, men and women do need each other.

Women sharing their skills, and their talents, are awesome! But when it's driven by pride and something to prove as a woman, then it corrupts, and negatively effects society, just as much as a man's when he is driven by pride. Prideful efforts are selfish. They're not about the humility of being of service to your fellow human being. It's about self-exaltation. This promotes societal decay.

A woman who puts her career before the Kingdom adds to societal decay. This, of course, goes for men too. If she puts her career before being a wife and a mother, it promotes societal decay.

We don't like it when men put their careers before everything else, why would it be better for women to do?

The Lord says to be fruitful and multiply. We're supposed to be productive (fruitful) before reproductive (Multiplying). God wants us creating, innovating and exchanging goods and services, but not forsaking Him, your spouse, and children. A woman is designed to nurture. She's biologically better equipped for it than a man. Too many women ignore this and don't want to apply that valuable biology to the upbringing of their kid, like it's beneath them. Being a career woman is more important than being a good mother, in their own eyes, but you better see them as a good mother anyway, according to them.

Circumstances arise that make it difficult for a mother to be there for those early years, and she may not easily be able to be there and has to work. That's a real struggle too, but it's not every case. Many prideful women just put being a wife and mother second. Women may not think it's fair that the man gets to go out and tackle the world. *Why is he so important out there?* Ok, women, it's not fair that you get to be home with the kids. But we thought that would make you happy; *being that they're so precious and all,* and not to mention they really need you far more than any job does. Biologically the man is better suited to hunt down what's needed for the wife and kids. Biologically The mother's direct presence is better suited to use what the husband brings home for her to put to use for the marriage and parentage. Many women have been deceived by feminism to find this as a degrading social construct.

I'm not one to strike a woman, or even the most rabid feminist, but a "solid right cross" is warranted. Again, Right-leaning people have been suckered into believing we're supposed to stay away from these issues. This results in being unprepared to counter and gives more ground to left-wing liberals to push us towards a democracy. From there, people will use the democracy to vote in totalitarianism because they will be suckered into believing that the state will give them all the security, education, food, healthcare, cell phones, internets, and whatever else they want. It will be the ultimate objective of feminism. Behold and hail the feminine power represented as the Nanny-State. She is the great giver and taker. She conceives rights and aborts them. She is the culmination of feminism; all under her rule.

The motto of this effeminate nation will be, "Love Wins!" written on a rainbow flag. And under this rainbow clad banner proclaiming that "Love Wins!" will be your pro-abortionists.

Killing children doesn't sound like love winning. The socialists and communists will be under this flag too; an institution of covetousness, theft, and envy - a system that resorts to violence and genocide to conform the population to it. That doesn't sound like love winning. Ideals of selfishness and self-righteousness that conclude in oppression and murder stand under the rainbow flag. If you believe in an unarmed citizenry that is totally vulnerable to an oppressive state then chances are you stand under the rainbow flag. If you are born a male or a female and you want to murder what you were born as because you think you're the other, and you want to force other people to accept your delusion, then chances are you stand under the rainbow flag.

If you're outraged that an unarmed black man (with a record mind you) has reacted violently towards a police officer and then was killed, while ignoring the fact that the black community commits more violent crime and murder against themselves than any other race in America, chances are you stand under the rainbow flag.

If you demand that people forsake the first right of the first amendment, (that being freedom of religious exercise), so as to submit to the lifestyle that disregards nature's ordinance, then chances are real good you stand under the rainbow flag.

All the ideals that stand under the rainbow flag institute oppression, disease, and murder. That's not love and that's not winning. It's delusional, and delusional people stand under the rainbow flag. This is the wickedness that flooded the world before God flooded it with water.

Y'all when God Let Noah know that the rainbow was going now serve as a reminder that the earth would never be flooded over again, it wasn't just a promise to Noah.

It was a reminder to God Himself.

Wait a minute, Zo! If God is all knowing, why would He need reminders? Well hello, that's why God is always in the know. He's smart enough to post reminders for Himself. And the rainbow, in this case, is one big colorful "Post-It", according to Genesis 9:14-17 NIV which says:

Whenever I bring clouds over the earth and the rainbow appears in the clouds, I will remember my covenant that is between me and you and every living creature of all flesh. And the waters shall never again become a flood to destroy all flesh. Whenever the rainbow appears in the clouds, I will see it and remember the everlasting covenant between God and all living creatures of every kind on the earth."

So God said to Noah, "This is the sign of the covenant I have established between me and all life on the earth." The Bible is basically telling us this: The dynamics of weather are designed by God. And this auto-run distilling system hydrates the earth. But if

God so wills it, He can override the weather program He designed and change it's routine from hydration to judgment.

As the storm clouds gather over the wickedness man commits on the earth, that's God looking at our wicked behavior and saying, *That is it! You've chosen to abuse your free will. You live for depravity and violence, and are evil towards each other. The world will be cleansed of the wickedness in a bath of My wrath.*

See? God got rid of the wicked people and now there's wicked people today who heckle, "If God is so good and powerful why doesn't He get rid of all the wicked people?" Well, He did, and wicked people today mock and call Him a murderer for it. They might want to reconsider asking that question, because wicked people ask that in their mocking, and are basically asking God to rid of them. And He will, as it is written, they are next.

As I was saying. God sees the dynamic of the rainbow that He said would remind Him that He would never flood the world again. Y'all, the Rainbow is a sign of God's mercy, but it's also a reminder of the wickedness that provoked the Lord to wrath and His judgment upon the wicked.

And today, people wave the rainbow flag in the face of His grace, trying to make a mockery of the sign He shared with Noah. The flag these people wave is on the tent pole that wicked ideals stand under.

The LGBT community wants to show solidarity with Muslims, yet the ideology of Islam says to murder and terrorize people who are not Muslim. All over, the people are lighting up structures with rainbow-colored lights. It really takes being "Like a Rainbow In the Dark" to a whole 'nother level. (Hat tip to Ronnie James Dio.) Because these people really are in darkness, parading their rainbows.

Jesus said it will be like the days of Noah, before He comes. How do we know that it's becoming like the days of Noah? Look at the rainbow flags. Standing under the rainbow flag is all the reasons why God Judged the earth in Noah's day. Full-on indulgence, you name it, from homosexuality to drunkenness to violence. Like it says in Luke 17:27, *as we look for the return of the Lord, folks will be gettin' their eat on, their DRANK on, their marry on, and so on.*

It will be like the days of Noah.

None of these things themselves are sinful. What will make them associated with the wickedness of Noah's day is that people will seek fulfillment in these things, abuse, and distort, them, while more and more forsaking God and despising Him; stuck-up, snooty people who think they're too good for God.

Marriage was created by God and it's not a sin. Trying to redefine it is. The rainbows we see paraded today are indicators of the sexual confusion, immorality, and perversions of Noah's day.

The rainbow for Noah wasn't just a promise, but a prophetic reminder of the wickedness that was and will be again before the next global judgement.

People seek marriage for false fulfillment. This is idolatry, dang it! No gratitude for God and His guidance for a fruitful marriage = Marriages that are fragile. These people expect to be fulfilled by their spouse, which is an unfair expectation, and will treat each other cruel. They'll idolize their children and put them before their spouse and God, and end up leaving children with broken homes. You hear it all the time and it almost always brings a curse on a marriage.

The most important thing in my life are my children.

Marriages usually don't last long with that mind set. The most important thing in your life should be the one who blessed you with children, next it should be with whom God blessed you to have the kids with. This demonstrates solidarity and security for your kids; an example for them to follow, to value their spouse.

Otherwise it leads to divorce.

The single parent ends up trying to assume the role of both mother and father, to spite the other parent, as if to show them they can do it without them. It's no wonder why we have people growing up confused about their sex being influenced by parents like that. On a side note, It's weird how parents can be so forgiving and gracious with their knuckle-headed kids, even into adulthood, but don't have the same patience and grace with the one they created them with, and just throw their love away. They always think it's the other spouses fault. It was never anything they did. Kids learn this and we wonder why we have kids growing up who can't take personal responsibility and want to blame everybody else for why they suck so much. This is what happens when people marry for false fulfillment and without God as their foundation. Does this happen with Christians? Yup. The devil was allowed influence in the Garden of God, he can get between a Christian marriage too, but we still have a choice to let God influence our marriage also. Let Jesus be the snake stomper in your marriage.

Eating is not a sin. Seeking fulfillment in it is. The Lord said it's written, man can't live off bread alone, but by what proceeds from the mouth of God. Bread sustains us temporarily. (Even though the weight it puts on us seems to last forever.) The Word of God sustains us eternally, but people seek fulfillment in eating, as we see the epidemic of obesity, eating disorders, and diet related diseases. People are obsessed with food. Cooking shows are served up everywhere! A sign of the times of people eating, drinking, and marrying. Food is quite fashionable now days.

And then, of course, we have the drinking. Me-linneals; the all about me generation, is drinking so much wine they're changing how it's sold. Me-linneals pride themselves so highly on their pursuit of information that like the wine it's gone to their head, leaving little room for God. God isn't sophisticated enough for them. Wine is what they seek to satisfy their need to feel a sense of sophistication and prestige. (Even though Jesus was sophisticated enough to yield a masterful selection of wine in a moment, that would normally take wineries years to render.)

But they'll drink wine without reverence or remembering, or being grateful for the One who bled for us while rainbow flags wave today, like the rainbow that followed the judgement of the same wickedness of Noah's day. And we don't learn.

Just like even righteous Noah didn't learn. Right after the flood the wickedness started again. Noah got Drunk; drinking wine without regard for God, and his son Ham tipped into his tent and pulled an Al

Franken on 'em. The wickedness of Noah's day is returning with rainbow flags raised in mockery of the judgement of God.

CHAPTER VI
FIGHTING FOR THE PURSE

"I have never understood why it is greed to want to keep the money you have earned but not greed to want to take somebody else's money." Amen to Dr. Thomas Sowell.

Now let the Almighty drop the mic with the foundation of that observation.

"Thou shall not covet." Boom.

Greed is evil. That's obvious... Or at least it should be obvious.

"Woe unto them that call evil good, and good evil; that put darkness for light, and light for darkness; that put bitter for sweet, and sweet for bitter!" Isaiah 5:20 (KJV)

We all detest greed. That should be so easy to agree on. The problem is agreeing on what greed is. Collectivist models, socialism, and communism; these are institutions of covetousness. Covetousness is worse than greed. The Ten Commandments don't explicitly say "Thou shall not be greedy."

It says to not covet.

The aforementioned institutions are based on the justification of coveting the fruits of another person's labor.

The greater good or the common good is the selling point that suckers the multitudes.

That crap-load disguised as compassion results in serfdom.

Throw that "greater good" line out there and people forget that they're being stolen from because they like the idea that they're going to get some from the people they've been encouraged to believe deserve to be stolen from.

Students are taught these envious collectivist ideas in school. They're taught to hate the wealthy while taking classes to embark on a career that will make them wealthy. And to those that manage to become wealthy, there will be another class coming up right behind them who will be taught to hate the alumni who have gone off to become wealthy.

Lots of people think it's the government itself that's rich and has enough money to take care of them. They don't understand that the government derives its treasury from the labor and inventions of the people, foreign and domestic. It's not presently taxing according to our original tax model, but the point is, the government does not generate its own money. The only way the government can generate its own money is when the government owns the people. If the people and industries are the property of the government then the wealth would be government produced and owned.

But in this republic, our government is not supposed to own the people or the industries; therefore they do not own our wealth. The people generate it.

Everybody detests slavery. Well, many people think they do. Even the Democrats who represented the Confederacy had those among them who claimed to hate slavery, but they would still manage to find a way to justify it. They certainly hated the idea of themselves being slaves, and as much as they hated the idea of themselves being slaves it just didn't generate enough empathy to say, *Hmm. Slaves probably don't like it either.* Nope. Instead, they just convinced themselves that their slaves liked it. (After the slave was broken, of course.)

And that mindset carries on today; that people should be happy to live in a nation that lovingly takes the fruit of someone's labor and sweetly gives it to someone else. *See? That's not greed! Look into that sweet socialist face! Does that look like a greedy person to you?* Hell yeah, it does!

But this is a fight between the collectivist and the capitalist over the purse, and the capitalists aren't putting up a very good fight. The collectivists have gone past reaching into the purse and pocket of the individual and are diggin' into our boxer shorts! Richard Pryor would say, "People ask, 'Why are black people always holding onto their crotch?' Because y'all done took away everything else! Brotha be checkin'!" And it's white Democrats who, to this day, are driven by covetousness and have always felt entitled to what belongs to another person. On top of that, these swindling white democrats depend mostly on black suckers to do it!

To reiterate Malcolm X, "Blacks who vote for democrats are political chumps and traitors to their race." I'll remind you. Malcolm didn't like anybody, but he especially loathed the Democrats!

I get jaded by people who ask, "Why can't we just be Americans and do away with the two-party system" Or people who say, "The two-party system is corrupt! We need a third party" I see. Obviously, the remedy for two corrupt parties is the addition of another. The more the merrier, I suppose.

Hey! For kicks, you can call it the "No Corruption Party"! I'll guarantee you that soon it will become as corrupt as the other two.

As far as just being American and doing away with the two-party system, good luck with that. What, pray tell, will determine the "Americans" we will be? Ya do realize that people have varying ideas of what it means to be American, right? You have those who understand we are a constitutional republic, and those who want America to be a democracy. Those who understand this is a constitutional republic understand that greed becomes a bigger problem when the State is given power to tax income. Those who want America to be a democracy think greed is controlled by giving the State the power to tax income. And the core of democracy is what's popular. And it's popular to vote for what you feel entitled to, and feel justified to do it at the forced expense of others.

Things like this are why we have a two-party system, because there are people who would rather stay here and force other people to live according to what they believe America should be rather than moving to another country that fits their ideals. We side with parties that reflect what we've learned to consider right policy. The elected representative of that party is supposed to uphold the ideals of the people who elect them from that party.

Some officials try to preserve what our republic is, others try to transform it. One of those areas they try to transform is in taxation. It is flat-out un-American to tax the people's income, and it's unconstitutional.

Oh, by the way, it's institutionalized covetousness, greed, and theft.

These people of the collectivist, statist, left-wing, Democrat, liberal, socialist, and communist mindset are relentlessly covetous. They live to get into the pockets of others and there are politicians of this type who want to get into office. Democrats are covetous people who know there's a big voter stock to be had of covetous people. Democrats wanting office stoke the flames of covetousness saying, "Such and such makes too much money! Don't you think you're entitled to it?"

And their covetous constituents say, "Yes! Give us their money!!!" Yet none of them see that as greedy.

This is the land of the free, but we're in a fight for what free means. That's another reason why we can't all "just be Americans". You have people who understand that this is the land where we have the God-given right to life, liberty, the pursuit of happiness, and property.

Then, you have those who believe the land of the free means they have the right and freedom to other people's lives, other people's liberty, the pursuit of other people's happiness and other people's property.

So which version of America will it be? It seems like it would be an easy decision, but Democrats have been effectively influencing the people towards their idea of America. How do they do it? Do you think they do it by limiting themselves to pundits, talk radio, and politicians?

No. They do it through entertaining illustrations. They give people a picture of what their fears look like, and they make those fears look like Republicans, business people, Christians, military, the NRA, and Law enforcement.

Conservatives have barely begun to support the production of counter-illustrations to this. This is why the left wing has been able to get as deep into the people's pockets as they have. They constantly promote the idea that greedy people are people who just want to keep the money they earned, and don't want to share, *and not sharing your own money is worse than stealing* to them.

So when you don't share your wealth you're stealing from the poor, or rather if you don't submit to the state stealing from you - you're stealing from the poor. Jesus doesn't want us forsaking the poor, but helping the poor by making it legal for the State to institute covetousness, greed, and theft was not what Jesus had in mind for helping the poor.

I know, I know. How is keeping your own money that you earned stealing from the poor? If you're a rational person you ask that question. But Democrats aren't rational people, and in their irrational minds, they believe that a person who keeps the money they earned without the State making a claim on a percentage of it is stealing from the poor. The poor didn't earn it. They didn't work for it, yet the person who did earn it is stealing from them. That's straight up Looney-Town.

We're in a prize fight for America against rubber-room residents. These people are kooky and dangerous. Like, Mike Tyson, kooky-dangerous. That kind of "bite your ear off then tell you he wants to have sex with you" kind of dangerous. And Mike Tyson has been known to bite the ears off of his opponents and yell at men, telling them he would make them love having sex with him. Democrats harbor this kind of cray-cray.

Democrats act like the world is going to end if they can't tax people. They are fiendishly fixated on other people's stuff! Democrats continuously use the "Reduction in social security" scare tactic to vilify any effort to cut taxes. Taxes on social security itself is a reduction on a person's social security benefits. I don't see democrats complaining about that. That's how obsessively covetous democrats are. They demand other people's money for social security. And when people get the social security they were already taxed for - they get taxed again on what they were taxed for in the first place.

Fear-mongering Democrats don't care about a reduction in social security Benefits. Democrats only care about scaring their way into other people's pockets. If they did care, for starters, they'd cease taxation on social security which in itself is a reduction on social security benefits. I guess they justify doing this with the thought that taxing social security benefits will perpetuate the benefits. Kinda like a cow sustaining itself on its own milk.

Yeah, that works out great.

Democrats are like pets. You can put two bowls of food down for two animals and one animal will insist on coming to force its way into the bowl that another animal is eating out of. They are like animals in the wild that feel entitled to come and feed off the kill that another animal worked for. It reminds me of Richard Pryor who said, "Buzzards aren't like what you see in nature shows. They pull up in a truck!" And that's what Democrats are like; Buzzards that pull up in a truck! Bussed into the voter booth to vote for the right to scavenge what others worked for! Bussed into other communities to belligerently protest and make demands; Bussed-in Buzzards. That's how Democrats roll.

I know I keep going on about this but it's a flipping tragedy that conservatives aren't more supportive of building a market of entertainment that's well-fortified to respond to the propaganda the Left puts out through music, movies, teleplays, etc. The liberals give so much absurdity to work with. It's ready-made comedy to put in a sitcom! It's ready-made irony to put in a psychological thriller. It's ready-made struggles to put in music. It's ready-made material to convey to the masses in the mediums people love best to receive points of view: ENTERTAINMENT!

Conservatives, for the most part, have sadly ignored the importance of this. Liberals succeed at getting their hands into the people's pockets because they produce creative and emotional content that plays on people's fears and self-righteousness. It works. But for all the common sense and critical thinking conservatives boast of, they overlook these tools that work, and just struggle, complain, and stay frustrated,

Too many conservatives in media are too busy sucker punching each other instead of being unified to counter-punch the Left.

Conservatives are their own worst enemy.

If liberals are as stupid as we claim, how are they able to get away with so much evil? It's got to be due to us letting them. They can't be smart enough to do all this damage on their own, right? We're in the ring with a swollen eye, busted nose, and a fat lip. Why? If liberals are so dumb how can they land all those punches? It can only be because conservatives aren't putting up their dukes, and countering, yet instead are letting liberals land free shots. Then, when conservatives go back to their corner, other conservatives who are supposed to be in their corner are reaching around and punching their own fighter in the face. How else can you explain it? Liberals can't be this smart to make us have to work this hard to promote liberty unless they have help from us to do it. I thank God for the conservatives I know who aren't part of the self-sabotaging acts of conservatives and who do see the importance of supporting the effort to represent in the culture.

Yes, we got a victory with the election of Trump, and the majority of the house and senate, but the cultural response to this is ridiculous! Democrats are going bat-guano goofy again! It's amazingly ironic how selfish, self-focused, self-righteous, and all things selfie that Democrats are, yet they do not see how belligerent, spoiled, tantrum-throwing, and vulgar they are. It's like they've got a bag of microwave popcorn for a brain going off in their skull.

A lot of them got this way because of constant influence through various media. Where were conservatives to counter that influence? How do you think people learn this stuff? Don't you think we ought to have a defense detail right there with interdiction media to counter that influence? There needs to be a budget to scout good talent to present these ideals in well-produced media.

If the Left were to only give their ideals for collectivism through pundits, and talk-radio, it wouldn't survive. It takes too much B.S. to sell that. They'd have to do a lot of contorting to stretch around the fact that it robs the individual and that kind of platform would be too easy for folks to catch on to them, and they'd reject that worldview.

They deliver it with the distraction of entertainment that numbs the critical-thinking and stimulates their imagination in the area of fear and self-righteousness. They are given an illustration and picture of what their fears are, who they should fear, and be prejudiced against. Now they're hooked on who to hate. They're fueled with self-righteous indignation and they want more ammo to fuel their crusade. They want to look like they're really in the know and "woke." That's when they tune in for parrot talking points from the left-wing talking heads.

They demand other people's money to pay for the psychology and poly-sci courses so they can seem really intellectual and say, *Yeah, I'm like, taking poly-sci and psychology n' stuff. Wanna come over and smoke some weed I bought with my tuition money?*

We keep losing youngens to so-called progressivism, atheism, collectivism, etc. because we don't give them something engaging enough to shield off the influence of the Left as the Left comes out swinging when the school-bell rings. And after several blows to the head, another zombie is made. Then the school-bell becomes the dinner-bell as they come out with a hunger for the people's purse.

Entertaining, engaging liberal created mind-rot is at the student's fingertips to keep them under the socialist spell as they walk around like zombies staring at their phones. They'll take occasions to look up long enough to shout at someone out of the prejudice they've been taught as they blindly accuse people of racism, sexism, classism, and whatnot.

If these people are going to stare at their phones, why not give them something to stare at long enough to inspire them to get un-brain-chained from the false-fulfillment land of liberalism?

If conservatives would fund creativity to promote conservative illustrations the way they fund politicians we wouldn't have as much of this nonsense. The fight to protect the people's purse wouldn't be so hard. It would still be difficult and ongoing but it wouldn't be this hard.

We'll always have some nuts out there trying to force their view of America and try to get the State to force a collectivist economy, but it wouldn't be as bad. That's all we can do. We're not going to bring about a perfect society. We will not live together in perfect peace until Jesus permanently drop-kicks Satan's behind into the lake of fire. Until then we can try to minimize the nut-baggery to a nominal degree where we don't have as much of an entitled, snowflakin', melt-downy, and covetous society as we do today.

It's like driving a car. It's normal to burn gas and produce heat, and ideally, you always want to be able to keep your gas gauge higher than your heat gauge. That represents a pretty stable and healthy economy, being able to keep refilling your tank and an engine running at the ideal temp. Even when things happen like a natural disaster or an attack, and the country has to shift gears, the transmission should engage more smoothly.

A certain amount of friction is expected and inevitable with running an engine. So yes we're always going to have some friction in our republic, but we've gotten to where the engine has too much friction and is running really hot. We don't have to have this much friction. Like a car engine, we will have some, but we have to try to cool back down to that nominal operating heat level. Life itself generates heat, yet heat helps to facilitate life. That's a natural circuit. But we've got a fever going. A lot of this friction is coming from bad additives being poured into the American engine. Collectivist ideals and political correctness are a bad additive that gunks it up.

Left-wingers screw up the way kids are raised – kids who grow up wired to add to the gunk. It's bad enough that the Left puts in policies that fade out the father, often leaving the mother to raise the kid in confusion as she proclaims to be both the mommy and the daddy. It gets even worse when the PC Gestapo control how people discipline their kids. You can't spank your kids. That's a no-no to them

I offer that spanking is no good when that's the only time a parent pays attention to their kid. Steve Harvey's comedy act featured him boasting about how "Black folks beat the F*ck out of their kids" as if to say that's what makes us grow up proper. I guess that's why blacks are so miserable today, and despise each other so much. We laugh about it, sure, but there's a lot of misery under that laughter too, growing up with mother's who were hurt and angry about a man who treated them like a dog and leaving them with kids who would bear the wrath of her pain.

But, in general, it's politically incorrect to spank your kids. The Bible says "Spare the rod and spoil the child," meaning that your child will become spoiled if you don't spank them. And man, do we have some spoiled, entitlement-minded, selfish folks today. We've always had these people. That's not new, but we're going through another cycle where it's now fashionable.

Since the dawn of civilization people develop cultures on what they think they're entitled to. It reaches critical mass and then that culture collapses. The policies of entitlement ultimately make people turn on each other. In America, 2018, it's the hip thing to do, to be a part of a culture that feels entitled to other people's stuff. The cycle of Democrats is surfacing again. It was the fashion of the 1800's for them to be entitled to enjoy the fruits of other people's labor with slavery. Today it's demanding the fruit of other people's state instituted social serfdom.

But political correctness set this in motion with kids decades ago: When a kid feels they're entitled to do things they're not supposed to do, even after they've been warned not to do it, oh well, spanking is prohibited. This is dumb. Spanking sends a clear message: Breaking the law hurts. And chances are a kid will grow up to understand that if breaking the law hurts them, it's probably because breaking the law hurts others. The kid is learning a very basic and impressive lesson in empathy.

Spanking a kid without showing a kid affection and loving support will render a screwed-up kid. But not spanking your kid when they disobey will render a screwed-up kid too. This is a hard-sell because everybody thinks they're parent of the year and their kids are just perfect. Well, somebody's perfect kid is part of a legion of perfect kids that are getting on a lot of people's nerves, calling everything racist, and not knowing what bathroom to use.

For years the accepted response to a kid getting out of line has been- "time out" or to give your kids more chores. Really? Chores as punishment?

The reason we're becoming such a lazy culture that hates work is because we've been raised to associate work with punishment. Punishment coming in the form of chores yields a poor attitude towards work when they're older. I know that's a hard-sell, because everybody thinks they have a good work ethic. And if they are the exception who admittedly doesn't want to work, they believe they have a good reason, or even a good reason to not have to give you a reason.

When I was teaching martial arts, I had a new student ask me if they were all in trouble (because part of the training for the students was to participate in keeping the school clean.) I had to explain to her that training in a filthy school would be punishment. Training in a clean school is a blessing.

Spanking your kids along with being affectionate parents who pay healthy supportive attention to their kids won't tend to have the later side effects of the aforementioned. It still can have those side effects because of other influences, but not as likely.

Taking away privileges or things like doing chores are bad replacements for spanking. Taking away privileges when growing up is a bad way to punish because when they get older they make negative and even perverted associations with privilege.

Am I wrong? Look at the attitude people have toward privilege today. Perhaps you have seen the mentally and emotionally damaged trend of "#CheckingYourPrivilege"

Not only is their attitude negative toward privilege, Left-wingers have perverted it into a racial stigma. What's even worse is that the Democrats are the ones pushing the stigma of white privilege when Democrats are the ones who instituted white privilege in the first place!

Replacing spanking with taking away privileges has backfired and brought people up to be more entitlement-minded than ever! More people are thinking they're entitled to whatever they desire while telling other people to check their privilege. What do they want to do? They want to punish others by taking away their phantom privileges.

Republicans defeated the Democrat apartheid institution of white privilege, but the people aren't being allowed to let the bigoted scars that the Democrats inflicted on America heal. Democrats keep those wounds open and accuse others of it. So, to this day "privilege" is evil while the accusers demand privileges as rights for themselves. Democrats haven't changed.

Ironically, Democrats who saw fit to beat their slaves to keep them in line are now the party against spanking.

Some folks wonder when is a good age to stop spanking. I'd say when they move out. I don't care if you're 18 years old. If you live under my and my wife's roof and you cross the line and disregard the rules of the house and transgress against the family while knowing the rules, it's whoopin' time. None of this, *I'm going to ground you or take away your car privileges, or your iPhone* jive. No! Whoopin'! Act like a child and you'll get treated like one. Chances are if you lay down the law earlier and the kid grows up knowing that breaking the law hurts, it's highly unlikely you'll be spanking a teenager or young adult.

I don't care if you have got a little hair on your chest and made the varsity football team and gotten bigger than me. I'll call up some homies from church to help hold your big behind down if I have to. You're gonna get this whoopin'!

Like if I was to find out that my high school football star behaved inappropriately with a cheerleader. Whoopin'! I'd even let the girl's daddy whoop 'em too!

Not trying to stigmatize footballers. I guess I don't have too. Too many of them give the sport a bad image themselves. I'm just giving an example of inexcusable behavior that taking away an x-box just won't do to resolve. Whoopin'!

But like I said; not sparing the rod, early on, along with healthy affection and healthy support and the constant display of solidarity and love between husband and wife will most likely make spanking a teenager ridiculous itself.

Not only will the teen most likely not cross the line, because of the apprehension of getting a whoopin', the very idea of betraying loving parents whom they love hurts them even more. They've come to a stage in their life where they comprehend accountability. Out of love, they wouldn't want to dishonor their father and mother and cause them grief. Kids are going to make mistakes before their parents. Parents are going to make mistakes before their kids. And grace for certain first transgressions is ideal. But for repeat offenses or certain transgressions, even if it was the first offense that they should have obviously known was wrong but they did it anyway? Whoopin'! The entitlement mindset must be purged! Because that's what got them into trouble! They felt entitled to something.

Daughters too. Daddy's little girl my Kung Fu-Kickin' foot! No little girl is going to have me wrapped around her finger like some little princess that can get away with whatever she wants. Whoopin'! (I know, Know. I would most likely be the biggest softy of a dad a daughter and a son could have!)

But for real, I know it's a lot easier said than done, but we've watched the results of how people are turning out and that's hard too. As my mom would say, "Better me whoopin' you than the police or a prison inmate."

If a son or daughter hasn't learned to act right by the time they leave the nest, then the law of the republic can take away their rights and privileges by due process. That's the appropriate time to use the punishment of denying rights and privileges. If they haven't learned how to act right in society, quarantine them from society.

Democrats pave the way for prison. Democrats and prison go hand in hand, unless you have the democrat white privilege of the Clintons. But consider what we've examined: from democrats putting in policies that have exacerbated the dynamic of single parenthood, to the entitlement mindset they indoctrinate kids with, making them feel like they're entitled and that justice is due them. These kids take to the streets with the attitude that they're owed and they feel justified to take from others, sell destructive substances to others, or feel entitled to a street, and if you enter the turf they feel entitled to, you could die. Turf-wars are not a new thing. Too bad after all this time we haven't gotten down to the root of it.

Democrat programming has cultivated this in this age. They'll deny it, but Democrats are the ones who have paved the way for prison.

This is proven by the fact the Democrats want prisoners to retain the right to vote. Prisoners are just another voter stock for Democrats to tap into. I'm not going to waste yours or my time giving references to where I get these conclusions, because if you don't want to believe it, my sources will not impress you anyway.

I observe it in the real world, and after observing it, I research it to see if there are stats on it. Sure enough, the statistics match what I've already observed and the fact is more people who are convicted are registered Democrats. I know that doesn't impress Democrats because Democrats tend to not think they're guilty of anything, and they believe that people who are prisoners are actually victims of the criminal justice system. The justice system is the real criminals as far as Democrats are concerned.

Meanwhile, Democrats forget that the justice system is filled with liberal democrat activist judges and legions of liberal democrat attorneys. So, if they want to blame the high population of prison on somebody then look no further than the Democrats.

Democrats are always trying to accuse Republicans of being crooks, while the reality is that most convicted crooks are Democrats, and the justice system that Democrats accuse of being crooks are mostly Democrats.

Yeah, I know. The reason most convicts aren't republicans is because they haven't been caught or got special treatment. Special treatment from who, though? The Democrat judges and attorneys in democrat run communities where incarceration rates are the highest? Ok.

If you're a liberal, let that sink in. While you believe that Republicans are crooks, face the reality that actual crooks are overwhelmingly Democrat voters, if they have bothered to register to vote at all. Why? Because it takes being crooked to be a Democrat. That's just what Democrats are; crooked. The system libs think is so crooked is overwhelmingly Democrat. I know, democrat denial makes them believe that prisoners are being unjustly locked up by a crooked justice system, but that wicked justice system is mostly democrats.

I agree with you. The justice system is corrupt. Democrats have corrupted the justice system, and have cultivated a prison population. If you want it to stop, stop listening to them and stop voting for them. Humbly ask the Lord to be your filter for discerning what truth is. Employ the Word of God to know better about what policies and representatives to vote for and stop being prejudiced against the Republican Party. Have a healthy guard of Republicans, yes, because there are deviant Republicans, but I'm talking about the fundamentals of being a Republican in this republic. Ditch your prejudice for that. Conservatives usually aren't convicts. That alone should actually tell you a lot if you're halfway reasonable and not drugged with denial.

And who are the people that occupy prisons? Covetous people who justified to themselves that they were entitled to something that belonged to someone else. They coveted and felt entitled to someone else's money, car, identity, or body for sexual gratification. These people felt entitled, and entitlement is the mindset of Democrats. These thieves go into office to represent other covetous democrat voters to make it legal to steal from job creators and workers. These are the people we're in a fight against for the purse of America.

Democrats are the party of Judas Iscariot. The one who came off like he knew what was better for a woman to do with her property than she did. A woman wanted to anoint Jesus with her perfume. Judas protested like he knew what was better for her to do with it. This is just like Democrats who assume to know better on knowing what to do with other people's property.

Judas assumed he was more righteous than Jesus as he claimed she was wasting her perfume. (Wasting it on Jesus? Bad call Judas.) And that's just like Democrats to tell the rest of us that we're wasting time and resources on Jesus. He doesn't belong in the public. *Separation of church and state*, etc.

Judas covetously made the case that he knew what would be better to do with the equity of the perfume, just like democrats assume to know better with what to do with our property. Judas then pretends like his concern is for the poor and that's why he's justified for coveting the woman's perfume under the guise of rebuking her. Judas didn't care about the poor. Neither do Democrats. The truth is, Judas was stealing from the treasury. And Democrats, just like Judas are stealing from the purse of America while assuming to be more righteous than Jesus.

"Why wasn't this perfume sold for three hundred denarii and the money given to the poor?" <u>Judas did not say this because he cared about the poor, but because he was a thief.</u> As keeper of the money bag, he used to take from what was put into it. "Leave her alone," Jesus replied. "She was intended to keep this perfume to prepare for the day of My burial. ... John 12:5-7 BSB

Jesus said we will always have the poor. Notice Jesus didn't say people will always be poor, but that we will always have them, then He said, "but you will not always have Me." How true.

You will always have the poor among you, but you will not always have me." John 12:8 NIV

Some people are born in poverty and manage to make the best of opportunities to get out. Sometimes those opportunities are good sometimes the opportunity is seized in evil. Some people were born well-off, or became well-off, and on the other side of that, maybe something happened that landed them in poverty. That doesn't mean they're mandated to stay there. There will always be people moving in and out of the state of poverty. Some may stay, some may never return, but there will always be someone occupying the state of poverty.

Jesus was right, and then He said, "but you will not always have Me."

Also true, as we see more and more people trying to keep the people separate from Jesus. Even before the birth of Jesus people tried to separate people from the Word of God. They would kill the prophets. They killed Jesus, too. Today, Democrats are more interested in the poor than they are in Jesus. Not because they care about the poor, but because the poor are the means to get votes, and to leverage policy to tax the rich more.

When you don't have Jesus and the Word of God, you will justify covetousness. Today, the poor will always be with us because Democrats need them. The poor are more valuable to Democrats than Jesus. We will always have the poor because Democrats make it harder for businesses to hire them. We will always have the poor because Democrats make it harder for businesses to maintain prices that make it easier for people to make ends meet. We will always have the poor because the Democrats keep them prejudiced against the rich. This affects their work ethic, and their ability to keep a job as they despise having to work for "the man."

Reflect again on people who are in prison. If they registered to vote, they are most likely Democrats, and they hate rich people. But why do they steal? Because they want to be rich themselves. This isn't so much that they hate what they want to become. They just hate it that someone else is rich and they're not. A lot of times when Democrats do get rich they hate other people who are rich. Why? Because Democrats believe that other rich people achieved their wealth dishonestly, but it's a projection. They can't help but be suspicious of other rich people because the rich democrats themselves are covetous, dishonest, and greedy.

Left-wingers chant over and over again, separation of church and state, yet invoke Jesus to shove the idea that Jesus would be for taxes, State provided health-care, social assistance, etc.

The truth is, Jesus practiced privatized healthcare. He didn't tax people to provide healthcare. He wasn't sponsored by the State that took the people's money to provide healthcare. I'll remind y'all, by the way, the State tortured and killed Jesus. So liberals who claim Jesus would be all about State provided healthcare are sadly mistaken.

Liberals think that Jesus wants us to pay taxes because He did. Jesus paid a temple tax, not a state tax. Big difference. Liberals think that 'render unto Caesar means Jesus wants us to pay taxes. No. Jesus asked them to show them a coin when they tried to trap Him with that tax question. Jesus exposed their hypocrisy because they were paying tribute to a false god, which is idolatry. That's why Jesus asked to see the coin because the coin had a graven image of a "deified" king on it. The inscription on those coins said, " Tiberius Caesar, Worshipful son of the god Augustus."

That's what Jesus wanted them to pick up on. That's not some wild speculation. Jesus Himself draws ours and their attention to the coin to see the commandment violation of the engraved image of a false god on the coin; the coin that they will use to bow down to paying tribute to a false god. This is an affront to the One True God, Jehovah, who's come to us as Yeshua.

Liberals are so covetous that not only do they miss the fact that they are violating the commandment to not covet as they demand the State tax people more because they feel people are making too much money. They also overlook that it's theft to do that, which is a violation of another commandment, and they overlook the violation the Herodians were committing when they tried to take Jesus on with the question of taxation. But libs don't see that. All they see is somebody else's property that liberals feel entitled to.

... "Show Me a denarius. Whose image and inscription are on it?" "Caesar's," they answered. So Jesus told them, "Give to Caesar what is Caesar's, and to God what is God's." And they were unable to trap Him in His words before the people; and astonished at His answer, they fell silent.... Luke 20:24-26 BSB

Caesar is false, so his due is false. God is real, so His due is real. Caesar has to take from people what God gave them in order to provide, which means the people are giving Caesar what belongs to God in the first place. The people are able to have these things because God is the one who facilitates their ability to get these things in the first place. So they're not supposed to be rendering unto Caesar anything. It's to God we owe everything. Does that mean that God wants you to take everything you own and drop it at the church steps? No. That wouldn't be practical. How you pay your due to God is by using what He blesses you with to be fruitful, providing good products, services, and citizenship, and to give Him the glory for it. He doesn't want you to part with the resources He blesses you to have, like the State does. He wants you to keep and use your resources and bless people with them. Unlike the State that takes your resources and uses them as the State sees fit. Are you seeing the difference of what it is to render unto Caesar what is Caesars and to God what is God's?

Liberal so-called Christians try to lean on verses like

Romans 13:1:
Let everyone be subject to the governing authorities, for there is no authority except that which God has established. The authorities that exist have been established by God. NIV

This is true. And when that authority governs according to the righteousness of God then they are to be obeyed. However, if the authority deviates from the position God blessed them to have then yes, we are to challenge that abuse of authority. According to liberal's misinterpretation of scripture, Hitler should not have been resisted, or Mao, Stalin, Lenin, or any other dictator.

Liberals don't understand what it means to square scripture by scripture. Squaring scripture by scripture balances out the protection of people's God given rights. Liberals only see the scriptures they can cherry-pick to justify intruding on other people's rights. This also involves them overlooking the commandment to not take the Lord's name in vain. Don't involve the Name of God to justify sinning against others.

Liberals want us to be subject to the godless government that they want. They want separation of church and state and freedom *from* religion, not *of* it. Yet they all of a sudden get religion, as they throw verses like Romans 13:1 at us.

They forget that the government is made up of people too, and if they are making laws that are apart from God then they are in error. We're supposed to be watchful of them and challenge them when they're wrong.

So watch yourselves. "If your brother or sister sins against you, rebuke them; and if they repent, forgive them. Luke 17:3 NIV

We are supposed to be obedient to good law, challenge bad law, and most importantly know the difference. Unfortunately, many don't. Because they don't know God. His ways are not our ways, but He helps us understand His Word if we humble ourselves to Him.

Without humility, entitlement gets super ugly. The entitled are very hypocritical. What's worse is that we're all infected with a sense of spoiled entitlement. Some feel a little entitled. Some, a lot. For example: Chances are when you get a monthly bill. You're offended. You roll your eyes and sigh, maybe even curse because you received a bill, like, "How dare somebody bill me for using their product or service!?" Like you're supposed to be able to use whatever you want for free and never be charged. You'll call customer service and ask for extensions and tell them why you can't make payments at such and such a time even though you expected them to not keep you waiting with the product or service you wanted, now you're going to make them wait for their payment.

Would you want your boss to do that to you after your services have been rendered? You provide your company with a service, and you send them a bill of your employment. That invoice is your time card for example. How would you feel if your boss rolled his/her eyes, and sighed and even cursed because he/she received a bill from you for your service and be like, "How dare they send me a bill?!"

You wouldn't like that. And you wouldn't take too kindly to him/her saying, "I'm not able to pay you at this time," or asked you for an extension. No. You want your full payment at the time agreed to for the service you provided, yet we grumble about having to pay for bills sent to us by others who provide a service or product to us. We tend to be entitled hypocrites.

CHAPTER VII
PUNCH DRUNK

Take a hit. The hit in this case that leaves people punch drunk is by puff- puff, not punch-punch.

I guess we could call this puff-drunk. And with that, we'll get right to the typical talking point of the pro-legalize drug crowd who contradict themselves with their prohibition arguments and alcohol comparisons.

Pro-legalize people hate prohibition and hate it that there was ever an effort to make alcohol illegal. They will defend alcohol until their opponents are under the table. But this is what's strange. When people say that drugs should not be legal, the Pro-legalize drug people all of a sudden make the argument about how many lives alcohol has ruined. They'll make the claim of how evil it is that alcohol is allowed to be legal because the government can tax it. No. Alcohol is legal because people threw a hissy fit over prohibition, and demanded alcohol be legal.

They stigmatize the very thing they defended. After carrying the "spirit" of the anti-prohibition sentiments and the demand to keep alcohol legal, they turn around and make alcohol out to be a life ruiner to make drugs look more benign compared to alcohol, and also a tool of government greed to grab more tax revenue. These are their arguments to legalize drugs. Weird, right?

Don't get me wrong. I don't think of myself as some throwback of the Dry Party. Jesus himself drank wine and shared wine with His homies. I don't object to alcohol being legal.

Mark my words--I will not drink wine __again__ until the day I drink it new with you in my Father's Kingdom." Matthew 26:29 NLT

For I tell you I will not drink __again__ from the fruit of the vine until the kingdom of God comes." Luke 22:18 NIV

(Notice there are two testimonies declaring Jesus saying He will not drink wine again. This means He has drank wine before. You won't read of Jesus being drunk, because that's not what wine was meant for.)

So drugs should be ok to be legal because the pro-legalize it people say it's not fair that alcohol is legal and it has ruined millions of lives, but people of this mindset demanded that alcohol should be legal because it's so wonderful. Now it's made to look evil to make drugs look wonderful to make it "sensible" to make drugs legal. Wow.

The other big thrust to legalize marijuana was the medicinal marijuana argument. I've been saying this was a joke for years. People who smoke pot and want to make it legal don't give one scoop of cat poop about people suffering who could use the discomfort relieving aspects of marijuana. If marijuana did not get stoners high, and **only** offered discomfort relief (as in pain relief, anxiety and as a stomachic, and such) these people would not care about marijuana, and certainly wouldn't care about it for medicinal purposes for people with illnesses. They even used vets suffering from PTSD to push legalizing medical marijuana. Anybody willing to be honest knows that marijuana makes you paranoid! How is that a good remedy for a person with PTSD?! (For the record I don't object to CBD. CBD isn't the part of marijuana that gets ya stoned. It's properties for Anti-Inflammation and, anti-anxiety is worth consideration. But if CBD didn't come from weed for stoners to get high with they would not care about it and the people who suffer from ailments CBD could be used to treat.)

These pot-heads do not care about them. These fakers used them for sympathy votes, and medical marijuana was just a stepping stone for them to make marijuana legal for recreational use. They will not stop until drugs are federally legal. This is not my speculations. This is reality. In California, the ongoing fight was for medical marijuana. Now recreational marijuana is legal in California. Guess I wasn't imagining things when I spoke of it in my audiobook, Weapon of A.S.S. Destruction. (American Socialist States.)

These people argue how smoking weed is healthy for you, while many of these liberal pot smokers hate cigarettes because smoking is bad for you. Somehow, only inhaling tobacco smoke is bad for you but inhaling marijuana smoke isn't. Do you not see how absurd this is? If you're high of course you can't see it. The denial is enhanced like the appetite stimulated to the munchies.

But the pro-pot smokers contradict themselves again. They stubbornly argue that smoking weed isn't bad for you like smoking tobacco is, but when you check out pro-marijuana articles they're turning towards the growing market of vaping, and their selling point is, "Vaping is the Healthy way to toke." If vaping marijuana is the healthy way to toke marijuana, then that, by their own admission says that smoking marijuana has been unhealthy all along.

But these people are deluded by their selfishness. Their addiction to instant gratification gets in the way of good judgment. These people repeat the same talking point, "How is me using marijuana going to hurt you?" You cannot give a selfish person the answer to that.

Consider this. People who steal either don't see or don't care how it hurts another person. When you sin against someone you have already justified to yourself why you deserve the satisfaction of doing it, and that the person being stolen from either deserves having it done to them or that your sin against them won't hurt them, like a person embezzling from the company because they think the owner won't miss it.

A person who does drugs has already justified it to themselves. They're not going to see how it harms others. They don't see that it impairs their judgment. They stay in denial, for example: They keep pushing this BS argument about how more people die in Alcohol-related car accidents not in marijuana-related accidents (Remember Alcohol was good enough to be made legal, now it's made to look evil to play up how good marijuana is to make it legal) And that's their big seller. What they don't tell you is marijuana-related car accidents are increasing.

The reason why they're able to say people aren't in car accidents involving being under marijuana influence is because they don't have a device that measures a legal limit that determines if a person is too high to drive or not. These selfish stoners don't care that their judgment is impaired and these jackasses are going to get behind the wheel stoned and they are going to become a liability more and more.

They're proud of it too. You can smell them smoking weed as they drive past. So yes. It does hurt other people.

As I mentioned before I'm not opposed to alcohol being legal because Jesus Himself drank wine, and He drank it in fellowship.

Before I address the pro-drug drones who selectively believe in the Bible just enough to try to use it to make their case for moderation, I want to look at Christians who don't accept that Jesus drank wine, and is too holy (by their human so-called standard of holiness) to turn water into wine for people to drink.

They're more comfortable in their human formed piety in believing that Jesus would never turn water into wine but rather into fruit Juice, or grape Koolaid or something. By trying to over-moralize Jesus or fit Him into your flawed human idea of morality you put limits on Him. Jesus does not need our help being Holy.

The miracle of turning water into wine qualifies as such because those who make wine know the time it takes to yield a fine wine. Anybody can squeeze some grapes in a cup and have some juice, real quick. But making wine takes mastery. It takes time. And winemakers and drinkers know that. Jesus did it in an instant, tho'.

By trying to over-moralize Jesus you take away from the amazing implication of His miracle.

This pious approach also spurs more rebellion from those who are defensive about their indulgences. The Bible tells us to enjoy our wine with food.

Go then, eat your bread in happiness and drink your wine with a cheerful heart; for God has already approved your works. Ecclesiastes 9:7 NASB

NOTE! This is not approved by God when people seek fulfillment in these things.

Notice how wine is enjoyed with food. This alone can tell you that God doesn't want you drinking until drunk. Food isn't enjoyed while drunk and throwing it up or even hoping you can hold it down. Wine wasn't meant to be consumed for drunkenness. The Bible lets us know that early on with Noah that drinking wine for drunkenness is wrong.

Jesus said to "Do this in remembrance of me." Drinking to a point of drunkenness is not a good way to remember things. A person just consuming liquor is on their way to drunkenness, and are at the very least usually hoping to achieve a little buzz. A person having a drink with their meal compliments the flavor of the meal. The pairing brings out the flavor, and also a sip cleanses the palate to keep each bite tasting new. A person drinking wine with their meal isn't necessarily looking for a high.

People drinking fermented drink in earlier times did so because it tended to be safer than drinking water. Again it was for necessity, not to indulge in drunkenness. This is why it doesn't work to use the so-called Biblical model of moderation.

A person having an alcoholic beverage with their meal isn't pursuing drunkenness unless they're being foolish. Drinking to a point of drunkenness which will cause one to defeat the purpose of enjoying their food is foolishness and wasteful. It also intrudes on fellowship.

But here's the BIG difference between alcohol and drugs. A person can consume alcohol without getting drunk. As we've just covered, drinking wine with food is for the purpose of complimenting the meal, not drunkenness.

The ONLY reason to do recreational drugs is to get high. PERIOD! The only reason to smoke, vape dope, eat weed in recreation is to get high. If you partook of marijuana and it didn't get you high you would feel gypped.

Getting high separates you from God. The Lord said, "I am the way the truth and the life." He didn't say getting high is the way. Tying to twist scripture to say that God approves of getting high is taking the Lord's name in vain. Like this for example :

Then God said, *"Behold, I have given you every plant yielding seed that is on the surface of all the earth, and every tree which has fruit yielding seed; it shall be <u>food</u> for you; Genesis 1:29 NASB*

Stoners try to make this far-reaching leap to say that God made plants for us to get high on. The scripture clearly tells us that it shall be FOOD for us. Nowhere does it tell us to get high with it. Just because weed makes you really want food doesn't mean it is food. Some aspects of marijuana are consumable, and that's fine. But these pot-heads wouldn't care about any other benefit of marijuana if marijuana didn't get them high.

These people are selfishly trying to use God to justify their sin. And to you stoners that try to twist this scripture like the ends of a joint, you know darn well that even if the Bible used the specific words, "Do NOT use marijuana to get high" You would still choose to use marijuana to get high. By the way. God also created the Tree of Knowledge of Good and Evil and said Adam and Eve must not eat of it. Eve actually was allowed to touch it, Because Adam and Eve's job was to tend to all of the plant life in the garden. You can't really tend to a tree if you can't touch it. The fruit it drops still have to be removed and its leaves have to be raked it has to be watered, pruned, and what not. They weren't told to neglect the tree. They were told to not eat from it.

Eve didn't understand this as she was being blinded by the greed of becoming equal to God, and was losing trust in God due to the accusation of Satan claiming that God was holding out on her with power; that power being the knowledge of good and evil. But Eve should have sought counsel from God with her husband. She should have interrupted her conversation with the devil, called and trusted in God for understanding concerning her directive. Adam, himself should have stepped up to remind her and trampled the serpent right there with the Word of God.

The tree wasn't for them to decide what to do with it. It wasn't for them to make justifications on what it was good for. Their job was to tend to it. Eve lost sight of her job description. She figured that if she can't eat from the tree, she must not have to tend to it. Why should she have to take care of something she can't enjoy?

The point is, potheads are trying to use God to justify their vice. Just because God made something doesn't give you license to sin with it and invoke Him to sin with His creation or twist His Word to make your vice acceptable. He made the tree of Knowledge of Good and Evil also. It doesn't mean they were supposed to sin with it.

These people use the argument that they work fine when they're high. Even people who work in prestigious professions claim to do their job just fine when they're high. These are the same people who claim to hate greed the most by the way. These people disgust me. They are the most selfish and greedy. Getting high on company time? They're so greedy, they can't even wait to get home to get high on their own time. Mind you, pot smokers boast quite often that they work just fine when they are high. What was their big argument before that, especially voiced by Libertarians? "That marijuana should be legal for a person to have and enjoy in the privacy of their own home."

These are supposed to be the real champions of keeping government small, right? But they don't realize that it would take even bigger government to make sure people ONLY smoked pot in their homes. I warned of this years ago and said it was foolish - years ago. The proof is in the fact that pot smokers say they WORK just fine while they are high. This means they never intended to just smoke weed at home. They are getting high on the job. Libertarians who used the argument of "People should be able to enjoy marijuana in their own home" have either been really naive, deep in denial, or just used that argument to be manipulative to push to get marijuana legalized. Pot-heads lied about smoking weed in their own home. They intend to smoke where ever there's air.

Part of the reason why some of these pot-heads are able to keep a job is because it's becoming harder and harder to fire people. The Obama administration falsely bragged about how much jobs were going up. We know that was false because the Obama administration bragged about increasing unemployment benefits. Why would you need to push unemployment benefits up if unemployment was going down?

These benefits cost employers. Plus that, a person can become just as much of a liability by firing them than keeping them. Accusations of racism, sexism, sexual orientation discrimination, harassment, etc. A person can be a horrible employee getting high on the job and still not get fired. Look at all these entitlement minded tantrum throwers. Often time if they have a job, they hate it. They participate in things like BLM, OWS, ANTIFa. Almost every one of these people smoke weed.

It's funny how people delude themselves into thinking weed makes you peaceful and mellow. When you see these protestors belligerently obstructing traffic and even setting communities on fire, you can be sure that almost all of them smoke weed. And to those pot-heads with more high profile jobs - making more money than many only dream of, as they do their dream jobs, these people are just greedy. Whether it be attorneys or entertainers or politicians. If they're pot smokers they're greedy. They've been blessed to achieve their dream jobs. Some have beautiful spouses and children. They get to see the world, etc. But it's not enough for them. You'd think that would be an amazing high in itself. Nope. They're greedy. They have to get a fake high. The real blessing isn't a good enough high for them. These people disgust me.

These are the same people who try to make others feel guilty about the hungry people in the world as they satisfy their munchies following their indulgence with Mary Jane. They'll judge others and make claims about others not needing what they have. Did these judgmental pot smokers need that weed they bought? No. Could that money have been used to feed the poor? Sure. I'm not trying to be a Judas like liberals are, I'm just holding up a mirror to them.

And to any pro-legalize weed republicans and Libertarians who think liberals are so stupid. You just let it sink in that it's pretty much blues states where recreational marijuana is legalized. You know? Where there's a big population of those silly liberals.

But here's another reason why I take issue with Libertarians trying to co-opt the Republican tent and are selfishly corrupting what it means to be conservative. The irony with libertarians is that they tend to be very nationalistic and isolationist. They're very vocal about people staying in their own country, and not coming into ours to change our way of life. Yet libertarians demand pushing their way up into the Republican tent and making us assimilate to them. I'm not talking about Christian "small l" libertarians, but Libertarians.

I'd appreciate Libertarians a whole lot more if they stayed in their own yard, but like illegal immigrants, they just push their way up into the Republican zone and want to take over. This is a big part of why people can't tell anybody apart. Libertarians pretty much believe what liberals believe. Libertarians just don't want to have to pay taxes on it and that somehow makes them qualified to take over the conservative camp.

Liberals and libertarians believe the same things. A Libertarian just doesn't believe in collectivism. But both tend to believe that it's another person's right to marry the same sex, abort their children, legalize drugs, legalize prostitution, reject the Biblical foundation of the constitution, despise the Jews, and believe that acknowledgment of Jerusalem as the capital of Israel is evil Zionism, and oppose American intervention.

Considering that Libertarians believe that people should have the so-called right to abortion, and the Democrats have used the abortion industry against blacks as their number one target, it would make it a good idea to distance from Libertarians. Democrats are at the root of this bigoted campaign.

But because Libertarians insist on co-opting the conservative camp, the pro-legalize abortion stance that they share with Democrats, that has targeted chiefly targeted the black community, gets smeared on Republicans which adds to people assuming Republicans are racist. The animosity that

Libertarians and Democrats share against the Jews and Israel gets wiped on republicans when Libertarians insist on co-opting the conservative camp. Then republicans get seen as anti-semitic when we're the ones standing for Israel! When we have anti-zionist Libertarians among us, Trump can acknowledge Jerusalem as the capital of Israel and people will still see Republicans as anti-semitic bigots.

Because many Libertarians tend to be neo-confederates due to their overzealous sentiments for state's rights they are infected by their affinity for the Confederacy which was created by the Democrats. And the Libertarians are the usual culprits dragging the democrat created confederate flag amidst republicans wiping that stigma on us. And Republicans are guilty of ignorance and vanity to let this happen.

These things are a huge reason why so many people think Republicans are racist because they're seeing Republicans through Libertarians. What's worse is that a lot of people calling themselves republican are giving over to Libertarians, and Libertarians tend to be agnostic, atheistic or if they call themselves Christian they often still put their idea of liberty over the Giver of liberty. They're prideful and their confidence is in how informed they think they are before their confidence in God All Mighty.

I keep seeing all these Republican groups acting like they are obligated to rebrand as a Conservative/Libertarian movement? Why? I'd have more respect for Libertarians if they'd just be Libertarians.

Republicans are being duped by Libertarians into believing that liberty is all that matters. This view leads to oppression and murder. When liberty is your highest ideal, you will ultimately take the liberty to take liberties with other people's liberty. Libertarians never see the big picture that this effects other people. They don't see how abortion takes liberties with other people's liberty. They don't see how same-sex marriage takes liberties with another person's liberty.

The heathen scoffs at the idea of going to hell. They even welcome the prospect of Hell because Hell is the ultimate liberty. None of God's stuffy rules. Therefore, hell would be the realm of ultimate freedom. This is what happens when liberty is the highest ideal. However, unlimited liberty means that a person has no freedom from what another feels free to do. By what authority can you tell another person what they can't do to you or take from you etc. They have total liberty to do so.

Oh. You think they have to abide by some arbitrary code of conduct. Nope. That would be in contradiction to total liberty. One can try to argue all they want with the premise of, "Liberty; as long as it doesn't harm another person." That's a bunch of garbage. Because by what, pray tell, are you going to define what is or what isn't harmful to another person? When a person seeks pleasure, and if their pleasures mean enough to them, they will convince themselves and others that their interests don't harm others (when they really do).

And if it's total freedom, then there's no rule to tell them otherwise, and they don't have to accept that their activity is harming another person. Am I wrong? People justify harming other people every second of every day. The premises of "Total liberty; as long as you don't harm anyone" is false. There has to be a supreme law, written by a Supreme Author that guards the balance of liberty. The Libertarian idea of liberty, believing each person will abide by their own moral fortitude and naively assume that others will abide by it too is sadly deceived.

Think of it as: My idea of right, wrong, and morality differs from yours, and my view of what I'm about to do is justified, and I don't recognize the code you live by. It's my law against your law. This really turns out to be *my lawlessness against your lawlessness*. The zeal for liberty turns into chaos. This is the course of anarchy. People will try to say that the founding fathers were anarchist. No, they weren't. They didn't rebel against the crown to be emancipated from laws. The rebelled against the crown of bad laws to establish good laws that would protect the balance of liberty, and the only laws that could do that had to come from an immovable Law Writer so that these rights would be certain and inalienable. That way people can't just intrude on somebody else, and call it liberty. People try, sure, but there's laws against that.

So when people sell drugs to people that overdose on them, you do realize that the dealer doesn't feel responsible for the harm they sold. They feel justified for the liberty they took. The pimps and sex traffickers don't feel responsible for the damage they do to the humans they sell. These people are only interested in their liberty to do what they do. Legal or not. When liberty is the highest ideal people will ultimately abuse each other.

The Lord who blesses us with liberty has to come before liberty. This is what preserves liberty. People wanting drugs to be legal are people who think that liberty is in the drugs or in doing the drugs. To them, liberty is being "free" to get high, and getting high is an escape. They think It frees them from reality when what it really does is chain them to a fantasy. That chain gets shorter and shorter, and then the user becomes too bound to be fruitful in the real world.

These people put getting high over the Lord. Those who say it should be legal are people whose highest ideal is liberty, not the Lord. This leads to the wrong dependency. Libertarians claim to be all about independence while insisting on legalized dependency on dope. I reckon that would be called Dopendency.

Drug users tend to end up dependent on their drugs. It's funny hearing pro-legalize drug people claim that drugs should be legal and responsibly regulated. That's not very anarchy, but ok. This is the argument of Libertarians as well. So despite wanting small government, they're ok with bigger government to regulate people's drug habits. Hmmmm. They don't see that government actually gets bigger. Sometimes the best way to keep government small is to keep certain things illegal.

Libertarians think I hate them. I don't. And I'm far nicer to them than they are to me. Libertarians tend to find it incomprehensible that anyone would find fault with them. That's really conceited. As y'all may have noticed I've been clearly making my concerns known about Libertarians. I repeat. As y'all may have noticed I've been clearly making my concerns known about Libertarians. And they're usual response is, "Why do you hate Libertarians so much, Zo?" As if I woke up one day and just decided to allegedly hate them. And the only reason they can come close to any such conclusion is because they must have read my concerns. But rather than considering my concerns, they typically just respond with, "Why do you hate Libertarians?" Even though I don't. And even after I expressed my concerns, they just conclude it's hate. It's like with LGBT. I don't hate them at all. I simply disagree and have clearly stated why. But to many in the LGBT, they just conclude it's hate. Thank God I've actually spoken to folks who are gay, and when they actually hear what I have to say, they agree that I'm not coming from a position of hate at all.

The Republican party was founded to abolish slavery. The Libertarian wants it to be legal for people to be slaves to their vices while believing they're in control of them. Their view is conflicting with the very founding of what it is to be republican. Why are we giving the Libertarians a platform?

Part of their ideals include legalizing drugs. Drugs are a trap disguised as an escape. Drug use is another form of slavery. The Republican party was founded to abolish slavery. Anybody claiming to be a Republican and is pro-legalizing drugs is pro-legalizing another form of slavery and is in contradiction of what it is to be republican.

If a person wants to use drugs, that is their business. I think Libertarians would agree to that, and the best way to keep it their business is to keep it illegal. Doing drugs illegally helps to better ensure that people will do drugs privately. They will be more apt to keep it their own business.

But the truth is people don't want drug use to be their own business. They want to be very public with it. They have always deceived themselves and others that they wanted their drug use to be their own little private affair. No. They want the liberty to get high at work. They want the liberty to get high and smoke weed at family attractions. Get high in front of your children at Disneyland or county fairs. They're so greedy they can't even just enjoy where they are. They have to get high too.

These selfish people are so enslaved to their vices they don't wait to get home to just get high in private and make it their own business like they've said. No. they want everybody to be witnesses to their little rebellion kick. They're so cool as they get high in front of others. This is liberty to them, and what a waste of it.

CHAPTER VIII
SUCKER PUNCHING THE 2ND AMENDMENT

There are those who question the claim that the NRA was founded to help freed slaves. The NRA website doesn't speak of it, but it's a matter of putting two and two together. The Republican Party itself was built on abolition. The Republican represented Union fought to end slavery. Eventually, those vets became the NRA. The NRA was established primarily to improve shooting techniques. Why was it so important for them to sharpen their skills? Because they still needed to defend against sore loser Democrat Confederates. (Just like we still have sore loser Democrats today) That was who the union was at war with. Who else would they need to improve their skills against? In this case, it would be the terrorists the democrats created; the KKK. The NRA doesn't try to boast or pander to this because they try not to get trapped in the quicksand of race-baiting. Even if the NRA affirmed their history, Democrats still wouldn't be satisfied and would try to manipulate it. (That doesn't mean the NRA shouldn't put up a protective measure against the charge, because some things guns don't help defend against. The NRA may need to learn that at some point. Sometimes it takes learning how to aim a camera and a microphone instead of aiming a gun so as to create creative and compelling content to promote a counter influence in the culture.)

Democrats have to twist the history of the NRA because they don't want people to make the connection that Democrats didn't want blacks to have guns then, just as they don't want blacks to have guns now. And they've suckered people into thinking Democrats have changed.

We can see proof of Democrats twisting the recall of past events today. Any event that happens where multiple people are killed, the Democrats blame the NRA. Even if a gun isn't the murder weapon, the left wing media will broadcast the stigma that it was the NRA's fault and, of course, Christians.

For example, in November 2016 there was a knife attack at Ohio State University.

In the excitement of liberals thinking they'd be able to blame guns for a violent attack, the liberals experienced a spell of premature eFACTtuation. Yup, they "went off" without knowing even a nominal amount of facts in a sad display of factual inadequacy. (Chortle)

So the knifer, whose full name I won't include in this piece because I don't want to take up a bunch of time saying it, like reading the story of Tikki Tikki Tembo. Anyway, the knifer got a bullet in his akbar when a gun was used to save the day by Officer Horujko. But, considering the dyslexic worldview liberals have, somehow the Knifer became the shooter who went on a shooting spree. Slashing people with bullets I suppose. Is that like a new thing on the market now? Slasher rounds? Butcher knife Bullets?

And while liberals are always trying to assign some sort of phobia on us Christian Conservative Patriots that's going to supposedly make us go Psycho-Destructo, it's the left wing that always ends up doing it. Like the knifer nut. Who said:

"I wanted to pray in the open, but I was scared with everything going on in the media. I'm a Muslim, it's not what the media portrays me to be. If people look at me, a Muslim praying, I don't know what they're going to think, what's going to happen."

He said he's not what the media portrays him to be? That's nuts. The left-wing media has been the ones trying to mitigate what people like him are and instead has made the Christian Republicans out to be the boogie-man. The knifer-nut actually was what he accused others of seeing him as. So according to the Muslim-Knifer's so-called reasoning; he was afraid that people were going to see him as a murderous Muslim… So he had to go murder people. Ass-alamu alaykum.

This is the loony-ville that liberals live in. Do you think liberals ever wave their finger and those COEXIST bumper stickers in the Muslim's faces? No! They can't even pull their heads out of their mud-pipe long enough to see that the assailant used a knife, and want to call this a shooting.

So no. It's not at all a stretch to say that even if the NRA posted their history with helping blacks protect themselves from the terrorism of Democrats, the Democrats would still reject it and twist it. But just because the NRA hasn't posted it doesn't mean the NRA denies it. I've not known the NRA to refute the claim. We already examined how democrats twist and switch things around.

They go from being the "separation of church and state" party that wants God removed and replaced with what they qualify as "science", to all of a sudden being so concerned that church-goers were attacked. They vilify Christians at every turn yet are trying to further drive their gun control demands by all of a sudden making church-goers out to be the most innocent victims of the self-thinking gun-goblin. Even though, before that, liberals saw Christians as people who bitterly cling to their guns and their Bibles. Even Obama took low-blow opportunities to stigmatize Christianity for slavery and Jim Crow.

Christianity doesn't condone slavery. People, being liberal with what the Bible actually says, pushed for slavery. And by the way, Muslims were enslaving people long before America was founded, and still do it today! So Democrats, spare us your fake outrage about a church being shot up. Democrats have been directing violence against churches for a while now. You can have all the anti-gun laws you want, people will still find another way to attack a church. Democrats, being anti-gun, is just a front to throw the public off the fact that it's Democrats who overwhelmingly do the shooting. People will be disarmed while Democrats exempt themselves from the laws they expect the public peasantry to abide by. You know? Like liberals having armed security. Democrats used bombs to attack predominantly black churches too, and it's actually NOT legal to bomb people either.

I hear these Fruit loopin' liberals asking, "What's it going to take?" As they try to make the point to ask "How much gun violence is it going to take before we ban guns?"

Wrong question.

What's it going to take for liberals to understand that constantly promoting their entitlement victim mentality is what gets people killed? They push this propaganda in the culture that people are owed, entitled, and justice is overdue; somebody's gotta pay! They push this poisonous propaganda over, and over, and over again, and then have the nerve to try to be outraged when someone snaps and takes what liberals have been pushing into their heads and unloads violence on innocent people?

Does sex kill people? No. Selfish people who want pleasure so bad that they don't care what disease they can catch and pass on kills people. Do liberals want to ban sex too? No. Instead, they say have more sex and make sure you do it with anybody available - same sex or opposite sex. Heck, manipulate your gender to have just as much sex as a supposed woman as ya did as a man.

Double your pleasure! Triple your pleasure! Be a Try-sexual. Try anything!

Drugs kill people, but do liberals want to ban drugs? No. They want to make drugs legal.

Does abortion kill people? Absolutely, but liberals don't want to think so. Even when the pregnant woman dies from an abortion procedure, liberals just say, "That's because the abortion wasn't performed safely." First up, an abortion can be performed in the safest, cleanest facility in the world. It ain't safe for the kid that's getting butchered. But libs say that abortion is ok when it's done safely. Well then, how come libs don't say guns are ok when handled safely? *But guns are for killing people!* left-wingers screech. Not exactly. Guns also prevent people from killing and help preserve life. The specific purpose of an abortion is to kill someone. Liberals say, "If you Republicans have your way a woman will have back alley abortions and she most likely will get killed." They're making my point; terminating pregnancies unnaturally is deadly, no matter how you put it. So why insist on keeping this deadly practice legal? Liberals don't care about life. Their lust is for control.

This is how loony liberals are. They think that a mass shooter will be afraid of strict gun laws. Nah. A mass shooter/murderer has already decided they are already going to meet the use of deadly force by law enforcement. They already know they will be judged with fire and have decided that it is worth it to murder people even though they most likely will face the law in its most strict sentence; death on the spot.

Humor us Liberals. When a mass murderer decides that it's worth it to be shot dead where they stand just so they can kill innocent women and children, what law do you think is going to stop them? That's how loony libs are, and I am sick of the success of willfully stupid people forcing us to be ruled by their stupidity.

People are now saying, "Even churches aren't going to be a safe space anymore. Is that the world we live in now? Are Church members going to have to have armed security?"

If liberals would actually study the Bible and consult with the Author instead of cherry picking they'd know the answer. Note to liberals; the church is generally seen as a "Gun Free Zone." That doesn't stop people from murdering innocent people in church now, does it? That might register with y'all at some point. "What's it going to take?" as libs like ask.

Church wasn't founded as a safe space, folks. When Jesus held church His disciples were armed. Not only were they armed, they were skilled with their weapons, and ready to fight. The reason why Jesus didn't let them fight was because the only way that Jesus could prove to man that He is the conqueror of death was to be killed. Not dying isn't the ultimate proof of immortality; coming back from the dead is.

The world is messed up because of the selfish choices we make. God gives us the means to defend ourselves from others who ignore the very law of God who says don't intrude on the rights He gave us. If there are people who will ignore the law that says do not murder, doesn't it stand to reason they will ignore gun laws too? People have the right to protect themselves from those who choose to do them harm.

And to all those nuts like Hillary Clinton who are desperately trying to make some brilliant point about "silencers," well, they're just being shallow and stupid. A person who wants to commit mass murder wants to be heard. Not "silenced." They want a big booming "release" to reflect their catharsis. They don't want to go out with a whisper. They want to go out with a roaring curse upon the blood of whoever offended them. So trying to accuse the NRA of being facilitators of mass murder because of silencers is absurd.

But liberals believe that silencer crap. Yet all these loudmouthed liberals have to do is look at their own behavior. "Live out loud and hear me roar." Liberals want people to be forced to hear them. They're determined to not be silenced, yet they think a mass shooter (which American history shows have pretty much all been far left wingers) are going to use a silencer.

I'll remind y'all again, practically every act of politically motivated violence in America since the Democrat Party was founded has been perpetrated by Democrats and left wingers. A few examples would be;

Democrat John Wilkes Booth who shot Abraham Lincoln.

Then there are the Democrats in The New Orleans riot, 1866, Democrats attacked Republicans, most of whom were black parading outside the Mechanics Institute in New Orleans, where a reconvened Louisiana Constitutional Convention was being held. Over 100 blacks were killed. They were virtually unarmed... Just the way the Democrats like it.

Charles J. Guiteau, who shot James Garfield. I list Charles because even though He campaigned for Garfield it doesn't mean he couldn't flip a switch and turn on him. Judas was a disciple of Jesus and was an accomplice in His murder. Even Guiteau's daddy thought Chucky was possessed by the Devil. Guiteau was just a nut with a defective weener. This might have contributed to him going daffy. He was a political opportunist that latched on to a political figure that he thought would get him an appointment the fastest. Guiteau considered himself the Stalwart of Stalwarts, but ultimately he was about as Republican as David Duke. His political views were obscure, but he was a religious sexual fanatic who got kicked out of sex cult by cult leader, Oneida. Between not being able to be welcomed in a sex cult and not welcome to have a job in the White House - it seems that Chucky G. had a bit of a problem with entitlement issues. He was obsessively entitled, actually, and that puts him in the left wing camp.

William McKinley was killed by Leon Czolgosz a Democratic-Anarchist.

(Democrats were contradicting and confused then, and they're the same now.)

John F. Kennedy was killed by Lee Harvey Oswald; Communist.

There were assassination attempts on:

Franklin D. Roosevelt by Giuseppe Zangara; left winger (Italian anarchist who shot the mayor of Miami during a speech by Roosevelt

Harry S. Truman by Oscar Collazo & Griselio Torresola for the "Popular Democratic Party of Puerto Rico; left wingers

Malcolm X was shot by black-nationalist socialist, Talmadge Hayer, Norman Butler, and Thomas Johnson; all left wingers.

Martin Luther King was shot by James Earl Ray a Democrat.

Gerald Ford endured an assassination attempt by Lynette "Squeaky" Fromme, a follower of Charles Manson; left-wing cannibal. 17 days later the second assassination attempt on Ford came from Democrat activist, Sara Jane Moore, a Patty Hearst Fanatic.

Ronald Reagan had a less than polite run-in with John Hinckley, Jr., another registered Democrat.

But according to Liberals that stuff is old news. (Slavery is old news too, but they keep bringing that up. That is until it's pointed out to them that Democrats are the ones who fought, like the Devil, to keep it legal. Then they revert back to the, "That was then, this is now" thing.)

Well then, how about Jared Lee Loughner; a registered Democrat who made an assassination attempt on Gabby Giffords and also wounding 12 others?

"Maj." Nidal Hasan, a registered Democrat and Muslim that viciously murdered thirteen people and wounded 29 at Fort Hood.

Seung-Hui Cho, a registered Democrat, hate mail writer, murderer of 32 people, and wounded 17 at Virginia Tech.

Wade Michael Page, another registered Democrat, murdered 6 and wounded 4 at a Sikh Temple.

James Holmes, a registered Democrat monstrously murdered 12 and wounded 58 innocent people at a Colorado movie theater.

Christopher Dorner was a registered Democrat and a California cop killer who murdered 4.

Adam Lanza, another registered Democrat, viciously murdered 20 innocent children and fatally shot 6 adult members of the school's staff. He also wounded 2 at the Sandy Hook Elementary school. Besides shooting himself in the head he also shot his mother. He is the poster child of the loony-ville violent left.

But of course, Democrats don't look at that. Because that would mean they'd have to look at themselves. But they can't do that because they're too busy judging other people, most likely to distract others from realizing just how screwed up libs truly are. It's amazing how selfish these people are without actually seeing themselves.

Lastly. Liberals are the real profiling hypocrites. They breathed a sigh of relief when it was discovered that Stephen Paddock, the bigoted Las Vegas mass murderer was white.... Oh, the horror! So liberals profiled him as a Christian conservative. This also means that libs are the ones who profile brown Middle-Eastern folks as Muslims, and assume Islam is an actual race thing, (as if "whitey" can't be Muslim.)

As I've said a long time ago, liberals have a judgmental sickness, demanding to be in control of everything from gun control, to weather control, to population control. And in their sickness, they only see encouraging self-control as judgmental. Libs believe people can be responsible with all the things and ideals that poison them and demand others assume the cost of their irresponsible choices. And that always backfires, and sometimes it comes out as unfriendly fire upon innocent people.

Democrats are a backward breed. They insist that a country like Iran has the right to have nuclear power but don't believe people should have second amendment rights. They trust the irate state of Iran to have nuclear power and believe they'll be friendly and responsible but don't trust Americans to have guns to responsibly protect themselves against Democrats.

As mentioned before, Democrats use blacks to push their agenda. The gun control issue is no exception. Since Hillary Clinton insists on still being relevant we'll give her some attention.

Hillary has carried on with liberal nonsense saying that "The gun epidemic is the problem."

No, Hillary, that's hardly the problem. When you have black people who are the leading population of people who decrease their own population by aborting their children you can't blame that on guns. Much of the black community doesn't have a gun problem. Too much of the black community has a spiritual problem. They have been inflicted with an ideological problem, and they're addicted to the Democrat problem.

Hillary and the Democrat's ideas are backward and it leads to more oppression and murder. Hillary and Democrat's think that gun control is more important than self-control. Hillary and Democrat's believe that more state control is more important than self-control. Self-control isn't encouraged because it doesn't couple well with pandering. Democrats need to have something to blame so their voters don't feel like they're being held responsible and don't have to assume any responsibility for anything. They can have a false sense of happiness to say it's someone's, or something else's, fault. That's what Hillary did and it exposes what rots the proverbial village she thinks it takes to raise children.

Democrats will say stop and frisk is unconstitutional because it singles out black people. Well, of course, to Democrats it's unconstitutional. Democrats don't want black folks to be obstructed from killing other black folks. Democrats have to keep the population of their wards under control and use them as their examples of people to point to. This way they can blame others for the black plight, claim to be their champion and reap the votes for it.

You can't stop and frisk a black person. They might be armed. If they're armed you'd have to take their gun. The Democrats need that black person to keep that gun to kill other people with. One; to control the population of the "undesirables", and two; to point to the number of gun deaths. Mind you, they just want people to look at the number of deaths. They don't want people to be outraged about blacks killing each other per say. Just a body count.

Don't get me wrong, the murder of anybody is wrong. The tragedy of murder knows no color. #ALLLIVESMATTER! I'm pointing out the Democrat's policy of manipulation of color to institute their policies.

But Democrats don't want to see us as one people. They want "diversity" and want you to think it's a good thing, when all diversity is - is just a sugar-coated deceptive way of saying divide.

Whether a black person committed a crime against another black person or a white person, the outrage should be the same because no matter what, it's motivated by hate. To the white people who are outraged by such and say, "if this was a white group who did this to a black person there'd be outrage then." Well, that's not a constructive perspective, because for many decades whites were able to commit crimes like this towards blacks and justice wasn't so swift. The whites who were doing this would ultimately become the Democrat Party. The white people who wanted to maintain supremacy and apartheid over black people voted Democrat. They wanted diversity too; whites here, coloreds over there. So, white people saying, "If this was the other way around... " Pump your brakes. It has been the other way around.

I keep trying to tell y'all, you need to be more aggressive yet "finesse-full" in making the case that it was not white people in general who instituted the racism that blacks are still so angry about. It was Democrats. Like Democrats who didn't want blacks to be educated. And here it is today, Democrats oppose school choice for blacks wanting a better selection for their child's course of education. Who didn't want blacks to have second amendment rights? Democrats. Today, who insists on intruding on second amendment rights and use blacks to infringe on the second amendment? Democrats. They're the same.

Democrats hide behind the racism Boogie-Man (that they're the breeder and feeder of, mind you.) They say, *It's white people in general and that it's white privilege,* (When it's really the Democrats.) The areas of this country where this mess is happening are run by Democrats. And in their containment, these people are fed the same crap year in and year out. They're poisoned with dysfunctionality. Raised with no fathers, feeling abandoned, raised by bitter mothers trying to play both parents, and not knowing how to direct their resentment. There's males trying to learn how to be men from other boys, and girls having no idea of how a real man according to God is supposed to behave.

They take what's broken in the home with them out into the streets and take it out on each other, so they can feel some sense of power because they feel powerless at home. It feels good and powerful to subject another to their frustration. One of those senses of power that they're seduced and suckered by is black power. Ironically it's one of their biggest weaknesses.

Black power, white power, or whatever in-between isn't a show of strength, it's a mentality of weakness!

Anyway, that's the only power that they've been fooled into thinking that matters, and that the white boogie man is trying to take it from them. Year in and year out they're poisoned with this thinking. The truth that they're missing is that it's white Democrats who have been manipulating and stealing from them. And they still don't see it. (Invisible Empire)

But history will have a funny way of repeating itself. Black on black crime is fine in these Democrat run communities, but when it breaks containment and white Democrats start becoming a more frequent target, you're going to see Democrats get more aggressive with denying gun rights to blacks. Hmmm. Denying gun rights to blacks. Sound familiar? You're going see legislation enacted that seems to want to keep blacks over here and whites over there. It's already happening and Democrats are setting it up to where blacks are happy to do it. Democrats will have successfully segregated blacks again.

Democrats keep trying to keep blacks shackled to them and it ends up having a violent result.

We're going down that road again because Democrats refuse to let go of black folks, and what's worse, too many black folks refuse to let go of Democrats. They've got "brain chains" on them and when you just slap chains on people like that they can become toxic and violent. The Democrats have them trapped and they're ingesting then recycling the same old poison, the same insecurities, the same paranoia, and the same animosities. They stay stuck in these Democrat run communities with the keys to unlock the chains in their pockets, while feeling bitter that the white man keeps them down. But then when they try to better themselves and try to leave and grow they're accused of being sell-outs who want to be like the white man. This is the poisoned thinking that Democrats keep these people trapped in. As I've mentioned in the analogy before, like crabs in a bucket.

The coup de grace, of the Democrat's plan, is to implicate the Republicans as the guilty party that represents racist white people, and too many black people fall for it. Republicans need to understand that they are deceived by thinking that they've got superior firepower with whatever cache of weapons they have, and The Democrats just have the pathetic weapon of race-baiting. Please understand, there are times when guns are ineffective against other weapons. Satan didn't destroy mankind with a gun. He destroyed mankind with an accusation, and that's how Democrats are destroying the Second Amendment, Republicans, and the Republic; with accusations.

Republicans boast about jobs, national security, and economic policy. That doesn't mean squat if the people don't trust you, and if you haven't cleared the air about the prejudice they've been infected with. More jobs being available is great! But if a job opens up, and a person who is black takes that job but hasn't cleared their thinking on racism then that person is going to have people around him walking on eggshells. And if anybody complains about his or her performance then it's going to be blamed on racism.

This could be the same with Mexicans, Asians, and Middle Easterners etc. White people can find a way to make it about their race too. They can say they're being denied work because they're white. It's not far-fetched. The Irish are white and they were denied work too. Remember NINA? (No Irish Need Apply)

Sure, we can have more jobs, but more jobs have opened for women who've been poisoned with the pride and insecurity of feminism. Employers walking on eggshells who will be accused of sexual harassment just for holding the door open for a co-worker. Or even women insisting that they're not being treated equally. Great! More jobs are available, and you're going to have to deal with more people wanting to dress up as the opposite sex and represent your business, and if you don't allow it, you're discriminating. You're discriminating if your place of business has a theme or a uniform, but there's a woman who wants to wear a Hijab which would be non-conducive with your business. But now you have to let her wear her Hijab. But hey, more jobs, right? All of these things send us back to the problems we were already having.

Republicans are no better than Democrats in thinking that jobs are the answer. Jobs aren't the answer, Jesus is.

Remember how ridiculous it sounded when Democrats like Marie Harf said "We just need to give the terrorists jobs?" We republicans thought that was a doozy of a dumb statement. Because it was dumb! Yet Republicans think that jobs are the answer to our problems too. Republicans are boasting about how jobs are returning. They think that America is going to be saved with the return of jobs! The return of Jesus will be the savior of humanity, not jobs. Not the return of work, jobs, not Steve Jobs, or Job in the Bible, but Jesus. #JesusIsEnough! And until Jesus returns we need to return to His Word to help preserve the republic, because all though jobs are very important, it's not the answer. Don't get me wrong. Even Jesus will frown on people who just seek Him but don't seek a job. Jesus expects us to work. It's a commandment actually. However, If people are still sensitive to their insecurities from race, class, gender, religion or whatever, those things will go into the workplace and present a liability to that company, and money cannot fix that. That's a fix from Jesus. When people have these chips on their shoulders they also tend to feel very entitled. They will still feel like they're owed more. There will be politicians who will be sharpening their game to seduce the public peasantry for their vote who will institute policies that will burden the job creators. This will pseudo-satiate the envious and insecure who just want to see the rich get punished. And when the rich can't afford to hire as many they'll just be accused of being greedy, and around we go again.

This is a big reason why Republicans need to support the productions that will illustrate the absurdity of the Democrat's slander. You have to disable the weapon of race-baiting, class-baiting, gender-baiting and such. All this, if not addressed now, is how the

Democrats gain ground with pushing things like gun control, because Democrats gain trust by getting people to distrust others. Why should people trust Republicans with the second amendment when Democrats have convinced them that Republicans are a bunch of chauvinistic bigots?

Democrats easily convince people that Republicans are racist by accusing Republicans of making it difficult for blacks to get an ID. Again, this is Democrats accusing Republicans of what Democrats have been guilty of. Democrats resorted to terrorism with the KKK to keep people from voting, imposed poll taxes, and literacy tests to disenfranchise black voters, and even the whites that they thought were inferior stock. (Probably because they were republican whites) The tests were designed to be really difficult. Democrats didn't want blacks to be educated in the first place and then imposed an unfairly difficult literacy test on them just to say, "See?! They're too stupid to vote!" If you have the right to vote, you don't have to be tested for it, BTW.

Democrats insist that healthcare is a right. They'd be offended if you told them they have to be tested for it and be found with a pre-existing condition which could affect the obtaining of coverage. No. They assume they have a right. So they don't have to take a test. But Democrats were the ones who imposed a test on the right to vote.

The point is; if Republicans don't start illustratively covering multiple angles to refute Democrat accusations, we're always going to keep coming back to the same problems. We will only enjoy outstanding prosperity for a brief moment. And while the Republicans are complacent, basking in the glow of their bubble moment, the "Devil-crats" are going to be whispering in people's ears with accusations - using the same old jive on new suckers. Republicans haven't set safeguards in place to capture people's interest and inoculate them by delivering creative and compelling content in the culture before the left gets to them with their poisonous philosophy.

Remember when we had productions that showed it was a good thing for a good guy to be free to carry a gun because bad guys were going to carry a gun to break the law anyway? Shows that made the police more relatable to people; Police shows that called out crooked acting cops, but didn't depend on always making a cop look good by being a rogue amidst a legion of crooked cops.

The Democrat's objective is control. Make blacks distrust Republicans so they'll trust Democrats by default. Democrats use the loyalty of blacks to attract votes by shaming whites and making them feel that their redemption is in voting Democrat. They have to prove an admission of guilt by voting for Democrats who are going to give blacks everything they feel owed from these guilty whites.

Liberal whites are happy to do this because they love the idea of this making them appear like superior people. They're much better human beings in their eyes for such ideals.

And we know how Democrats have historically been with supremacy. Democrats succeed with getting as far as they have with this because they're always illustrating and making songs of their version of what their ideals look like, and behold... Prejudice! It's going to take the same to undo a lot of prejudice.

The Democrats are keeping people prisoners with prejudice. It's time again for a new abolition to set the "prisoners of prejudice" free, or we'll end up losing our liberty too; including the liberty to defend ourselves with the guns we were supposed to have the right to have. I would rather change this course before it gets to a point where it's going to take guns again to liberate people from Democrats. But I think pro-gun folks shoot themselves in the foot because they too often seem more enthusiastic about their Guns than the gospel. To them, the most important right is their right to their guns as it protects all other rights. This is sad, because it means they trust in their guns not God to preserve the right's that God Himself gave us. Our national motto is "In God we Trust." Not in Gun we trust. Yet pro-gun people trust in their guns more than God. Sure, people ignore the Word of God. They ignore guns too. A person may not care that they'll have to answer to God someday, but some may not care that someone might shoot them for their trespasses. They'll take the risk. Many don't. Some do. However the fear of the Lord does keep many people from trespassing too, and so do guns. Thank God for the ingenuity to make Guns! God Himself gave us the right to be armed before the constitution was penned.

God chose David and David armed himself! And while liberals tell us we don't need whatever amount of rounds for our firearms, David took a surplus of ammunition! Not only was David a really good shot, He had God with him! One stone would have been enough, but David grabbed five stones! Four stones more than He needed! Even dispatched by God, David STILL took a surplus of ammunition, plus a staff. Don't let some liberal put limits on how much ammunition we can have. The Word of God Himself gives us permission to have a surplus! But here is what I hope Pro-gun folks get. David didn't charge Goliath with faith and enthusiasm in his weapons. His faith and enthusiasm were in God!

1 Samuel 17:44-46

45Then David said to the Philistine, "You come to me with a sword, a spear, and a javelin, but I come to you in the name of the LORD of hosts, the God of the armies of Israel, whom you have taunted. 46"This day the LORD will deliver you up into my hands, and I will strike you down and remove your head from you. And I will give the dead bodies of the army of the Philistines this day to the birds of the sky and the wild beasts of the earth, that all the earth may know that there is a God in Israel,...

It's ok to be enthusiastic about guns, but it's better to be enthusiastic about the One who Blessed you with the right to them. But right now guns themselves are being used to deprive the people of their God-given right to them. Gun-control laws keep creeping up, along with the death toll. And when a person breaks the law and kills people guns get blamed. The people are suckered into giving the state more power to infringe on the 2nd amendment. Guns are going to become useless in protecting us from this erosion.

Now the anti-gun left is taking advantage of another instance; Conservatives turning against each other over why there are more shootings. There are some conservatives who believe it's possible that these shootings are being staged to get people to ultimately forfeit their guns or lead up to confiscation. And there are conservatives who believe it is a sick conspiracy theory and curse other conservatives for being heartless people who don't care about children for thinking such a thing.

I'm not into conspiracy theories. But I think the latter mentioned are given over to a self-righteous, knee-jerk emotional response. It's one thing to disagree with the speculation, but some of these people seriously over-reacted, and all it is is an exercise in trying to puff themselves up as a better person as they try to look like they care so much more than everyone else. To make themselves look like they care more than anyone else they attack other conservatives who consider that there are minors being used to perpetrate these actions or that people are being propped up to commit mass murder to forward an agenda. But how dare that be considered?! So, that means you hate children and don't care that they're being slaughtered? Y'all it is legal to slaughter the unborn by the millions, and people think it's ridiculous to consider that kids could be used to stage a shooting? Such as the Cruz shooting.

Kids were used in the Hitler Youth to advance Nazi Policy. We can see today in our own country how kids are used. Kids are used to sell drugs. Kids are sold into sex trafficking. In other places Kids are recruited with Boko Haram, kids are used as bombs, Pharaoh had children thrown into the river, Herod committed infanticide to stop the coming of Jesus, where do these self-righteous people get off acting like it's cruel to think that it's possible that people would harm kids or use kids to kill kids?

We're talking about Democrats, here. The party of the KKK, the party of Lynching, bombing, shootings, and do not care if children are the target. But we have some conservatives who are appalled that some other conservatives would call out minors for possibly being used to stage a shooting to promote a gun grab? These kinds of conservatives are the ones with the kind of denial that are shocked when their kid is arrested for drug possession, or have a drinking problem.

The music that is mostly listened to by kids is music that has a constant theme of devaluing life. Kids are exposed to all kinds of conditioning to make them more dysfunctional, but somehow guns are the culprit. Nobody likes to be at fault. Especially kids! And kids will be happy to blame guns, and blame the NRA! They don't know what the NRA is nor do they care! As long as people blame this NRA guy instead of them! Kids are more and more being brought up to not take personal responsibility. They prefer to believe that being responsible is when they make indictments against someone else. This is unchecked hormonal huff and puff. They're brought up by parents blaming each other for why they broke up. They're brought up with constant accusatory content being passed off as entertainment. Kids are brought up to assume everything is someone or something else's fault. Someone else should be made to bear the responsibility. That's too many of the youth, And thank God for those who haven't been infected with that kind of selfishness, and do try to be accountable. Peace and blessings to the parents of those brave youth who get in the line of fire so another can live. Shalom to all parents who had their children stolen from them. I pray that they understand that guns are not the problem. Influence is. Whether it's negative influence, or not enough positive influence, or negative influence promoted as positive influence; like teaching kids about fisting. That's a negative influence disguised as a positive, open minded, adventurous, brave, and introspective practice. Democrats are masters of dressing up negative influences to make them seem positive.

Liberals are going to use the kids they've brainwashed as tools to influence voters. And votes will be used to infringe upon the Second Amendment. Your guns won't protect you from that. If you put your trust in guns over God you will invite an unnecessary shootout. This "Come and take it" attitude, is a prideful call of those who value guns over God. Don't get me wrong. Don't let your right to property be violated. Be ready to defend yourself with fire if necessary! But the Fire of the Lord should be trusted above all. While you boast in your bullets, people are being suckered into depositing ballots that will put the squeeze on your rights. And you trying to reverse that by boasting in your guns ain't going to help, and when they squeeze your rights even further to the point when they're coming to your door to take your guns, and it becomes a shootout, trust me - you're going to be made to look like the bad guy with bad guns, and that will help the commie cause even more. Why? Because you killed and or died for your guns. Not for God. Not for country, but your guns. I so hope you prove me wrong. I really want to be wrong about that. But it sure would be nice to see Pro-gun folks show they know just as much about what the Word of God says as much as they can tell ya about their gun specs. Don't get me wrong, many can! But we need many more, because there is a legion of people out to remove the Word of God and guns, and without the Word of God, guns won't be much help. I say these things to preserve the Second Amendment. Pro-gun folks keep saying the Second Amendment protects the First. Meanwhile, they overlook that the First Amendment is being abused to eliminate the Second Amendment.

The Disciples of Christ were armed, and not only armed they were skilled fighters! Peter was so skilled with His sword that he pulled his sword and cut off a man's ear with one stroke! That is skill! You don't just pull out your sword and chop off a man's ear in one move without having some serious chops! Pun intended! Jesus knew Peter would do that and allowed it. Why? Because Jesus wanted Rome and the Sanhedrin to know that He had a very ready and willing Army to decimate them all. But then Jesus healed the man by restoring his ear. Why? Because He wanted all to know that He is God and that the only way they could take Him is if He let them.

Peter was serious and fully meant it when he said he would go all the way to the grave with Jesus! But Peter didn't know that the Plan was to be handed over. Peter didn't register that part. He thought there was going to be a fight! He was prepared to fight to the death. That is what Peter was ready to die with Jesus for! I'm sure you can relate. Die fighting!!! That's how Peter felt! But when he saw that Jesus wasn't going to lead them into battle against Rome and there wasn't going to be a fight, he ran. He didn't want to just hand himself over to die. If he had to die, it would have to be in a fight. Ultimately the time came when the temple was destroyed, and all the fighting skill the Israelites had couldn't save them. Why? Because they didn't have God with them. Jesus warned them of their rejection. He never told them to disarm. God raised Israel up to be an army as it is, and have been the most capable fighting force against the most brutal tribes in history. They put the sword to oppressive nations that brutally enslaved, sacrificed children, raped, cannibalized, engaged in bestiality etc. God sent them to punish nations that were the worst violators of human rights. Israelites were very, very, skilled with weapons! They were well armed! They still are! This was by God's ordinance Himself! It is our right to defend ourselves and to liberate others when their God-given rights are being stripped from them. But despite how well the Israelites were armed and skilled they lost touch with God and ended up in subjugation. But it is God that preserves Israel! The best way to defend our God-given rights ain't with guns, it's with guns with the sword of Truth affixed as the bayonet. Just sayin'.

CHAPTER IX
PUNCHING SOUTH OF THE BORDER

Liberals relentlessly resort to low-blows like race-baiting. Another low-blow Liberals are notorious for is invoking Jesus; cherry-pickin' posers who try to cite the Bible when it suits them to make some self-righteous protest. They try to come off like they're all compassionate, without exercising common sense. They try to throw Jesus in our faces to make their so-called point while giving Jesus the finger concerning everything else He taught.

But let's set the record straight about liberals all of a sudden becoming "All about Jesus" concerning the refugees, and invoking Him as the example of compassion. Jesus, Who is God, is the same Dude who kicked Adam and Eve out of the garden and did not let them back in. Why? Because they couldn't be trusted.

Jesus, Who is God, is the same Dude Who denied a bunch of Hebrews who were refugees from Egypt entrance into the Promised Land. Even Moses, who was also a refugee from Egypt was denied entrance into the Promised Land. Do you know why they weren't allowed entrance into the promise land? Because they couldn't be trusted.

The Hebrews proved over and over again they could not follow basic laws and would adopt and impose the ways and laws of other cultures that ultimately lead to oppression and murder.

God was like, *You are not bringing that nonsense into the promise land.* So don't go trying to use scripture to say that it ain't Christian to not let in all the refugees. Liberals hate the book of Leviticus, yet the Book of Leviticus says.

"The foreigner residing among you must be treated as your native-born. Love them as yourself, for you were foreigners in Egypt. I am the LORD your God." Leviticus 19:34 NIV

So yes, God does want us to be welcoming to foreigners. Immigration is awesome! But this is the part liberals overlook, where God says, "Love them as yourselves." If the foreigner is going to be among God's people, they have to become like God's people. The foreigner has to become like God's people to be a neighbor loved by God's people. That's right y'all: Assimilation. If the Israelites are going to love the foreigner like their native-born, then that means that the foreigner must become like the native-born, ergo, assimilate to the laws and ways of the native-born. the foreigner can't come up into somebody else's house imposing their own way.

You can't just assume to love people any old way you want and rightly define it as love. Loving your neighbor as yourself does not mean forcing your native countrymen to compromise their security so you can feel good about yourself. That is not love, compassion, or practical. Liberals don't understand. There has to be a vetting. Liberals talk about how Jesus is all about compassion and He would let them in. Wrong. Don't assume to interpret the compassion of Jesus. Jesus has the talent of balancing practicality with compassion. Libs, not so much.

Lefties are only concerned with the affairs of man. Jesus hates that. He called Peter Satan because of that. When people are all caught up in the affairs of appeasing men, oppression and murder follows. You think Jesus is all welcoming? Really? I say to you assuredly, people tend to die before Jesus welcomes them to cross the border into His Kingdom.

God would rather let Jesus die than to let us into His kingdom. That's how screwed up we are.

But you think Hippie Jesus would be all compassionate and just let anybody in. Liberals are trying to invoke the name of Jesus, and Jesus has already made it clear that He's going to be like, "Yo. I don't know you. You ain't crossing my border."

Then I will tell them plainly, 'I never knew you; depart from Me, you workers of lawlessness.' - Matthew 7:23 BSB

Liberals, of course, cherry-pick a similar verse that says the following to justify in their minds letting in illegal immigrants:

...Then He will say to those on His left, 'Depart from Me, you who are cursed, into the eternal fire prepared for the devil and his angels.

For I was hungry and you gave Me nothing to eat, I was thirsty and you gave Me nothing to drink, I was a stranger and you did not take Me in, I was naked and you did not clothe Me, I was sick and in prison and you did not visit Me.'... -Matthew 25:41-43 BSB

But that is an example of liberals not squaring scripture by scripture. Jesus says **"...depart from Me, you workers of lawlessness."** If strangers are **breaking the law** you don't take them in and feed them. The strangers are to depart; or shall we say, the departed lawbreakers are to be deported lawbreakers.

I pray to My Lord and King, Jesus, that I'm not one of those people He says He does not know. But the point is, Jesus isn't going to let people who would screw up His Kingdom in. You get in when you choose to accept that Jesus is the Law, and to know the law is to love the law. The law being Jesus.

You think vetting immigrants takes a long time here? Ha! God vetted the Jews forty years before they reached the Promised Land. Don't tell me that God just welcomes people in. Jesus has been vetting the human race for over 2000 years, since the cross, and will keep vetting us before He's given the go-ahead to let the new generation of refugees witness the Electric Exodus that will usher us into His Kingdom. Don't tell me that Jesus is just all accepting and welcomes people in.

Jesus IS accepting, but not the way liberals want. They don't understand that people aren't accepting Him, and just want to benefit from the blessing but not follow His way, which intrudes upon others. Peace cannot sustain that way.

It would be great if liberals would stop trying to use Jesus (Who they don't even really accept,) to make their claim about compassion. They do not care or understand what Jesus teaches about compassion.

Now, regarding the national security threat of illegal immigration. Muslims can lie and say they're Christian. Consider also, the KKK are a bunch of pagans claiming to be Christian. You don't think Islamo-terrorist won't pose as Christian refugees too?

It is heartbreaking to see these people are having to run for their lives from psychos whom you liberals claim follow a "religion peace". Yes, there are real refugees who are running for their lives, and there are real murderers among them.

We are to help our foreign neighbors, but you don't help your neighbor by gambling with the well-being of your family and the well-being of your neighbors. That is not compassion, that's just freakin' rude. It's not depriving Muslims of their right to enter our country. It's liberals depriving Americans of theirs when you demand we allow entrance of un-vetted people who follow a doctrine that deems us guilty for being infidels and due for the punishment of death.

There's a right way to discriminate and a wrong way. I'm calling out the most wrongfully discriminating people in America there are, and have always been since they were established: Democrats, and they just happen to be the ones who accuse others of the most of discrimination. Democrats instituted the discriminatory apartheid laws this country is still so bitter about. They still want to lecture us about discrimination as they insist on letting in the refugees of the most wrongfully discriminating theocratic system there is: ISLAM. As in submit to the doctrine of Islam or be taxed literally to death.

Liberals be like, "You're lying about Islam! They're not oppressive and violent. It's a religion of peace!"

Ok, so what are these refugees running from then? Libs want us to blindly let in refugees, many of whom are Muslim; following a doctrine that says to kill infidels or those who do not follow the doctrine to the letter. Libs don't believe any of them are fugitives from Islamic tyranny because they're suckered into believing it's a religion of peace... SMH.

But I can understand why Democrats want to let a bunch of Muslims in. Democrats who founded the KKK hate the Jews, just like Muslims do. So, Of course, Democrats are tolerant of the Muslims.

I understand, not all Muslims hate Jews. This just means they're not following their own religion. Their religion tells them to hate Jews. They're not willing to follow their own doctrine. They're trying to shape Islamic doctrine to fit their own ideals. Why would you follow a doctrine you disagree with? Part of why I'm a Christian is because I don't disagree with what Jesus said.

Some of those refugees are Christian, but you have to play a little bit of roulette as to which ones though. So I agree to let the Christians in first because the Christian faith doesn't tell us to murder people. That's fair, but not to Democrats. They just want to keep yapping about discrimination. That same old party of discrimination wants to lecture us about discrimination.

Democrats are the biggest hypocrites concerning discrimination. Look how they're all about the LGBT folks. They're among the worst discriminators. Homosexuals discriminate against the opposite sex. There are fine women out there who would love to find a husband to raise a family with, but they're discriminated against by gay men. There are even gay men who want to raise children. They want to be fathers. Women are like, *Hello!!! I am fully equipped to actually facilitate bringing forth a child for us to raise together. I'm built for child rearing.* But the gay guy who wants to be a dad looks at this basic essential qualification that a woman has and discriminates against her. Despite her qualifications, he says, *No. I want a man.* And it's the same discrimination with lesbians wanting to be mothers, but discriminate against men for spouses.

Men and women need each other to perpetuate our species. That is a natural biological law, but the darlings of the Democrat party; the LGBT, want to lecture us about discrimination, while they discriminate against the very biology of what reproduces life.

Transgender people discriminate against themselves. If you're a dude, you discriminate against your masculinity to try to be a woman, and vice versa for a woman. Left wingers are all about wrongful discrimination.

Bi-sexuals probably think of themselves as non-discriminatory and all-inclusive. Nope. Bi-sexuals are just another thing that liberals claim to hate; freakin' greedy. Bi-sexuals want both sexes. Democrats claim to hate greed, but are the most greediest and covetous thieves there are, as they're always trying to intrude on the fruit of others. They want others to give up their wealth, their space, and their security, just so liberals can feel good about themselves.

I laugh at how liberals try to quote Emma Lazarus and try to shake the statue of liberty torch at us, saying, "Give me your tired, your poor, your **huddled masses** yearning to breathe free..." Interesting. One of the liberal's main excuses for discriminating against the pre-born and denying them the right to breathe free is that the pre-born are guilty of being **huddled masses** of cells.

Another reason for liberals discriminating and exterminating the pre-born also flies in the face of that poem libs try to keep throwing in our face. "Give us your poor." Yet if a child is going to be born poor, libs don't welcome the child to the golden door.

Liberals discriminate against the impoverished pre-natal kids and have them destroyed. The liberal argument to keep abortion legal is that they think *it's right and compassionate* to keep children from being born poor! So they have the child killed! They claim to be **for the poor** but will impose the death sentence on a child who would be born poor. That's evil discrimination! Liberals claim that a child born poor is likely to be a criminal, so they deprive the child of life without due process of law and ignore the principle of being innocent until proven guilty. They give the kid death based on prejudice and profiling. They're evil discriminating hypocrites. Liberals execute babies before they cross the border of the birth canal, but call us evil for proposing a wall on the border to help prevent illegal entry.

It irritates me how liberals try to compare refugees and illegal immigrants to slaves in America. Liberals use blacks to push this thought, and too many blacks are happy to oblige so they can satisfy their need to lay a guilt trip on white people. For anybody butt-hurtin' about slaves being brought here against their will, nobody is keeping you here against your will today. Black folks have been free to go to that land they claim to have been stolen from for about a good 150 years now. What's stopping you? Nobody is forcing you to stay here. In fact, there's even occasional jackasses that encourage us to leave. They be like, "Why don't you go back to Africa?" Many blacks get mad, instead of being like, "Yeah, good idea. I've never been there, but yeah, I am free to leave here for Africa." Many blacks are mad because black folks got snatched away from Africa, but when someone says, "Well go back." Those same blacks get offended.

What's worse, too many black folks are loyal to the party that would wave pickets signs saying,

"Go back to Africa."

"We don't want you in our schools."

"We don't want you in our jobs "

"we don't want you in our women,"

"We don't want you in our country."

It is very true that black slaves did not volunteer to immigrate to America. They were snatched up against their will by other black Africans and by Muslims and sold to Europeans. They were brought here involuntarily, very true, but black folks have **voluntarily** stayed here. For all the complaining that afro-centrics do; cursing this country and paying all these accolades to the mother-land, they do not leave the country they curse for the mother-land they say they were ripped from, even though they have the freedom to. Why is that? What's stopping them? If you're among these, go to Africa and live like the kings and queens you think Africans live like instead of staying in America where you believe you're being treated so poorly.

So, for liberals yammering about some nonsense about blacks being brought to America against their will, blacks aren't making some huge exodus to Africa. That's because deep down everybody knows that despite how rotten racist Apartheid America was, being a second class citizen in America was still better than how blacks are treated by other Africans in Africa.

People are getting treated like crap south of our border where they have a collectivist system. Pretty much everywhere in the world where they have the collectivist model - they feel oppressed and want to come here, and then accuse us of being discriminating oppressors because we don't have the same oppressive system they ran from. How's that for irony? They don't understand that entitlement minded people such as themselves can never be satisfied. The state will take more and more from others to satisfy the phantom that demands more education, more healthcare, more rent control, more food vouchers more, more, more.

It's a phantom because the state takes more and gives back less, and the people can't figure out why they feel so oppressed and then want to come to America to curse us for not wanting them to illegally enter our country to accuse us of what they ran from in the first place.

They accuse us of denying them of what they think they have a right to. So they see us as evil. They don't understand that the reason why they feel oppressed in their country is because they felt the pain of being robbed by what others felt entitled to. A state that assumes to facilitate entitlements will be oppressive. This is a parasitic system that will suck the life and liberty out of people. They don't understand that here, you are entitled to the freedom to pursue these things, not entitled to be issued these things. There will always be those that feel entitled to more, and that leads to oppression and murder.

Liberals argue that people feel oppressed in our capitalist model. (We don't really have a capitalist model here. We were supposed to but we don't.) Regardless of that, and despite how people may claim to feel oppressed here in our even semi-capitalist model, they're not risking their lives to leave.

The liberal internet overlords definitely didn't like my observations in my audiobook, Weapon of A.S.S. Destruction. (American Socialist States) and have gotten in the way of it being seen by their stock that they want to keep control of because my observations were making sense to some of the people they wanted to keep control of. I reckon they'll do the same with this book.

But again, I ask the question I've asked a long time ago. If America is greedy, racist, and unfair, why would people want to come to evil America?

CHAPTER X
"I'M THE GREATEST"

Make America Great Again! #MAGA is boldly posted by Trumpers all over social media. I can dig it. But in order to make America great again, you have to define the time when America was great. Pride keeps people from doing that. This means pride will get in the way of truly making America great.

Being the greatest is not the same as being great. I agree that America is the greatest nation in the world, but that doesn't make it great. Facebook may be greater than Myspace, but Facebook isn't great. Facebook is run by bigots that discriminate against ideals that don't match those who run it. They're fools that claim to hate discrimination yet that's what they do. They're hostile to those who actually detest discrimination, and are tolerant of those who do discriminate against others. Facebook may be the greatest social media platform but they're not great because they don't live up to the ideals of equality that they claim to be the champions of. America is kinda like that.

However, the foundation of America is great! It's not only great, it is the greatest foundation to build *a great and greatest nation*! What gets in the way of that is people instituting what is contrary to what America was founded for: Free acknowledgement of God, the rights He alone gives mankind, and the protection of those rights.

What's this point of greatness that people are talking about? Is it economic greatness? Is that what it all boils down to: after manufacturing, innovations, and such? Does it come down to how much revenue we have that makes us great? No wonder people think Republicans are just all about money and think we don't care about anything or anyone else. Is that the point that we're trying to get back to? Was what *made America great* when America was doing great economically? Maybe a period between the Civil War and 1913? The Gilded Age, I reckon. I dig the Gilded Age. It wasn't great just because of the economy but because it was a time when it was more close to what America was founded to be. It was a time when there wasn't so much government over-reach, and perverted laws in place to make it legal to deprive another person of their God-given rights.

Democrats lost the Civil War, and could no longer disregard personhood and make another person property. Slavery used to be lawful. It was "lawful" to disregard the supreme law of the land.

That would not be great.

When America stood up for what America was founded on, that being to acknowledge that God is the granter of rights and that we're all created equal and are inheritors of these rights, that was a moment when America was great.

When it was "legal" to treat women as second-class citizens and not allow all women suffrage, that law was antithetical to the supreme law of the land that says we're all created equal. Women should have the right to vote. If women were not given equal rights then that would again be so-called Americans not living up to the promise of America. That is not great.

Now, the God-given rights of American men and women, regardless of race are acknowledged to all be protected according to the U.S. Constitution. I understand a lot of people don't feel that way. These people want to stay in their bitterness, but the fact is it is no longer "legal" to deprive people of these rights. There was a time it was "legal" to do these things. It is no longer "legal". (It was never legal according to the Constitution, but people took liberties with interpreting the Constitution or justified ignoring it)

When all man's God-given rights were acknowledged, America had a flash of greatness! Then, some so-called Americans went right back to interfering with the promise that made America great.

Another thing that makes America great is our right to property. But the Sixteenth Amendment was imposed, which contradicts our right to property. This interferes with the promise of America. This is not great. How can America be great if it's legal for our government to steal from us? We already had a tax model in place that would fund government functions and it did not intrude on the people's right to property. But the people got greedy, and the government reflected the people's greed. That's not great.

To make America great again isn't just making money and products. You can't be a thief and be great. Thieves aren't great. There was a time when America stole people's liberty and deemed it legal. That's not great. America rectified that. That is great! Americans then allowed for a government that deprives people of property. That is not great. No matter how much money or industry America excels with, it cannot be great because theft is not great. Abolish the government's power to tax people's earning. Stop allowing greedy people to drag us into the forfeiture of more power to the state to lord over us and steal our ability to thrive because these greedy people think they're going to gain from it.

These same people call America a thief, and in a way they are right. They're the thieves in America who covet the earnings of others and vote their power away. The collectivists are bent on dragging others with them because they think the state is going to punish the wealthy and that's going to make their life better. Leftists are the thieving Americans they accuse America of being. As long as we have to be governed by "legal" thievery, America can't really be great.

America can't really be great when it's legal to kill pre-born children. It's in contradiction of the right to life, liberty the pursuit of happiness, and property. The prenatal kid has a right to live, but it's been made "legal" to ignore that right. That prenatal kid has a right to liberty, but it's been made legal to ignore that right. That kid has a right to property, but it's been made "legal" to ignore that right. (Since the poachers of the abortion industry snatch off the kid's body parts - which are the kid's property by the way - and the abortion industry sells them.)

That prenatal kid has a right to pursue happiness, but it's been made legal to ignore that right.

America cannot be made great until it is not legal to be in contradiction with the supreme law of the land.

All the bigoted blood of intolerance that America has on its hands to keep it from being greater for the past 150 plus years has been drawn by the Democrats (and deviant Republicans whom we have to thank for legalizing abortion.) Democrats can't even "coexist" with or tolerate a pre-born kid, but they want to lecture us about coexisting and tolerance. They can't even tolerate that kid for nine months after which the kids will exit naturally. I thought the left was all about natural stuff. Then these so-called "pro-choice people try to justify abortion by saying "Conservatives claim to be pro-life but don't want to take care of children after they're born." Don't even try that cop-out on us. If you're claiming to be pro-choice then you need to be pro-pay for your own choice, not pro-make somebody else pay for the choice you wanted to make. That includes the baby having to pay. Making the baby pay the death penalty for your choice is straight up evil.

So for those who ask "When has America ever been great?" I kind of agree with the question, because Democrats have been long intruding on what could make America greater. But when Republicans stepped up to stop democrat evil, that's an example of when America has been great.

Even in America's worst times it still has been the greatest nation on earth. For those who say I'm preaching to the choir. That's kinda off. Have y'all read my hate-mail? If I'm preaching to the choir where's that hate-mail from? Or even worse being shadow-banned so even haters can't see my work.

And it's not like preaching to the choir is a bad thing. The choir not doing the right thing with the right preaching is a bad thing. Liberals preach to the choir all the time, and they're constantly in our face with what they've been taught. So many others get infected by liberal loony-speak, and the collectivist choir grows. So, I hope y'all will share my efforts and support Creative Christian conservative content producers so the Kingdom Choir will grow and reduce the Borg Collectivists in our time.

Preaching to the choir is bad when you preach crap to the choir and the bad choir takes that crap to spread around the world. Or preaching to the choir is bad when you preach good stuff to the choir and the choir doesn't take that good thing and spread it around. So if you just watch my videos, for example (which I think have a pretty decent message), and you don't spread the vids around or recommend this book, then that would be an example of what's bad about preaching to the choir. You didn't do anything with it! Ha! The choir just sat there with what's good while the liberal choir grows from spreading what's bad. Don't be complacent. We got a great victory. Now we have to keep the victory from liberals who are losing their "minds" on par with a zombie apocalypse and trying to infect others.

"Freedom isn't free!" People on the right keep saying that, but a lot of those same people don't like to put their money where that saying keeps coming from. Freedom costs. And I really hope I can get more of y'all to support and contribute to the building of my production company, Bronze Serpent Media, so I can do my little part to create media to compete with the liberal narrative. Show support so the field grows stronger with more creative Christian conservatives to compete in the culture.

Bronze Serpent Media draws its name from Moses being instructed by God to make a bronze serpent and put it on a pole. Despite the sins of the Israelites who brought upon themselves snakes striking them with fiery venom, the Lord said if they look at the bronze serpent they will live. This is a picture of Christ for the exercise of faith He would come to speak much of. The bronze serpent was to be an image of a venomous serpent, (because the venom of a serpent is needed as an anti-venom.) The Lamb is injected with the venom. (Christ bearing our sins) The Lamb's blood creates the antibodies to treat envenomation. (Christ's authority to forgive sins)

Notice, the Israelites were not told to worship it, pray to it, bow down to it, burn incense to it or whatever. Just to look at it. (But eventually, they started doing the aforementioned anyway despite the commandment not to.)

And John would come to say, "Just as Moses lifted up the snake in the wilderness, so the Son of Man must be lifted up" -John 3:14. BSB

Bronze Serpent Media is a production moniker under which I produce audio/video productions. Whether it be music, movies, teleplays, comedy, action/adventure, sci-fi/fantasy, mysteries, suspense/thrillers, etc. (That's the objective, anyway.) Bronze Serpent wants to deliver such productions with style and guts to invite people to dig the Lord, instead of glorifying what is apart from Him.

Liberals get lots of funding to make media that rots. I hope y'all will be just as supportive in helping me make media that rocks! Part of making America great again is making great media again. Entertainment Media is what's been used to bring America to the mess it's in now. I hope you'll support media to help reverse that.

Thank you all so much who've been supporting all these years! I hope more will come through and realize the legion we're up against. It took eight years to land a good punch to that legion, but they're not down for the count. They're getting back up already, swinging more wildly in a way that will lead us back into an all-out war.

As Christians and Republicans, we have to reclaim what it is to be radical. Being a radical isn't about shaking things up. It's being grounded, rooted, solid, leveled, and adherent to a core when things are shaken up and breaking down. Or there's radicals whose core is chaos which renders oppression and murder. There's right radicals and wrong radicals. To be a right radical you have to have a right root to bear right fruit. Right Root Fruit. That's just fun to say.

Republicans were founded as the radicals of the U.S. Constitution against the Democrats who were the rebels against the U.S. Constitution. To make America great it's going to take being radical. When the Republican Party was founded they were considered radical because they were rooted in the charter of our God-given republic. They were crazy enough to fight for it against the selfish who were a sacrilege against our Constitution and the God-given rights of man. And it does take a little bit of cray-cray to stand up to the selfish, because selfish people tend to be quite belligerent.

It's a lot like how capitalism has been poorly defended, because Republicans poorly define it, which is why they poorly promote it - being a radical has the same problem, as well as the usage of the terms "left-wing, right-wing, and fascists". All this stuff has been obscured. To make America great, the record needs setting straight.

People are deceived by these things because Democrats run the institutions of the highest influence: The school systems, news and entertainment media, even Google. People get a lot of their info from

Google searches, and Google has perverted the already evil meaning of fascism to a slanderous definition. Google defines fascism as a *right wing* ideology, when it absolutely is not. Fascism is a collectivist ideal, and the people are rallied into bundling together to forfeit power to the state to dictate how people will be socially dependent. That has nothing to do with the right wing, absolutely nothing.

But these childish people understand fascism to mean control, and being controlled to them is not allowing them to do what they shouldn't be doing. They only consider it as imposing a morality onto them. That's what they think fascism is.

What they feel entitled to supersedes morality, and to them it is immoral and fascist to deny them their desires that they want facilitated at the forced expense of someone else's rights. Like forcing doctors to treat their STDs or provide them with birth control via government fiat.

So if you say people can't come into our country illegally, the liberal will call you a fascist. They see you as a control freak who won't let others do what they want to do even if it's wrong and illegal. But the true fascists are them because they want illegals to come in so they can bundle them together with them to give the state more power to force us to be socially dependent, and make it legal for them to do things at the forced expense of someone else's rights. That's Fascism.

Conservatives shouldn't be letting liberals get away with this but they're doing it right now. Google has deceitfully changed the definition of fascism to influence millions. These left-wingers have again falsely switched a definition and people are going to believe it. Just as the Republicans party wasn't founded to be liberal. Liberals always say Lincoln was a liberal, yet

Liberals always say "War is never the answer." For Lincoln, war was the answer. So if he was a liberal he wasn't a very good one. He was a radical, and a liberator, but not a liberal.

Today we think of radicals as people who've gone 5150. No. radical means root, grounded if you will. Stable. Do these left wing nuts out there calling themselves radical look stable to you? If they're rooted in anything it's rooted in wrongness.

The Abolitionists who came together to form the Republican Party were called radical republicans. Why? Because they were rooted in the Bible and the U.S. Constitution. The Democrats were not. The Democrats were so uprooted from the Bible and Constitution that they took the liberty to make their own Constitution of the Confederate States, so they could keep the slave market going. Who says the Bible is outdated and needs to be changed, then ironically says you can't trust the Bible because *according to them it's been changed?* Democrats.

But in America, who has adopted the switch of what it is to be radical? Democrats. They embrace the book, Rules For Radicals by Saul Alinsky. His book isn't for radicals. His book is for rebels against righteousness. He dedicated his book to the first rebel against righteousness: Lucifer. Lucifer wasn't a radical. He was a rebel for a wrong and selfish cause. The book by Saul Alinsky is deceptively called Rules for Radicals but it is really a book for unruly rebels, but it's effective marketing. There is only one truly righteous Rule-Book For Radicals: The Bible. It's the Book of Righteousness that the Republican Party is supposed to be rooted in.

Unfortunately, there are even Republicans today who reject that.

The Word of God is the Word of true liberty that tells you to not even think about infringing on another person's rights to satisfy your own selfishness. The Bible tells us, *I don't care if you think it's right. It isn't. I assure you that what you think is right is selfish, and it will infringe upon the rights of someone else.*

Or as it's written,
There is a way which seems right to a man, But its end is the way of death. -Proverbs 16:25 NASB

The Republican Party was founded, and rooted in the liberating Word of God. The law of God is that we are to be free. Jesus is the ultimate liberator and the Truth that makes men free. The Republican Party was founded on abolishing slavery, and to liberate according to God's design of freedom. That's what made them radicals.

We need more of those radicals today. We need Republicans today who want to reclaim what it is to be radical, rooted, grounded, and stable in something stronger than ourselves, and be conservative with its Word so as to preserve liberty. Not these pseudo-conservatives who say, they don't see what Christianity has to do with conservatism.

Their attitude is, they'll define conservatism by their own standard, or by the standard of another flawed human being. For instance saying, "I'm a Reagan conservative or I'm a Goldwater conservative," etc. However, at the end of the day, anybody can find a fault with Reagan or Goldwater.

That's why I'm a Christian conservative. I find no Fault with Jesus. Therefore I base my conservatism on Jesus who had no fault, I don't base my conservatism on men who do have faults, especially my own faulty self. Anyone who does just bases their conservatism on anything that could change at any time according to the imperfect ideals of men. I don't care how good you think you are.

ISIS think they're good men too. Nazi's thought they were good men too. The Democrats think they're the party of the goodest people there is. But no, you don't have to be a Christian to be a conservative. There's no law saying you do, and Jesus wouldn't want us to make it a law. It should only be a free-will choice, but if you can't even consider that there has to be a fixed foundation to build a platform on, then you aren't really a conservative. If you think that being a conservative means you can be a conservative based on what you think is good and right then you're being selfish and self-righteous. That's not conservative.

Even Andrew Breitbart, who was not a Christian, acknowledged the Judeo-Christian foundation of the Constitution, and wouldn't change it because that is the safest and most stable foundation for liberty. You don't have to be a Christian, but trying to dismiss or remove the Judeo-Christian foundation is a really bad idea. So is claiming to be a Christian but taking the Lord's name in vain to assume that it's ok to do things apart from what He'd approve of, or saying that you keep Him separate from your political views, which makes no sense - like trying to sniff the letter five.

These people be like, *I Believe God is all knowing, but He doesn't know anything about politics. Wait outside the voting booth, Jesus. You don't know how this works. I mean, I'm a Christian cause I kinda believe you created the universe and all, but I just don't think you're Word is wise enough to consider when casting my vote. Voting with you in mind just isn't progressive and stuff.*

Such things are among the reasons why there is so much fracturing on the right end of the spectrum. But for me personally, I just think it's practical to pledge my allegiance to the One who establishes the eternal Kingdom, and by His light and law helps us preserve our republic.

I see Christians, even Republicans, who keep following the applause line of "God is neither a Republican or a Democrat." (Democrats favor this more than anybody because they are the ones who want to keep God out of how people vote the most. Republicans should totally set themselves apart from this Democrat way of thinking.) Stop clapping for that stuff! It's just pastors pandering for applause to the self-righteous sentiments of their congregation who want to be made to feel like they're enlightened because they're casting judgment on both sides as failures. This feeds that holier than thou ego.

And both sides do fail, but one of those parties, the Republican Party, is actually based on the right approach that squares with the Bible and the U.S. Constitution. The problem is Republicans not having the constitution to adhere to the Bible and the Constitution, or Republicans who aren't being radical; Rooted in it - whereas the Democrat Party is inherently at odds with the Bible and the U.S. Constitution. They weren't formed to be rooted in the Bible or the Constitution in the first place.

And if a pastor is not explaining what those platforms are in the effort to have a people ready to vote to preserve our God-given republic then that pastor is doing their congregation a disservice. All that said applause line sentiment does is discourage people from voting, or weakens them voting in a manner conducive with preserving our God-given republic, and makes them useless in maintaining the freedoms that we have.

True. God is not a democrat because God doesn't make law based on our selfish majority votes. We're a republic with representatives and we are ruled by a constitution of laws.

Well, if we're Christians, Jesus is our representative, and He is the law, and if you're a Christian then you understand that you're life is under His rule, and you are under the rule of He who Is the Law. When Judge Dredd says, "I'm the law" Jesus be like, "That's cute."

The Republican Party was founded by abolitionists and its highest objective was to abolish slavery. Let's look at the very first commandment in the Ten Commandments.

And God spoke all these words: "I am the LORD your God, who brought you out of the land of Egypt, out of the house of slavery.... - *Exodus 20:1-2 NASB*

God, Himself is letting us know that He is the ultimate abolitionist! What God is saying is that it is a COMMANDMENT that man be free! The Republican Party was founded to honor the commandment that all men are to be free.

That is the rule of law we live under. It is the Law of God that we are to be free. It is the foundation of the law of this republic that we are to be free. It was on the Word of God that the Republican Party was founded to abolish slavery so all men could enjoy their God-given right to be free. That's the rule of law we live under, so legislated by our Highest representative; Jesus. That sounds pretty Republican to me.

If Christians aren't clear on which platform stands closer to the Bible and the U.S. Constitution then we will have the Godless ruling over us. There's nothing great about that.

America will never be perfect because there are no perfect people, but despite being imperfect we can still be a great nation. We've done great good, but we've also done great evil. America wasn't founded to be a great evil. We will always have people who violate good law. That's not what would keep America from being great though. What keeps America from being great is when America keeps making it legal to violate the rights of man. You can't buy your way out of that with a great economy.

Liberals disagree that America was founded to be good since they believe America is this evil group of people who stole this country from the Indians. They ignore the fact that the Indians were taking land away from each other before the white man showed up. Indians, pillaged, raped, enslaved, and made human sacrifices, but liberals want people to believe they were all these peace-pipe smoking hippies.

For all the guilt liberals try to make us feel about supposedly stealing their land, I have yet to see these liberals relinquish their property to the Indians, and "go back to wherever their ancestors migrated from." Hey! If all the liberals were to actually put their money (and I mean their own money) where their guilt trippin' mouth is and leave the country for the land of their ancestors then that would be a huge step in Making America Great!!! We can dream, right?! I mean if the Dream act can be passed where other people can come here illegally and dream then we can dream too. Just Sayin'.

CHAPTER XI
ORTHODOXER BOXER AND THE SINISTER SLUGGER

When examining the word, orthodox, we have the prefix, ortho, which means; straight, normal, upright, correct, or simply, RIGHT! And dox, from the Greek, doxa, meaning; belief, opinion, or doctrine. So, orthodox, turns out to mean, "the right belief." America was founded on an orthodoxy. It was founded on the right belief that we are all created equal and endowed by our Creator with certain inalienable rights; Life, liberty and the pursuit of happiness, (and property as per the constitution.)

This is a right belief. The sinister however, or the left believers, are enemies of the orthodoxy, or the right believers.

I'm not talking about religion. No religion is orthodox. No religion has the right doctrine. Only the Bible, the Word of God alone is the orthodox. It's not just orthodox. It's beyond a belief. It's the Truth. If God says "man cannot build a temple for God" what makes you think man can build a belief system for God? Just a note, I think people overlook that Jesus didn't tell Peter to build a church or a belief system. Jesus said, He Himself would build it.

*And I tell you, you are Peter, and on this rock **I will build my church**, and the gates of hell shall not prevail against it. - Matthew 16:18 ESV*

We don't have to accept the orthodox. That's one of the things that makes it so right. It wasn't meant to be a law that we accept it, but accept the Lord freely. The left-wing promotes a prejudice that right-wingers want to force us into a theocracy. This is slanderous, absurd and contrary to the Word of God. They don't understand that as Christians we serve Jesus; the original Freedom From Religion Foundation.

Left wing liberals, true to sinister form, are the ones who have been insidiously instituting their religious beliefs and establishing their theocracy while they distract people with their slander about the Christian right wanting to establish a state religion. It's a wicked weirdness with liberals. When Republicans try to defend people's rights the Left says we're trying to push our religion on them, and say we're trying to force a theocracy. Democrats have always been hypocrites about this, but it's always the same Godless point of view.

Democrats in the 1800's shoved their twisted version of Christianity down the people's throat to justify slavery. This, of course, was a perversion of scripture, but Democrats pushed their twisted renderings of scripture to justify slavery. It was still Godless. And it's Godless today, as the Democrats who used to push perverse renderings of scripture onto people now say, they don't want the Bible pushed on them.

When do they feel like the Bible, (or religious morals as far as they're concerned) is being pushed on them? When you tell them they can't intrude on other people's rights. If you don't let democrats infringe on another person's rights they will always cry that we're trying to push our religion on them. But when it comes to Islam, which is the basis of Sharia, the liberals are tolerant of that.

The mandate of their political correct ideals will usher it in if gone unchecked. That's why it gets on my nerves when "conservatives" say, "Who cares what these people think?"

That dismissive attitude is how the infection spreads. They scoff and say *who cares what these people think* and then have the audacity to be outraged when an illegal immigrant murders an American citizen. That's what happens when you say, "Who cares what these people think?"

What these people think turns into sanctuary cities. What these people think turns into them forcing us to live by their religious beliefs concerning the environment and evolution. The sinister slugger or the left-wing has punched their way through with media, and the education system, and are wearing down people's faith in God, and beating their ideals of their so-called science into the people's heads, while you say, "Who cares what these people think?" These people you scoff at are teaching your kids what to imagine, and you're paying them to do it! Notice I said "What to imagine", not what to think. People's imaginations are being tapped into, not their reasoning.

Conservatives say, "Liberals need to get educated." Liberals are getting plenty educated! Unfortunately, they're getting degrees in delusions. These delusions have them imagining things like, "Separation of Church and state." Are you getting it on how their imagination is being stimulated, not their reasoning? The only way you can look at the constitution and say "Separation of Church and State" is if you imagine it's there.

They're imagining things like the glaciers melting and covering the earth with water while telling Christians that the Biblical flood is an imagined story. The whole Bible is imagined to them, But according to their religion, we are going to drown in a global flood as a judgment for our infidelity to their religion of environmentalism.

It's been proven that their data is cooked to make it look like we have a global warming crisis looming to fuel their imagination.

TV, music, movies, and the education system. They are constantly feeding and feeding on lies and are calling it being informed. As Reagan said, "It's not that liberals are ignorant, it's just that they know so much that isn't so." These liberals to which conservatives keep dismissively saying, "Who cares what these people think" have people imagining that a kid in the womb isn't a human being. You can't apply reason and come to that conclusion. They don't want embryonic stem cells from another species, but from aborted babies. Why? Because they're human. Why are they poaching kids in the womb to sell their body parts? Why can't they just reserve that for another species? Because they need the human tissue. Speaking of experimenting on another species, liberals act like their "science" is all benevolent and superior, yet it's scientists that do experiments on animals that liberals are so horrified by.

When it comes to poaching kids in the womb or using their stem cells, all of a sudden the liberal conveniently recognizes their DNA as human. With it being evident that the being is human, that means they have to imagine that the kid is not human. This, of course, puts them in contradiction with themselves. Is the kid human or not? This is when selfishness wins over. Selfishness tends to cancel out reason, and thus imagination takes over and solidifies their denial.

I know I keep saying it, and y'all are probably sick of me saying it. But I'm sick of conservatives not doing much about it. I'm sick of seeing liberals push their propaganda through entertainment, and conservatives not supporting the same measure. They've got plenty when it comes to politicians though. Liberals get support to promote their republic-rotting propaganda while conservatives in media have to beg, beg, beg to get a morsel of support to produce competitive media to preserve our republic. I'm so thankful to the supporters I've had. It breaks my heart that because they're so rare their support doesn't get me that far, and the conservatives who do have the bank who could add to their efforts would rather just put their money behind another politician. It's like a politician makes their contribution valid and official or something.

There's nothing valid and official about supporting entertainment to promote American preserving values to them. I go on and on about this because over and over again liberals are using imagination to wreck the republic. Conservatives say, "Fight fire with fire!" Liberals are pushing their imagination imaginatively, and it freakin' works! Their worldview is total BS, but they successfully get into people's head with it because they have imaginative delivery systems!

If only conservatives would support imaginative delivery of the truth! If liberals can get as far as they have with their imaginative delivery of BS, then just REASON how far conservatives could get with imaginatively delivering the truth.

Is what I'm proposing not reasonable? Is it not logical? Is it not Practical? With all the common sense that conservatives are supposed to be trained up with as the Orthodoxer boxer, how is it that the Sinister slugger is landing so many punches?

We've seen that sweeping Republican victories are followed by great disappointment. Reagan presided over the years that conservatives wish we could go back to. Had conservatives stayed on top of the game and were supplying and demanding productions to counter what liberals were pressing you wouldn't have to be wishing to go back there, we'd still be enjoying those things that you miss today.

Conservatives say, "Be ever vigilant", right? Why aren't they ever vigilant with supporting counter illustrations in media? This is what the left is doing to screw people's minds up. Why aren't we more supportive with using the same measure to unscrew up people's minds"

You can't reason that tax increases are better for the economy. You have to imagine that. You have to imagine that tax increases are sustaining when in reality they are not. Tax increases lead to increases in the cost of living and we're back to square one with people demanding more.

You can't reason that increasing minimum wage is better for the economy. You have to imagine that. You can't reason that you are pro-small business while demanding minimum wage increases that small mom and pop businesses can't afford. You have to imagine that you're the good hearted pro-mom and pop small business liberal.

As a conservative, do you see the liberal worldview as reasonable? No! They're in imagination land! Reason doesn't register with them. They're taken by their imagination. You're going to have to use or support the use of the vehicle of imagination and creativity to deliver reason to them. This is not free! It takes money, time, and stamina! Liberals are relentless. Conservatives are quick to throw up their hands and say, *Who cares what these people thin? I'm out.*

You can't reason that a man can be a woman, and a woman can be a man, and that there are multiple genders, or that there are neutral genders, etc. This is not reason! This is straight up imagination! These people are making their imaginations policy for us to have to abide by. And often the conservative answer is, *Who cares what these people think? Why are you even wasting time on this?* So common sense to a conservative means ignoring an infection and just letting it get worse? Ok. And it has gotten worse, hasn't it? Or is it just our imagination? Many conservatives are obviously upset about what's happening to the country but want us to ignore the people who are influencing it. Just imagine they aren't there, I guess. However, I totally agree that we should ignore their ideals, but we shouldn't ignore the fact that a lot of people don't ignore them. They have fans who enjoy their productions. It's not a good idea to ignore that reality.

Support the creation of media that distracts people from the liberal influence. You can't just tell a lot of people that they can't have something because it's bad for them. You'd better have a decent alternative to help take their mind off of the bad stuff they enjoy.

To be a liberal you have to imagine that the world is warming up enough to melt the ice caps when the winters have been freakin' cold.

So to my conservatives, I have to ask, is it reasonable keep saying, "Who cares what these people think" while getting more frustrated by what their influence is doing? Are you just imagining that they're just going to disappear and stop just because you close your eyes? Isn't that burying your head in the sand? I thought conservatives hated that?

But I hear Republicans say it all the time. "Just ignore them," which means bury your head in the sand with your butt up in the air waiting to get screwed by liberalism.

Republicans claim to be against cutting and running, but people are cutting and running out on the party. They want to preserve the republic but are having a hard enough time preserving the Republican party. Like I said, People on the right keep saying, "Leave Commiefornia!" Isn't that cutting and running? Are we so fragile that that weenie liberals are making conservatives flee the state like a refugee? Right-wingers wave their Molon Labe flags while telling us to leave California for libs to take.

It's not like California has become a caliphate. I'm still free to express my concerns without getting butchered by a regime. However, It will be that way in the states if we keep cutting and running.

People on the right want folks to leave California, and just leave such a big territory of the messaging industry to the Godless. Los Angeles means the angels, folks. Angel means messenger. Los Angeles is the city of messengers. It is a city that is at least true to its name as it is a city where so much messaging is generated, and you want us to leave California and let that messaging go unchecked? Is that practical? Is that reasoned? You can only imagine that the problem will just go away, conservatives.

The city of angels is filled with evil messaging delivered through imaginative media, and there's hardly any support for good messaging through entertainment media.

Jude 1:7-8
...7 In like manner, Sodom and Gomorrah and the cities around them, who indulged in sexual immorality and pursued strange flesh, are on display as an example of those who sustain the punishment of eternal fire. 8 In the same way, these people--who claim authority from their dreams--live immoral lives, defy authority, and scoff at supernatural beings.

Angels and Angelinos have abandoned truth. One of those Truth abandoning Angels is Satan, and his name means the Accuser. The slanderer. And what do these libs use the industry of messaging to do? Slander, and promote make-believe. You can use make-believe as a vehicle to promote truth. You can creatively tell truth. But liberals use make-believe to promote make-believe. It results in things like being forced to endorse a person's delusions of gender-bending, to things like having our second amendment rights stigmatized by pompous celebrities who love making movies with guns. If these libs can make movies featuring gun slinging liberals, how come the NRA doesn't have a creative writing team to compete with a counter-narrative with movie or teleplay formats? Liberals can make movies where the good guy uses guns to take out bad guys, and then turn around and say guns are evil. But the NRA can't put their resources behind the production of movies or teleplays where the good guy with a gun takes out bad guys and at the end of the day people are at least left with the impression that guns are useful? Just sayin'.

Fundamentalist Christians take Jude to mean fallen angels came down to earth and had a bunch of freaky sex. Even though Jude says the people were doing that. The only thing the people and the angels have in common is where they are going. They both committed a great sin to God, but they didn't commit the same sin.

In like manner, Sodom and Gomorrah and the cities around them, who indulged in sexual immorality and pursued strange flesh, are on display as an example of those who sustain the punishment of eternal fire. Jude 1:7

Los Angeles is a city that hosts and boasts a culture of sexual indulgence and immorality, like the people of Sodom and Gomorrah. Bear in mind that Los Angeles is the city of Messaging. The sin of the angels in Jude was that they left their first estate. The fundamentalist insists that they came to have sex with women and that's why they fell. This isn't possible because Satan and the angels fell before Adam was created. Which means woman definitely wasn't created yet for them to fall from heaven over. And in Sodom and Gomorrah, the great sin that they were committing was that they sexually engaged with "Strange flesh" Meaning flesh they could not naturally procreate with or with whom wasn't their naturally qualifying spouse. Meaning men and women weren't married before God in accordance with His design for marriage and they were having sex with the same sex, relatives, children, beasts, and even the dead. That, however, wasn't the sin of the angels that fundamentalists are charging these angels with. They believe the angels fell because of women (even though angels fell before the creation of human women.) But they're also trying to use Jude to make the claim that angels fell because of women, yet Jude is making it clear that the people of Sodom and Gomorrah weren't destroyed because of men having sex with women, but because men were having sex with men and whatever else. So again, this issue of angels being in a fallen state due to having sex with women, doesn't hold up.

The sin of the angels in Jude was that they deviated from their position of truth. Truth was their position, their station, their dwelling. It was supposed to be in truth. They deviated from that. They rejected truth. They were seduced by the prideful selfish message of the angel, Lucifer. The angels that fell with Lucifer, now Satan, fell and are ultimately doomed to eternal hellfire because they abandoned their station of truth. They were in pure truth, and chose to reject it. If they reject truth they cannot speak truth, and the angels very job was to recognize truth and speak truth, report truth, message truth, dispatch judgment from truth. The station of Lucifer as the highest cherub was truth. His pride interfered with him acknowledging truth, and the lie that was born within Him was that He deserved to ascend above God. He abandoned His estate to try to take God's throne.

Los Angeles, the city of messengers is filled with messengers that reject truth, and broadcast messages of untruth. And it's poisoning our republic more and more, and you want us to cut and run and let that go unchallenged?

I see people lamenting over FOX News, and how liberal it's becoming and whatnot, and I'm like, *is FOX news the only thing we've got? That's a shame!*

Liberals push their ideals through entertainment, and many conservatives still watch what liberals produce. Why? Because it's entertaining! Conservatives give just as much money to liberals to keep doing what they do as liberals do. Why? Because people want to be entertained!

So we know that liberals and conservatives are listening to left-wing propaganda because they are both attracted to the entertainment factor. But both liberals and conservatives don't listen to right-wing propaganda, because it's just talking heads, and that doesn't go that far to entertain.

If you're a conservative you'll enjoy just hearing conservative talk, sure. You don't need it to entertain you because it already makes sense. But would you listen to liberal ideology if it didn't entertain you? Heck no! But you'll pay money and put up with it long enough to be entertained by liberals though, despite the propaganda they push. And sometimes we even lose conservatives to these libs. They're often the ones that still want call themselves Republicans but are "fiscally conservative but socially liberal."

So if conservatives will watch liberal entertainment because they can't resist the need to be entertained, why the shark-snot are we not supporting the production of imaginative entertainment to capture liberals attention long enough to deliver a dose of reason?!

Christian film content camps like Pureflix are doing a great job of cranking out productions! But the problem is they insist on being apolitical. This makes for wishy-washy messaging. When you try to avoid politics your church audience will stay in their church bubble and let their God-given freedoms get voted away as the laws that appease secularism are instituted to rule over us.

It's not reasonable that a person should have to turn away from the law of God and be made to serve the demands of the Godless. The church, trying to be apolitical, is why a business can be sued and shut down if they won't forfeit their faith and accommodate people demanding services validating their same-sex lifestyle. That's not reasonable. That's the church imagining that God would be ok with this and it doesn't matter because *He's on the throne.*

I've never seen touched by an angel before, and recently I watched one episode, and I was appalled. It was full-on wishy-washy - love you straight to hell kinda stuff!

It was the kinda stuff that liberals wanted to hear but not what they needed to hear. On the flip side of this is conservatives doing entertainment without God, which ultimately just ends up being the same stuff a liberal would produce.

American Conservatives are definitely more friendly to the Bible than liberals are but conservatives and the church really alienate each other when it comes to working together to promote the gospel. It's ultimately the gospel that preserves our republic. If conservatives really want to preserve the republic then they have to be more dialed into the gospel. Conservatives show that they have more affinity for the country than the Kingdom. It hasn't registered with a lot of them that the best thing for the country is the Kingdom. Christianity without conservatism is wishy-washy, and just a form of feel goodism and it leaves people making up an idol they call Jesus who accepts them for whatever they are and do.

We've got Christian based entertainment getting out there, but not so much conservative produced entertainment getting out there, and there really needs to be the union of the two.

I know this sounds silly, and juvenile and has probably even gotten a few eye rolls if you've managed to read this far, But these people who you say need to get educated are getting an education, and the education a lot of folks are paying for has them believing that

Castro was good, Che Guevara was good, Chavez was good, Palestine is good, etc. You cannot reason that these people are good, you can only imagine they are.

I see conservatives often telling liberals that they need to get educated.

But educated in what? Are they supposed to learn what you think they should have learned? How are they supposed to do that? They're not going to really get taught that in college and the culture because conservatives haven't supported a counter-narrative to creatively intercept their attention when the liberal influence comes for them.

You can't reason that state provided health care is the better model for the people. You can only imagine that. How does one reason that Obama-care is fabulous and think it's evil to repeal it? How does one reason that the Affordable Care Act is Affordable? People were needing financial assistance for it. If other people are being forced to pay for the financial assistance of it then the ACA is just imaginarily affordable. You can't reason that the Affordable care act isn't fascism. If the government is going to fine you $100.00 for not registering for the ACA - and on top of that, the fact that you were too poor to afford this federal HMO anyway, then you would have to imagine that it isn't fascism! Reasonable people know it's fascism!

I hope I've made the point that reason is being replaced by imagination. The irony is a lot of these people invoke Thomas Paine as one of their hallmarks of them being reasoned. Yet the people are not reasoned at all. They scoff at people of faith who believe in the most scrutinized Word in History, but cannot prove it wrong. Meanwhile their so-called reasoning and science always has to be updated. This means they're constantly imagining that their ideals work. That's not reason.

This is what we're up against. We're up against people's imagination, not reason. Conservatives think they can reason with these people. You can, but not in the limited manner in which conservatives do it. Imagination is typically shaped by emotion. What liberals think is right is just imagined, but their idea of what's right is not really reasonable. It's ok that imagination is shaped by emotion governed by God. The problem is that there are people who are really emotionally unstable, and they shape their imaginations with that. Their ideals are based on their imaginations woven with unstable emotions. These ideals become instituted as policy, and the result is a more unstable society. That's why we keep hearing this term "Snowflake" because these people are melting down and dragging society into their meltdown.

Y'all, ever since America was founded there have been people here who have not understood what America was founded for. There have been people here who took "the Land of Liberty" to mean the liberty to intrude on another's liberty.

They put themselves in a class that is entitled to do so. These are the culprits of class warfare. It's still that way today. I marvel at how we're having such a hard time selling freedom, while people are buying oppression like it's the next iPhone. Yet these people see America as oppressive while they vote for what's oppressive and imagine that what they're voting for is liberating.

This has been the back and forth battle in America since it's founding. To this day, somehow a form of oppression is legalized. And it's usually done by playing to people's imaginations, not their reason. People can become very effective with it. They can make their ideals look quite reasonable. The devil himself masquerades as an angel of light,

And no wonder, for Satan himself masquerades as an angel of light. It is not surprising, then, if his servants masquerade as servants of righteousness. Their end will correspond to their actions.... 2 Corinthians 11:14-15 BSB

The Devil makes a lie look like truth. He makes what's unreasonable look reasonable.

The Devil was able to convince Adam and Eve that God, the Truth Himself, lied to them. Let that sink in.

People have that talent today. They tell people that America, the land of the free, is a lie. It's the land of slavery, and get people to vote to give up their freedom in the land of the free! That happens with people who are unreasoned. They are duped by imagination. Isn't it weird how people go on and on about how much they demand freedom, while they invest in oppression?

Oppression sells itself like street drugs, while freedom is harder to sell than a dental appointment. As mentioned before, drugs are oppression disguised as freedom.

Oppression comes disguised as freedom. It's like freedom in drag. And this promiscuous drag-queen attracts people, because it promises to put out. Straight men, drunk with the idea of getting what they want, gravitate to it without caring about the consequences. Gay men gravitate to it for obvious reasons, women gravitate to it because supposedly it's "liberating" hip, cool, open minded, and empowering to be sexually adventurous with different partners regardless of gender.

(While despising men for their bed bouncing, yet seeking to feel empowered by behaving like what they despise.)

But yes, oppression is a seductive drag-queen. While freedom is that pretty girl or the handsome guy next door. Freedom has all the right qualities, but there's a catch. Freedom wants commitment. And we know how too many Americans feel about the C-word. Oppression is the drag queen that makes you believe there's no commitment. It lures you in making you think you're gonna get something for free, and when you get in the sheets, well... Aren't you in for a surprise? Though you didn't want commitment, you may find that you ended up stuck with something anyway.

Then you're going to demand that someone else pay for the choice you made. And now oppression is using you to oppress others; using you as a carrier to spread the disease - all because of the desire for instant gratification.

Freedom, on the other hand, doesn't do instant gratification. You have to work at it. And when you work at it, it doesn't force an expense on to anyone else.

But too many Americans are sold on the idea that somebody else should work at it so they can enjoy a roll in the hay with freedom. In someone else's barn to boot. When they feel they're being denied that, they only see freedom as oppression.

In their imagination, freedom would not deny them the liberty to intrude on another person's freedom, so they are convinced that the drag-queen, called oppression, is freedom and embrace oppression.

That's how we ended up with a president like Obama for two terms and why people are still throwing a tantrum that Hillary or Bernie isn't president. Woe to those who don't know good from evil, light from dark, bitter from sweet. Man from Tran.

"Woe to those who call evil good and good evil, who put darkness for light and light for darkness, who put bitter for sweet and sweet for bitter." -Isaiah 5:20 NIV

People demand freedom but embrace oppression because too many people think that freedom is something they should enjoy at the forced expense of someone else. That's the sweet seduction of it. Because these deceived people fail to consider that they're going to be deprived too, but they're too greedily preoccupied with the prospect of what they think they're going to gain to even consider what they're going to lose.

Y'all, do you really think it's about the economy? A lot of these people vote for these Democrats because they want the satisfaction of seeing the business owner get sodomized by the drag-queen, called oppression. Then they get mad and cry out, "Corporate welfare!" when the business owners have to try to survive, so they end up getting in bed with the drag-queen state anyway.

They demanded that the businesses get screwed, and then when the businesses get into bed with the screwer they're still mad, and still demanding freedom while they're the ones who give the finger to freedom because they don't recognize freedom. They're blinded because they want to be a part of the collectivist orgy hosted by the drag-queen called oppression, masquerading as freedom. And those seduced by the drag-queen are suckered by the drag-queen 's slander. Because when the few of us who actually get how freedom works, and see's the drag queen of oppression for what it really is and we try to warn the people, saying, "Hey! That's not who you think that is" The-drag queen of oppression accuses us of being intolerant, closed-minded, homophobic, racist, and sexists, etc. And those seduced by the drag-queen of oppression curse us for it.

Too many people are sour-grapers, and give in to the influence to be sour-grapers to fit in. Complaining is a cheap, and easy way to fit in, and often done out of safety. They're made to feel like the American dream is just a dream. They're sold on this crap by people who get rich off of proclaiming the American dream is just a dream. Or they're seduced by democrat politicians who tell them that they will make their dreams come true by intruding upon the dreams of others who are living the dream. Democrats call that fairness.

Why are democrats able to get away with this? Because oppression has amassed legions of people who have been conditioned since kindergarten, through their grade school years, through college, via music, tv, movies, fashion, video-games, sports, etc. Its influence is constantly promoted.

But strangely enough, freedom doesn't seem to have that same culture behind it. There isn't much of a culture that demands the supply of promotional content for actual freedom. The real kind of freedom that has the balance that says, "Your ideas of rights and freedoms can't intrude upon another's rights and freedoms according to this fixed and certain set of God-given rights, and not by some moveable standards of what man thinks is right.

Sure, we show our support for freedom in how much we support the troops, and God bless 'em. But why are we so limited to support the promotion of freedom in the form of a person getting their limbs blown off or killed? Is that the only way we can show our support for freedom? Our military men and women deserve way better than risking their limbs and their lives and the cohesion of their families, fighting oppression overseas while we're letting oppression grow in our own home country. What an insult to them.

We don't do much at home to promote freedom, but instead, let oppression become more and more fashionable. We've got plenty talk-radio and citizen Journalists, bloggers and Vloggers, criticizing enemies of liberty, and we need them! But that's pretty much all we do. We pour out reason to people given over to imagination. We're critiquing and questioning the mentality of people with our reason when that isn't their language!

As a conservative, I agree that if you're going to come to America you should learn to speak the language. But you have to be able to convey that information to a person who doesn't speak English! You can't tell somebody who doesn't speak English that they need to learn how to speak English. They're going to have to hear that in a language they understand. If not, they're going to expect you to learn their language. And if you don't illustrate what oppression looks like then you will have people coming from other oppressive countries expecting us to accommodate them with their language and them assuming that we owe it to them to have to accommodate them with their language. That's why we have to press different buttons for different languages.

Reason is a foreign language to liberals. Ya dig? Conservatives talk, talk, talk, and criticize and complain about these liberals, thinking that liberals are going to understand reason! Liberals understand imagination, not reason. We've got talk-radio and talk-shows on FOX; talking reason more or less, which is great for people who understand the language of reason, but it's going to take some serious doing to translate that reason into a language liberals understand. It's going to take "doing" to create vehicles to deliver reason to them that they can register.

Sometimes your computer programs can't read certain files. What do ya have to do? You have to convert the file. Well, conservatives don't convert the file!!! They just keep trying to run the file shaking their fist at the computer and pounding the keyboard like the computer should just understand it. Convert the freakin' file! That doesn't mean change the contents of the file. It just means change the file type so the original content can be understood.

This is going to take doing, not just talking. We need some talk, it's helpful, but it shouldn't be this difficult. We need more than talk-radio, We need some doing. That "doing" is being more illustrative, to convert reason into language liberals or people who haven't really considered these things can understand. Notice it's called talk-radio and talk-shows not do-radio and do-shows? Talk, talk, talk. How about some walk, walk, walk! Enough with talking the talk and let's get to walking the walk. Make reason understandable. Make it illustrative. Employ imaginative vehicles to deliver reason.

It sucks to hear vets say "I went to war just so this crap could happen in my country?" Why is this happening? Because there is little demand for the supply of the promotion of freedom. The best we offer is putting our hopes in politicians we can't even agree on, holding our noses while we vote. Y'all if you keep your eyes limited on a politician, you can't expect freedom to be promoted.

But if you start showing the demand for it on the cultural level, the market for it will grow and it will start to pay for itself. I'm trying to get that started. We've already got talk-radio, we've already got news channels. Talk and news, Talk and news, Talk and news. That is missing huge demographics of people to relate the message to.

It's an ongoing effort, guys. Freedom has to be maintained. A republic, if we can keep it, remember? There's always going to be people trying to screw it up. We just have to keep DOING our part to keep them from screwing it up completely. Not just TALKING our part.

Freedom is a natural beauty. But freedom wants commitment. Are you committed? Can you go the distance as an Orthodoxer Boxer against the Sinister Slugger? Mohamed Ali talked a lot too. He talked a whole lot! But he still walked into that ring to show what he was talking about looked like! He talked about being the greatest and then he showed what that looked like!

You can't just talk about America being great, you have to show what it looks like in a manner that those who have an unreasoned idea of America can understand. If you don't support that then you will have more people trying to undo what makes America the great place it was meant to be.

As I've said before, conservatives tend to not be creative but are more practical, but it would be great if conservatives could see the practicality in being more supportive of conservatives who are creative to create illustrations to counter-punch against the sinister slugs of the liberal narrative. It's like there's no corner crew. It's like they'd rather put their support behind a politician who takes a dive every time the bell rings.

Am I lying? How frustrated have Republicans been for so long that their representatives let Democrats get away with as much as they have, and feeling sold-out? You keep saying you're sick of it and that we need to drain the swamp. Am I just imagining your frustration?

Am I on target or not when I use the analogy that it's just like betting on our GOP representatives to go in there and take the fight to the Democrats and then they take a dive against our bet?

They say it's compromise. It's compromise alright. It's compromising the stability of our republic. The people have been suckered on the idea that we need to compromise. That's not reason! That's imagination! They give rotten analogies like, "When the pilot is flying the plane you cooperate with the pilot." I tend to agree with that, BUT NOT IF THE PILOT'S PLAN IS TO CRASH THE PLANE! I don't want Republicans to cooperate with Democrats. Because cooperating with Democrats means to cooperate with people who want to destroy our republic. How is that Practical?

Democrats have a fantasy that this is a democracy, they have to destroy the republic to make that a reality. The problem is, if they succeed in making it a reality then they will be awakened to the shocking truth of what real oppression is. Not just because a democracy will result in oppression, but because it will be a reality! Truth and Reality itself is oppressive to liberals!

That's why most of them want to stay high all the time, and stay in their imagination all the time, because reality itself is oppressive to them. That's why they won't move to another country where their socialist ideals are in play! Am I wrong? How long have we been hearing these liberal Hollywood celebrities threaten to leave America? They could totally move anywhere else in the world where they're wonderful socialistic, communistic and collectivist ideals rule. But they won't do that because it would become a reality. Reality is oppressive to them, that's why they don't leave. These people are allergic to reality. They dang near sneeze out a new butt-hole they're so allergic to it. So they stay here imagining how oppressive America is while they make millions of dollars here. Are they reasoned? No.

Remember what I said about George Carlin? Are you getting what we're up against?

Does compromising with democrats sound practical to you? Boxers don't go into the ring to compromise with each other. They go in to compete with each other. For all the talk the GOP does about being pro-competition they do more cuddling up to Democrats than competing, and Republicans tend to be more competitive with other Republicans than with Democrats.

Boxers go into the ring to knock each other's heads off but even these ruffians tend to abide by the rule of the sport. That is their compromise; to box under the rule of law in accordance with the constitution of their sport.

Democrats, on the other hand, aren't just fighting Republicans, they're fighting the constitution itself. Why would we compromise with people who are fighting the constitution? Are you trying to help them fight the constitution? Stop compromising with them, because when you compromise with Democrats you're helping them fight the constitution. They are enemies of the constitution, and worse, enemies of the Bible.

We're talking about a party that hates the constitution so much that they made their own; the Constitution of the Confederate states. Compromising with Democrats is not a good idea!

To this day, Democrats believe the Constitution needs to be re-written. Just like they did in the 1800's and made their own confederate version. To this day democrats are trying to transform America. The Tranny-crats, remember? Trans is a big thing with them, and our Republican representatives want to compromise and make deals with Democrats? Dealing with Democrats means dealing out the republic.

Liberals want to live by what John Lennon imagined. John Lennon couldn't even live by what John Lennon imagined! What John Lennon imagined ultimately leads to tyranny. What John Lennon imagined would take a lot of taxes to fund a government strong enough to force everybody into this utopia John Lennon sang about. And we know how much The Beatles disliked the Tax Man. Quite a contradiction. But the magic word was "imagine".

CHAPTER XII
THE GLOVES ARE OFF

Actually, with Dirty Dukin' Democrats, the gloves have always been off. I do not want to be like these people. I don't like it when some of my more militant Republican compatriots want to stoop to the Democrat's mud humping level. They say we need to get as nasty as Democrats are do. That defeats the whole purpose of having our principles that are distinguished from their lack of principles. Being a low roader like Democrats is not a good route to go.

Do not give dogs what is holy; do not throw your pearls before swine. If you do, they may trample them under their feet, and then turn and tear you to pieces. -Matthew 7:6 BSB

Don't be seduced by the angry temptation to take the low road and become like Democrats. We already have a problem with people not being able to tell the difference between Republicans and Democrats. The high ground is a better place to fight from anyway.

Conservatives criticize Democrats for going off emotion. If you feel like you have to get low like them to fight them I assure you that your emotions have gotten the better of you too.

I'm not interested in going on the offense either. Not because I disagree with going on offense as a tactical principle, but because people who generally attack do so because they are motivated by sinning against another. Sinners attack other people. That's my reservation about being on offense. Sinners bring war. They bring the sin of wanting to steal. This offense leads to war. Sinners bring slander. This offense leads to war. They bring the sin if murder. This offense leads to war. Technically, we can't go on offense with people who have already brought a war against us. The Democrats have already brought the offense. The Republican party can never really go on the offense because the Republican party was founded as a counter-offensive to the Democrats who had already been intruding upon the rights of man and demanded the so-called right to be the offender against the God-given rights of man. The Republican party was founded to defend the God-given rights of man.

I don't want to attack anybody. I want to mind my own business. I want people to mind their own business. I don't want people trying to make their business my business. If you try to make your business my business and whine to me about how I'm trying to make my business your business because I won't let you make your business my business then it's on, because you are unreasonable.

I wasn't looking for a fight. I just want to pursue my happiness, and enjoy my fruits as my sowing yields them. I don't want to offend or be on the offensive, but I don't want to be ruled by the bad laws of other people's selfish delusions. This means an offense has raised up against me and others like me who have concluded that the law of God is the ultimate authority. Disregarding this warrants a counter-offensive.

I'm not at all trying to boast as a talented fighter. I don't think I am. But I studied the art of self-defense, not the art of offense. I'm not looking for a fight. However, in the manner in which I was trained, the assailant was meant to be left very, very sorry they attacked. Throws, take-downs, and seizures, that dislocate extremities, Hyper-extend joints or break bones before they hit the ground with enough force to knock the wind out of them.

Again, I'm not saying that I'm a master of these techniques or wired to be talented with such techniques. I'm just saying I've studied it. I'm thankful that it increases my chances of defending myself and decreasing the odds of me being hurt if attacked. What's the point of me saying this? Regardless of how well I may be armed, I don't want to go on the offensive with Democrats. Democrats have always been on the offensive anyway, and always think that they're being attacked when you tell them that they can't do what they're doing because what their doing is an intrusion on someone's else's rights.

By Democrats attacking first, they keep us on the defensive. And part of the reason why we stay on the defensive is because when we counter we don't make them very, very sorry they attacked us. There are people out there who bruise up liberals pretty good, but it's from one angle; some kind of talk forum. Democrats are kinda numb to that.

I was trained that when your opponent hits the ground, it's not over. You make sure they're not able to use an extremity. They are going to need a cast for something. You destroy their chance to continue to fight you. Destroy their physical ability and their will to continue. Discern which hand they would try to pull a knife on you with, and render that artery useless. Take their ability to try to come after you later by striping them the uses of their leg. Stomp and fracture bone.

When I taught self-defense, I made it a point to impress this upon my female students. Be mindful to not put yourself in a more heightened situation to be attacked. If a person crosses that line anyway, respond in a way so they cannot chase after you. Keep one of their eyes as a souvenir for their sin of looking on you with a covetousness that possessed them to do evil against you. These were just my teenagers! Ha!

Don't get me wrong, y'all. I also taught my students to gauge their opponent and situation. Does this warrant a police type response or military response? A woman by herself might want to use a more military response to make sure her assailant can't pursue her. A woman attacked where there's people close by would resort to a more police application to resolve the issue.

Sometimes with an opponent, all it takes is letting them fumble themselves to the ground; causing their pride to get hurt is enough to resolve a conflict. That's the most preferred. But then sometimes bruised pride turns into a broken bottle that they'll want to gash you with. The point is. Different tactics need to be employed - different angles. It takes more than just a talk forum. It takes different delivery mediums to follow through with the opponent to lessen their ability to attack. There will always be someone wanting to attack us. Sometimes you have to make an example of the bully to deter others from trying to get some. Another may try, but the likelihood is lessened. You can give a liberal a bloody nose in a debate, it may show others that they might not want to debate you, but it didn't change their perception of you. They still think you're evil, and want to influence others to perceive you with that prejudice. That's why I keep saying there needs to be illustrations that compete with the illustrations and mediums that liberals use to get in the way of what liberals are entertaining them with. This is a big way the liberals spread their influence, and we're not countering there.

Lt. Col. Allen West lets us know that in the Army they have a saying, "why do you kick a man when he is down?" The answer is simple, "because he's close to your foot." Don't start none. Won't be none. Republicans are on the counter-offensive which is good! Liberals have attacked with slander and Republicans are swinging back, but when the dust settles from this political round the Republicans are going to let Democrats walk away from their offense, and the Democrats are going to regroup in the culture to attack with more slander and prejudice promoting propaganda.

Republicans have to follow through culturally to interfere with the cultural contamination Democrats will be casting. Republicans talk about being ever vigilant. I hope we can walk it like we talk it and defend ourselves in the culture that makes it really hard for Democrats to get back up. Hit them from every angle. Let them find no rest, and minimize areas for them to flank. We're well fortified with the talk front. Bloggers, Vloggers, talk radio, and news channel talk. But we're not covered on the music angle, Sitcom angle, movie angle, sci-fi angle, etc. All these areas that liberals attack from we're not fortified to defend.

What I strongly suggest conservatives do is establish scout and artist development firms that find talent in music, comedians, actors, directors, writers, and pay them to listen to the conservative point of view. Not pay them to believe it but to listen to it. Make the investment to nurture talent in the Christian conservative view. Mentor artists in this! Give the option for them to want to give it a go.

If they're open to it, mentor them and hire them. YES! HIRE THEM to represent Christian conservatism in the culture. Fund productions to showcase writers, directors, and actors. Fund music of various genres to carry the Christian conservative message to their audience with. Send them on stage with shirts with stylized images of Frederick Douglas, and Abraham Lincoln. Make it the counter fashion to the clueless that wear Che' Guevara shirts. Blaze an image of the Cross on it with a message that boldly cuts down liberal worldviews with the Word of God.

A lot of people don't feel safe being conservative in entertainment because there doesn't appear to be any recourse for them. They want to be a career entertainer, and it appears the only way to do that is to assimilate to the liberal idea. But that's the nature of being a Christian conservative; If you're really for Christ and this republic He's blessed us with then you take the risk. And just as they should be willing to take the risk, then so should investors. Is not our King worth the risk? Is it not worth the risk to preserve this republic that He blessed us with where we're free to promote His Word?

More and more the Liberals turn people away from God. The more they succeed, the less liberty we'll have. You think that can't happen here? Just Keep in mind the Garden of God was on the continent of Africa. It's chaos there now. If America separates from God, America will unravel.

We're up against a legion of leftward thinking that is teaching that there's nothing special about us. We're not created in God's image. We're all accidents that came from nothing and evolved into beings that would ponder our origin. It's pretty common for us to have a sense of purpose or even wonder what our purpose is. We don't have a sense of "Accident". We have a sense of purpose. Why? Because the universe was created on purpose. It wasn't an accident. The more we allow leftists to promote the idea that life came from nothing then the value of life will keep reducing to nothing.

Halfway well-adjusted people want to amount to something, not amount to nothing. That's because our origin is in something. So, it's in our nature to persist in the nature of what we came from and mature into what we came from. We don't persist with the instinct to become nothing because that's not the nature of what we come from. Does that mean that we are to ultimately become gods? Nope!

We can't become gods because our origins include finite material. Man originated with the dust of the earth. A day will come when we will be rebooted with all new immortal gear. Does that make us gods? Nope. Because even though we'd be immortal the whole universe including us can only sustain the forever existence by the will of God. God can go on forever and still cancel His creation. Heaven and earth will pass away, but the Word of God is eternal. Because of His love, He will host eternity for us. If we were meant to be gods, we could facilitate that ourselves.

We were not ever meant to be gods. We can't give ourselves immortality. Only something that already existed with that ability could do that and produce a creature with the already existing information to endow the creature with. We can never do that. It's already been done. We can never facilitate an eternal dwelling because we have a beginning, Eternity has no beginning. So, it's impossible for us to be a god that can make an eternal dwelling. That something that is responsible for our existence is that Purpose. He is that sense of purpose we have. We can choose to accept that or not. I suggest we choose to be cool with it and turn others on to it because that is the way to preserve the balance of peace joy and liberty.

If we don't promote this for the preservation of our republic, it will accelerate in decline. Our republic can't last forever. It's made of finite material just like everything else, but we can be a generation that answered the call to be salt and light to preserve the liberty the Lord gave us, make it savory for others to crave it, and light the way to the One Who Blessed us with liberty. That's how you bless the next generation. The leftist promotes empty platitudes concerning the next generation. "Love the earth for our children and grandchildren." That's a long load of doo dooooooooooooooooooooooo, right thar.

As I've said before, these fakers talk about making the world a better place for our future kids. You mean those kids that haven't been born yet? You liberals don't consider kids that haven't been born yet human. You abort kids that haven't been born yet. The earth doesn't need protection from us. Those future kids you're talking about need protection from you.

Loving the earth doesn't make the world a better place for future generations.

Loving God with all your heart mind and strength and loving your neighbor as yourself is how you make the world a better place for your children and grandchildren.

But remember folks, these people believe creation came from nothing. That's why they see the human creation in the womb as nothing. These baby butchering bullies have had their gloves off for a while and fight with absolutely no honor. We're in a struggle between patriots and parasites.

Pious parasites at that! Parasites that really think they are better people! Isn't it ironic that Democrats have a worldview that wants them to implement parasitic policy, yet they justify killing the pre-born because they claim that the unborn is just a parasite? But they think they're better people. Even the liberal so-called Christian thinks they're better than Jesus at the end of the day.

The "liberal Christians" are usually the so-called Christians who will say, "Jesus can't be the only way." This means they have judged that there are other ways just as good a Jesus to get to heaven. They have judged that they know something that Jesus doesn't. "Um, excuse me, Jesus. I know You said 'You are the Way, Truth, and Life and that nobody comes to the Father except by You.' but I'm going to pretend that You never said that because that would make You really ignorant to the other ways to get to heaven."

Liberals scoff at and mock Jesus for the wickedness and suffering in the world. For all the money these Jesus judging liberals have together you'd think they would have solved the hunger problem long before now since they know so much better, but haven't. Bear in mind Jesus was winning all the battles the rulers couldn't win. Jesus was winning the battles against disease, hunger, blindness, deafness, and mental illness. He was winning the battles the rulers couldn't, and the ultimate battle for Jesus to win against was the greatest enemy of mankind; death itself. No ruler could do that.

Jesus proved He could solve all of these things. He was rejected for it, by the same kind of people who reject Him today. God did get rid of the wicked people. But the same people who charge God for not getting rid of the wicked people call Him a genocidal maniac for getting rid of the wicked people - just like they accuse America of being genocidal imperialist for defending against actual genocidal imperialist.

Liberals overlook a dictator who starves his people and threatens the world with nuclear war, yet look at our president in America where obesity is a more of a problem than starvation yet somehow our American president is the more evil threat to the world.

Liberals see us as evil for not letting in refugees and overlook the evil they're running from.

When America responds with military force to the evil that causes people to become refugees, America is accused of trying to be the world police. And since liberals insist American police officers love to shoot anybody who isn't a white Christian, it just means America is sending out the world police to shoot non-white non-Christians.

Remember how in my Audiobook Weapon of A.S.S. Destruction (American Socialist States), I made the connection between Democrats and Satan whose name means the Accuser? In full satanic nature, these liberal Democrats and leftists will look for any angle to accuse. That's just their nature. They can choose to be cured of it, but they have to be able to get over themselves enough to do it and petition the Lord to make them new.

One minute we're accused of trying to rob the world, the next minute we're accused of trying to police it. But I reckon that doesn't matter because again, according to the left, cops are crooked. That must mean America must be the crooked world police. But somehow, it's okay for the world to police us, especially concerning the environment, even though America is a leading clean air nation.

To the left, America is the worst offender and facilitator of the biggest threat to the world—climate change. Do I need to revisit the point of imagination and reason? There is no proof that climate change is going to destroy us.

but there is a proven entity following up on their threats called Islamo-Terrorism, but they're not a threat somehow to liberals. In fact, as far as they're concerned, we should be coexisting with them (terrorists). On top of that, what better way to set an example of how America should show the Islamic world that we are going to coexist than to invite them to an LGTB Parade!?

According to these people, it's America's fault the terrorists hate us, and the LGTB and liberals are the redeeming population of

America that will cause the Islamists not to hate us. Those poor Islamic victims. America should be ashamed according to Liberals. Liberals be like, "Why can't the greedy Israelis let the Muslims have that little piece of land called the Gaza strip?" To which I ask of the poor perspective liberals, why can't the greedy Muslims let Israel have their little piece of land that's dwarfed by how much Muslim territory surrounds it?

They accuse us of funding Israel so the evil Zionist Israelis can oppress with murderous apartheid upon the Palestinians. How are Palestinians able to look like they're the victims and us out to be the bullies who provoked them? It's not rational, is it? It doesn't make natural sense that people could be this backward. It's like a supernatural kind of stupid. That's not far off.

Does it seem strange to you that the Islamo-fascists and those blind to its evil promote themselves as victims when they are obviously the hostile bullies? Let's examine why Islamists are able to get a pity pat from the American left, and why it seems supernaturally stupid and how blind they are to them.

As Christians, we pretty much understand that Al Quran is basically a satanic manifesto in that it's a work meant to influence the rejection of Who Jesus says He is.

Here is where you can see these roots of how the victim mentality of Islamists gains so much ground with left wingers. Examine the fall of Iblis or the devil in Al Quran.

Al Quran is made to reflect the Bible to give it credibility. The devil himself can recite scripture and appear as an angel of light to deceive. Bear in mind Al Quran means "The Recital." And meant it's to be recited in action.

The Devil's light blinds. It doesn't light the way.

Al Quran will even tell you that Isa (The Jesus figure in Al Quran) was born of a virgin, he could heal the sick and raise the dead. Al Quran will even concede to the record that Isa ("the Jesus figure") was here. But it's a ruse to give Al Quran credibility.

And no wonder, for Satan himself masquerades as an angel of light. 2 Corinthians 11:14

In the Bible, Satan is introduced as the enemy who does something low that we can all identify with as low, even though many people miss it. I talk about this in my audiobook Weapon of A.S.S. Destruction. (American Socialist States) The low thing Satan did wasn't in tempting Eve. The low thing Satan did was falsely accuse God. That's his name. It means the accuser.

That accusation stoked Eve's pride in a feminist fashion. She got greedy, and as a woman coveted having knowledge equal to God. It is apparent Satan knew playing her feminist pride would work because he took the temptation to her instead of Adam who was right there and had relinquished authority to Eve, instead of being the spiritual head God made him to be and did not insist on the council of God.

The lowest thing you can do to someone without touching them is slander them. (Unless you're Darth Vader.) This is why Satan is called the lowest - as the serpent crawls on its belly. You destroy marriages, businesses, friendships, lives literally and figuratively with slander. Satan destroyed Adam and Eve with slander. He falsely accused God, from there was able to give himself credibility with Eve. (Remember, this is how democrats operate today; Gaining the trust of people by causing them to distrust others with slander.) Satan influenced Eve who influenced Adam to be the first mass murder-suicide couple. So, in the Bible, you clearly identify Satan as the enemy. Even if you only saw him as a tempter. You knew that even tempting people to do something they shouldn't is wrong. And we find that abhorrent.

But in Al Quran, Iblis or the devil is introduced to you in a very different dynamic. This is how the devil is introduced if you check out surah's 2:34 and 7:12

002.034   YUSUFALI: And behold, We said to the angels: "Bow down to Adam" and they bowed down. Not so Iblis: he refused and was haughty: He was of those who reject Faith.

007.011   YUSUFALI: It is We Who created you and gave you shape; then We bade the angels prostrate to Adam, and they prostrate; not so Iblis; He refused to be of those who prostrate.

007.012   YUSUFALI: (Allah) said: "What prevented thee from prostrating when I commanded thee?" He said: "I am better than he: Thou didst create me from fire, and him from clay."

In the Bible, Satan is introduced to you as an unmistakable enemy. Manipulative, and slanderous. Nobody digs that. Even people who are manipulative and slanderous get mad if they even think you're trying to manipulate them or accuse them of anything even if they're actually guilty.

However, in Al Quran, Iblis is introduced to the reader as a victim. And everybody can identify with a victim. This supposedly means *he really can't be the evil one.* You can sympathize with a victim. Iblis was commanded to do something unfair in his mind. He was commanded to prostrate before Adam.

"That's not fair. That's not justice, I'm the victim here!" And these Islamo-fascists are following the same template of Iblis; murderous agents who are able to keep pressing forward, because the so-called progressives don't see them as terrorists, but as victims.

Israel can be slammed by missiles; it doesn't matter to the left who are blinded by Satan's light. They only register that the Palestinians are the victims oppressed by Israel.

A belligerent victim mentality is a fuel they burn to go victimize others. The progressives in office will pander to people with a victim mentality to our peril, and it's going to cause chaos that's going to sink people into hell before it's over, the way Iblis wanted it. The PC-culture will yield to Islam in the name of fairness,

A big reason why Islam will dominate is because they will assert that it is unfair that their religious practices are being discriminated against, and Democrat policies will capitulate to them.

It's happening across the world with other officials infected with political correctness.

We're up against people who are terrorizing the world by "reciting" in word and deed the instructions in Al Quran. And it's working for them. You want to learn how to beat it? Apply the instructions in the Bible. It's the manual that reduces all this crap. We can't remove it, but we can reduce it. We're not perfect so we can't remove it completely, but we can sure knock back a lot of the nonsense in this generation with the Word of God.

I hope more people who call themselves conservatives come to realize that patriotism is great, but faith in the All Mighty is more important. Conservatives show great affinity for the country and want to "Make It Great Again" but they seem to have more pride in the country than hope in the Kingdom. Pride all around is the poison. It was the first sin against God.

It takes being grateful to be an American, not pride. Grateful to God is the place to start for a Great America.

It takes putting Kingdom before country if we want to preserve our country. Abolish any law that makes it legal to infringe on our God-given rights.

It takes putting Kingdom before color if we're going to have harmony. People need to get over their pride and insecurities about their ethnicity and the ethnicity of others. Humility before God fixes that.

It takes putting Kingdom before currency to restore, multiply, and stabilize the economy. God, the One who blesses us with the ability to earn money in the first place is our security, not money. That's why even our currency; the most passed around note says, "In God we trust" to keep us reminded. Lots of money doesn't stop, divorce, alcoholism, drug addiction, sexual abuse, theft, or suicide. These things take rich and poor alike. Mindful of accountability to God stops these things, not what's in your bank account.

It takes putting Kingdom before creativity and craft to promote works that inspires and influences a culture.

It takes putting Kingdom before creation to make it better for the next generation.

It takes putting Kingdom before chromosomes concerning gender to bring men and women into harmony with each other, reduce insecurities and the delusion of saying chromosomes are false agents used to promote a false bio tool used to promote a false biological premise about genders.

God is the greatest Law Writer. His law perfectly sets the parameters of how to live in peace. On top of that, He wrote the laws that maintain our universe. That's a powerful, proven law writer. So, when He gives us Christ to be our King, He gets no argument from me!

God has given us a perfect moral law that will be ratified with love when He writes the law on our hearts.

That will keep those who chose Him living in paradise, peace, and joy forever. Even work will be like a holiday!

But the icing on the cake is that we won't be subject to the laws that maintain the universe. Jesus already gave us an idea of that.

We will no longer be subject to the law of gravity. Jesus walked on water, and Peter joined Him.

"Lord, if it is You, Peter replied, "command me to come to You on the water." 29"Come," said Jesus. Then Peter got down out of the boat, walked on the water, and came toward Jesus.... - Matthew 14:28 BSB

Upon rapture and resurrection, the new body will be in the state of rightness with God because of Jesus Christ. We will be new bodied creatures in Him that won't abuse that kind of liberty. In our present state, if we were to have the power to manipulate gravity, great horrors would be afflicted upon others. Only those who have chosen Christ and welcomed His law on our hearts will be exempt from the law of gravity.

We will no longer be subject to the law of time and space.

*...**When they had rowed about three or four miles**, they saw Jesus approaching the boat, walking on the sea—and they were terrified. But Jesus spoke up: "It is I; do not be afraid." Then they were willing to take Him into the boat, **and at once** the boat reached the shore where they were heading.... John 6:19-21 BSB*

Jesus time warped them through space to the other side of the sea! No more of feeling like there's not enough time to get something done or get somewhere. You won't feel the need to time travel because everything is perfect, so there's no desire to go back and fix regrets. People dream about time travel to fix something in their past.

In the Kingdom of God, there's no point. But at the same time, the ability to move freely through time and space comes with choosing the Kingdom. We will be new creatures in Him that won't abuse that kind of liberty. In our state, there would be great horrors afflicted upon others if we could manipulate time. Only those who have chosen Christ and welcome His law on their hearts will be exempt from the law of time.

We will no longer be subject to the decay of the law of entropy. We're reborn imperishable. We don't decay into another state. God's Kingdom will not decay into chaos. Our health and well-being will not decay. We will be exempt from the law of entropy.

For you have been born again, not of perishable seed, but of imperishable, through the living and enduring word of God. - 1 Peter 1:23 NIV

This is the Law Writer we're supposed to be free to live under. It is the Word to preserve our liberty by. If it goes so does our liberty. The word of God is what we were founded on to have liberty.

We, therefore, the Representatives of the United States of America, in General Congress, Assembled, appealing to the Supreme Judge of the world for the rectitude of our intentions,... -Declaration of Independence

Who is the Supreme Judge of the world and where does this title come from?

And He will judge the world in righteousness; He will execute judgment for the peoples with equity. -Psalm 9:8 NASB

And men will say, "Surely there is a reward for the righteous; Surely there is a God who judges on earth!" Psalm 58:11 NASB

When God arose to judgment, To save all the humble of the earth. Selah. -Psalm 76:9 NASB

Arise, O God, judge the earth! For it is You who possesses all the nations. -Psalm 82:8 NASB

Rise up, Judge of the earth; pay back to the proud what they deserve. Psalm 94:2 NIV

Before the LORD, for He is coming, For He is coming to judge the earth. He will judge the world in righteousness And the peoples in His faithfulness. -Psalm 96:13 NASB

He is the LORD our God; His judgments are in all the earth. -Psalm 105:7 NASB

in joyful assembly, to the congregation of the firstborn, enrolled in heaven. You have come to God the judge of all men, to the spirits of the righteous made perfect, -Hebrews 12:23 BSB

For he has set a day when he will judge the world with justice by the man he has appointed. He has given proof of this to everyone by raising him from the dead." -Acts 17:31 NIV

Before the LORD, for He is coming to judge the earth; He will judge the world with righteousness And the peoples with equity. -Psalm 98:9 NIV

So, it's a pretty big stretch to say God has nothing to do with the founding of our republic. The signers who invoked the Supreme Judge of the world to be a witness to their pledge would disagree with those who say the signers did not intend for God to be acknowledged in the establishment of this republic.

We are in a spiritual war that has manifested as a cultural, political, racial, gender, class, territorial, religious, war; all theaters chosen to destroy our salvation.

Tragically, it seems the only theater Republicans seem to be interested in fighting in is the political one. The Democrats have long had their gloves off, scratchin', spittin' bitin', cussin' shootin', lynchin', bombin', and burnin', to change America into what they want. And everything Democrats want is apart from God. Democrats use multiple streams of influence to get people to turn away from God. The more that happens, the more we lose our republic. But I'm hopeful because the Word of God is eternal. The first order of God according to Him is to know who He is. I AM the Lord your God. What is it to know God? To know God is to love God. Why? Because God's first order of love for us is to be free; free to love each other as we would ourselves according to His authorship of love.

He is eternal, and He wants us eternally free from hate, slander, hunger, famine, disease, theft, poverty, death. Any form of oppression, the Lord will ultimately liberate us from. Unfortunately, there are many who believe the Lord Himself is oppression and they want to be liberated from Him. Some people don't recognize oppression and engage in oppressive actions thinking it's liberty. These are the "Freedom FROM religion" types. And they especially want to be free from the Judeo-Christian God because He is the biggest threat to their selfish desires. The desires they want are the liberties to ultimately intrude on another's.

Liberals want the liberty to do that, and their selfishness makes them fight real dirty and swarm in from multiple angles. One of the dirty and insidious ways they have been doing this is with shadow-banning.

Liberals can't have messengers promoting the Word of God. They can't have people promoting content that challenges their narrative and exposes who they are. I've long said it's not a good idea for conservatives to be dependent on their platforms. I'm not meaning to play the victim here. It's actually kind of an honor, but I don't think there is ANYBODY who's gotten the shadow-ban worse than I have.

The ratio of views of my content to the number of my page followers is way disproportionate. It's been that way for years. The Lord is my motivation. He said they'll hate us because of Him. And it looks like these online overlords really don't like me and do not want me achieving my goals.

They do not want me seen by people who would definitely support my work. They do not want me seen by the people they have brain chained. They don't want my commentaries to be free to reach people and let them decide if they agree or not. They're terrified that people will agree with this knucklehead named Zo.

For some reason, they don't want my music to reach people. They don't want my ideas for teleplays and movies to ever come to fruition. They don't want the competition. You'd think they'd be happy to just let my work be seen so the liberal locusts can come and chew it all apart, but nope. They're afraid the work I've been blessed to share will break the liberal spell on them. Think about that, ya'll. Compared to all the conservatives in social media who are expressing their grievance about their content being limited, these people are still getting hundreds of thousands of views and even millions. They get thousands of retweets. I'm lucky if I get ten. I've got tens of thousands of subscribers on YouTube. I'm lucky my videos get a couple of thousand views.

My name doesn't come up in Google cross references with other conservative commentators. Why am I such a big threat? Why shadow-ban me so much worse than other notable conservative commentators? Maybe it's because I'm the easiest target. But wouldn't that make them hypocrites; picking on the black little guy? I don't have an illustrious academic career to boast of. Why are they so threatened by me? It's not because I'm a black conservative. It's because God is my banner. That is what they're afraid of.

Check out the other commentators. They're really brilliant, and they lead with that. They lead with their intellect and how conservative they are. That's their banner. They're flag-waving Americans who want people to know how patriotic and how MAGA motivated they are. These are their banners. Their banners are how informed they are, and that's great, but none of these things make demons shake like the name of Jesus.

Liberals are driven by demons, and they are not as afraid of any conservative's intellect as they are of Jesus.

Liberals aren't afraid of me. They're afraid of the Word of Jesus. Liberals aren't afraid of church bubble Christians because liberals don't worry about them figuring out that Christ should be their political filter. Liberals don't worry about these people because these are the people who say, "It doesn't matter who is in office because God is still on the throne." Liberals don't sweat them. But conservative who's banner is the Lord that's what makes liberals nervous. Not the conservative.

Christian Conservatives even, who lead with their pride may trigger libs but they don't really scare libs.

One day the evil spirit answered them, "Jesus I know, and Paul I know about, but who are you?" Acts 19:15 NIV

That's because the Demon wasn't impressed by the exorcist trying to invoke the name of Jesus. The exorcists still thought it was by their power they could drive out demons. Their call on Jesus wasn't confident, and the demon could sniff it.

I'm no political, academic, intellectual powerhouse for liberals to be afraid of. It's the light of God they don't want me sharing with folks. God is my banner above any, and that is why they silence me more than any other conservative and cannot let my work surface. But God has the last Word. And He wants this new Canaan taken.

CHAPTER XIII
THE 10 COUNT

As a Christian conservative Republican, I find that the Word of God is the best preservative of our republic when applied. Salt is a preservative and brings out the savory flavor, but it can sting if exposed to the wrong places. Salt also works as an antiseptic. Salt is a lot like truth. Truth is delicious. Truth preserves, it cleans, truth feels good! But to some, truth is bitter, it stings like it was thrown in their eyes. Many people are like that- as they don't want to see truth. Salt and light are highly welcome by some, and rejected by others. The Ten Commandments are such a preservative. Apply them according to Jesus Christ and a society preserves and thrives, but some people are so wounded with bigotry and dysfunctionally that the truth just stings their sores.

The following is the truth that is so true that it's a law. Those who love truth savor it. Those who hate truth react to it like a slug when salt hits it.

Then God spoke all these words, saying, "I am the LORD your God, who brought you out of the land of Egypt, out of the house of slavery.... -Exodus 1:1-2 NASB

As you look at the Ten Commandments or the ten articles if you will, you can see clauses with the articles. The first commandment isn't just to have no other gods before God. There's other parts.

The clause to not have any other gods before God isn't the main thing. The article of God saying, "I am the Lord your God" is. If a person rejects the Ultimate Truth in the article of God being the Lord our God, then the clause of having no other gods before God is most likely not going to be obeyed.

I AM the Lord your God is the Ultimate Truth. It is such pure truth that it is the law. We have the free will to reject that truth and disobey that law. But disobeying the law has consequences.

People need to understand the following about free-will. The Godless believe God doesn't give us free will because we get punished for not believing Him. They're absolutely wrong. Free-will doesn't mean you are exempt from punishment from making the wrong free-will choice.

Not having free-will would be never knowing what it means to make a choice at all; a robot programmed to never know the difference. That is what not having free-will would be. Having free-will means that you are free to choose between right, wrong, good, and evil, or what you think is good or evil, and whether the reward is worth the risk. Free-will is a choice that renders rewards or punishments. Just because a person can be punished doesn't mean they don't have free-will. It means they have the free-will choice to decide if the risk they are taking is worth the reward. It's all fair because if an unlawful risk taker was a target of another person who took an unlawful risk at the first party's expense, the first lawless risk taker would want the second party punished too.

Not having free will would be us being created to be ignorant to choices. We have the free will to abide by the article of God declaring that He is the Lord Our God, or not. There is the free will choice between reward and punishment. Become On-High Heaven fabulous, or become an eternal booty Bar B Que. Many are foolish enough to think there is no judgment that awaits them. They'll find out the hard way that Jesus is the longest and strongest arm of the law, that will bring them to justice no matter how far they think they can brush Him off.

"I am the Lord your God." Without that article, there is ultimately nothing to follow the other commandments for. You could try, but they will be for reasons that will be subject to entropy. They'll decay and change. God doesn't decay or change.

It's like the rights to life, liberty, and the pursuit of happiness. You can't have the second and third without the first.

How can you have another god before God if you don't even acknowledge the truth about God being the Lord our God?

This is the very first thing that God wants us to get a grip on; that He is the Lord our God. The first article speaks to the One on the first page He breathed to us; In the Beginning, God...

After this Supreme article, the clause that says, "You shall have no other god's before Me" doesn't even come next.

After the Supreme article comes the clause, "Who brought you out of the land of Egypt,"

This ain't God bragging about what He did or hanging it over our heads. "Who brought you out of the land of Egypt," is a law.

The very first thing God wants you to get straight is that He IS the Lord our God, and with the establishment of that understanding He mandates that we are to be free. His ultimate objective for us is to be free. It is against His law to oppress another. We are meant to be free, and God ultimately deals with oppressors very harshly, as He has done to Egypt. The name Egypt itself means oppression or bondage. That's why the article says, I am the LORD your God, who brought you out of the land of Egypt, *out of the house of slavery.*

It is against the law of God to be oppressed. We were not meant to be enslaved. Our liberties are not meant to be taken by force. It is the law that we are to be free. And the full law of God is that we are to be free from things that plague us like disease, poverty, famine, war, and ultimately death. God will ultimately liberate us from all oppression. It is His Law that we are to be free, and the ultimate freedom is found in Him. That brings us to the third clause. You shall have no other gods before God, because there is nothing else in this universe that can ultimately liberate us, and the worship of other gods results in oppression. From slavery to human sacrifice. These things are not of God.

The haters will say, "Didn't God sacrifice Jesus." They seem to forget that God gave Jesus authority to come back. No other ritual of sacrificing brings the sacrificed back to life. Jesus wasn't sacrificed to remain dead. Jesus was sacrificed to prove that even death can't hold Him, and that He could liberate us from death even after His death.

A person who can't be killed doesn't prove they can conquer death. There would always be the lingering wonder if there is something that could kill that person. Jesus removed all that. He died. But death couldn't keep Him. A person that can't die isn't really proof of immortality. It just means something hasn't been found to kill that person, YET! But a person who was killed and then returned from the dead takes the cake. That person proves that they have the power to free all from death, and that person is Jesus. He ultimately liberates us from the ultimate oppressor; Death. This is why God lets you know that as Lord and God He brings us out of Bondage. It is His law that we are to be free, ultimately from death.

So trying to accuse God of sacrificing His Son in the same vein as other pagan religions of human sacrifice don't cut it. God wouldn't have sacrificed Jesus if He couldn't bring Him back to prove to us that Jesus is the conqueror of death.

So, God wants us to choose to be in agreement that He is the Lord our God. That is the ultimate Truth and Supreme article the first clause is that we are to be free. Oppression is against the law.

The next clause is to not have any other gods before God, because serving other gods leads to oppression and murder. This is idolatry. We are not to make graven images. It doesn't matter if it's an image based on celestial bodies, or atmospheric phenomenon, earthen objects, subterranean objects, or objects from the deep, or whatever you think is in the sky, on the earth, under the earth, or the water. Because if you can shape an idol you can shape what it means. That's not really a god. A god isn't something we can shape. A real God shapes us. Idolatry renders us trying to satisfy what's important to us, and even if it cost someone else by force. The values of idolatry change. God's values don't change.

God lets us know what the sentence looks like if you violate this commandment. He's Jealous over us, and He'll visit the iniquity of the fathers on the children, on the third and fourth generation of those who hate Him.

God's Jealousy is a protective jealousy. The same kind of jealousy you would have over your kids when you see them straying from the values you tried to instill in them for things that are not healthy for them. You would feel jealous. It would hurt you that your kid prefers something that you know would hurt them over what you know is better for them. But you let them live their life, despite your jealousy, and when they're hurt by what they wanted, they're going to blame you, and or expect you to bear the burden of it. If you don't care that God will be jealous that you prefer other things to Him, God will bring the punishment upon your descendants. Why? What do you mean why? Like you care? People who have no respect for God tend to not care about the next generation. Remember, they make fanciful speeches about making the world a better place for the children of the tomorrow, yet demand the right to abort them. God knows how we are. People who don't want to obey God tend to be the same people who demand the right to make a child pay the death penalty for somebody else's actions. Don't even try to judge God for making decedents pay for the crime of the father. This is God giving people a dose of their own poison. Noah did the same thing. He made Canaan and his descendants pay for the crimes of the father of Canaan, Ham. The one choosing to not obey God doesn't consider the consequences, but his descendants most likely will. "Why is this crap happening to me? How is it my fault?!"

The selfish don't care what happens to their decedents. That's why Democrats don't really care about the debt that the next generation inherits, and that's if they aren't aborted to inherit the debt. Just sayin'.

But God doesn't punish the descendants of the father out of cruelty. The reason why God does this is because the initial lawbreaker was short-sighted and didn't care about how his actions would affect others, and even when warned, that person still didn't care to listen to God, not considering the risk that his descendants would pay for his actions. He didn't value his children enough to avoid the risk and just obey God.

When the descendants are faced with the iniquities of the shortsighted father, the descendants are more likely to think twice about rebelling against God. They're seeing confirmation. They're seeing God wasn't kidding. Chances are they may want the cycle to break, and come to God for mercy. They might see that if the iniquity of their father is being visited on them then their iniquity will be visited on their children, and if they really aren't selfish and value their children then they'd better humble themselves before God if they don't want their iniquity visited upon their descendants.

Furthermore the commandment to "To have no other gods before Jehovah God and to not make for yourself an idol, or any likeness of what is in heaven above, or on the Earth or in the water, or under the earth, and to not worship them or serve them", also means do not let anyone MAKE YOU. The commandment isn't just to not do it. It's also do not let anyone make you worship other gods. We are not to allow ourselves to be coerced, compelled, seduced, or whatever into making an idol of something else over God. Has that happened throughout history and happening today? Yes. We can see Liberals have been trying to force us into their replacement of God for a while.

The third clause says to not take the Lord's name in vain. This means do not sin against God or man while invoking God to justify it. For example; *God says that slavery is ok, therefore we can force people to be our slaves.* God did not say it is ok to force people into slavery. That would be taking God's name in vain. Or saying things like, *Jesus accepts me for being gay. I'm still a good person.* Homosexuality has never been condoned in the Old or New Testament. God as Jehovah and as Yeshua never gave the ok for homosexuality. He maintains His rule against it. Or things like, *God gave us weed to smoke.* God never told us to partake in pharmakeia. Taking medicines to help with physical pain or mental/emotional disease to help return to a state of normalcy is not a sin. Taking drugs to remove you from normalcy is. Taking drugs recreationally or for the assumed practice of spirituality is a form of violating the commandment to have no other gods before God. It is a form of witchcraft. It is an exercise in trying to receive a state of being that is a departure from yourself and from God. Trying to invoke God to justify doing things apart from God and sinning against God and others is taking God's name in vain.

"You shall not take the name of the LORD your God in vain, for the LORD will not leave him unpunished who takes His name in vain. -Exodus 20:7 NASB

Like I said, claiming to believe in God just to use His name to sin against others really ticks Him off.

Jesus revisits this clause in. verses like Matthew 7:23 BSB

...Many will say to Me on that day, 'Lord, Lord, did we not prophesy in Your name, and in Your name drive out demons and perform many miracles?' Then I will tell them plainly, 'I never knew you; depart from Me, you workers of lawlessness.'

So you see? This isn't me trying to make some wild interpretation. This is the Bible flat out telling you that taking the name of God means, people invoking the name of God while sinning as if it's ok, because either they think that God would be accepting of it, or they have just engaged in idolatry and made up some god they call Jesus who gives them permission to sin.

The Sabbath clause. This commandment has come to mean "Closed on Sunday." According to this Clause, we're really screwed. Many believe the Sabbath clause is just for the Jews.

How do we come to the conclusion that this Clause is just for the Jews? According to that so-called logic, The commandment to not murder is only for the Jews too, and the rest of us can go murder anytime we want. *Even on the Sabbath, cause that doesn't apply to us either.*

But here are the clausal components of this section: Remembering it, keeping it holy, doing no work, and working six days. Like I said, we're screwed.

Remember the Sabbath? We can't even agree to which day it's supposed to be on. And how are we supposed to remember a Sabbath day and keep it holy on days named after pagan gods?

How are we to do no work on the Sabbath? The Pharisees tried to indict Jesus for performing works on the Sabbath. They charged a man for working on the Sabbath just for carrying his mat! This tells me that even the scholars didn't understand what the Sabbath met. I further back up this claim by the fact the Pharisees themselves were doing work by following Jesus around trying to give him a citation! If a man carrying a mat is considered work then surely the hypocritical Judean authorities were in violation of the Sabbath if they're following people around policing them! If they were really consistent they should have all picked up stones and busted each other's heads open on the spot, but that too would be working on the Sabbath too, now wouldn't it?

Also, there's a very important clausal element to this section that people overlook.

The commandment isn't just about resting, the clause also tells us that we're to work six days!

Working is a commandment too! And we're supposed to work six days a week! We're screwed!

We want Friday and Saturday to do us! And leave Sunday over for God! "After football of course."

Come on, God! Five days a week, maybe, but six?! Many folks would even prefer four ten hour days!

On top of that, only in a perfect world with a perfect economy, where everything from farming, to manufacturing, to retail, etc. worked perfectly, could everybody work six days a week! There could be no sick days, no snow-ins, no power outs, etc.

Bene-Yisrael had no excuse to not keep this command because Adonai was right there as a pillar of fire by night and smoke by day. Under His reign, He could provide everything they needed to work six days a week and be able to straight chill with Him on the seventh. Just follow His instructions!

And I reckon that is the thing to remember about the Sabbath; That it takes God to have a perfect world. But His presence has been forsaken. We live in a world where it's almost easier to work six days a week than it is to rest on the Sabbath. Your boss may need you to work on Sunday or Saturday. You might not even be able to get the job unless you can work weekends. What if Sunday is the only day you have off and you need to catch up on stuff? What if you have to move?

The Sabbath reminds us that we are not in a perfect world and that in order to have a perfect world it requires total obedience to God.

If we all loved God, and loved each other the way He tells us to, going to work would be a party every day! People would be happy to go to work six days week! You couldn't stop us! Imagine going to work where everybody pulled their weight! No gossip, no throat cutting, no embezzling, no power tripping supervisors, no trifling employees. We are naturally wired to be purposeful. We want to perform tasks! It's the B.S. involved with being at work that is what's often so draining! Also, working on a job that we don't feel like we were meant to do is draining as well. We hate the idea of serving to make "the man rich". That's a poor and selfish attitude. You wouldn't want employees having that prejudice about you if you come to own a business. And it can suck working around cynical people like that. I like working around people with a service attitude. That "Git 'er done" spirit! I used to be a grumbler about "working for the man." But the Lord fixes that! I work on a job that I don't feel is my calling, but doing a poor job and grumbling isn't going to get me any closer to what I feel like I've been called to do. Showing gratitude and giving excellent service gets you closer to what you feel like you were called to do. And when you are doing what you feel like you were called to do, it makes working six days a week that much easier!

Imagine all being obedient to the Lord, and operating in love! Work itself would be like a holiday! And then it gets better as ya come home to your family whom you have missed all day! And being that they are obedient to the Lord, the party starts all over again; Loving spouse, and joyful kids! This world awaits us in God! Jesus told us He went to prepare this place for us!

So the Sabbath section isn't really understood. But rather, it reminds us that a better world awaits us in Christ. According to how we understand the Sabbath rule everybody deserves execution due to failure to abide by it.

The rules concerning the Sabbath almost seem unfair, and even absurd; be put to death for not resting after working six days, if you could even work six days?!

Let's review the word, "remember". Remember the Sabbath. Remember that a day is coming when we will be gainfully employed! Jesus will preside over an economic policy that will have a 0% unemployment rate! Remember the day of the Lord! Keep it sacred! Keep it Holy! It is the day where we get what we claim to want! Not just rest from work, but from war, famine, disease, poverty, drama, and death! If we really want to be free from these things then set apart a day to remember the One who will bring us that day! Show some freakin' gratitude to the One who has proven He will make it happen! He is worthy of at least one day a week to give thanks and praise too! He is worthy of eternal gratitude, and as for my wife and I, we want to give Him thanks eternally! Remembering the Sabbath reminds us that we cannot make a perfect world. It takes God. We are supposed to have this world! This is the world God meant for us! Not the way that it is now, in the reboot we inherit the land forever, and explore the universe for vacation homes! God does NOT take kindly to the world He meant for us being messed with. That's why He says disobedience of not setting apart time to fellowship and learn from Him is punishable by death! Because people who don't regard Him are elemental to what brings about mass death. We're supposed to live FREE from all these problems, remember? So, when people do things that lead to oppressive problems that afflict your neighbors, then you've gotten yourself on God's shmutz list. Again, even though we cannot maintain the clauses of the Sabbath, it IS the state we are meant to be in! But since we fail at it, The Lord takes that opportunity to show His grace. It isn't like God made up some rule that we cannot follow just so He could punish us or make some convoluted way to show that He is merciful.

Remember. We want a world where we're gainfully employed, prosperous, no poverty, no strife, no famines, no wars, etc. We're supposed to live free of these things! So let's not view God as making some rule we can't follow when it's a rule that guards something that we want! God wants to be able to bless us with these things, and burns against those who get in the way of what He wants to bless us with.

The next clause is honoring your father and mother. As I said earlier, notice it says, "father and mother". God knew that there would be those who would try to distort parental roles. That's why God didn't say "honor your parents." Because people would definitely take liberties with what that means, thus claiming a kid can have two daddies or two mommies. People do that anyway, but they don't have an excuse to because God made it clear; Father and Mother.

Chances are when you talk to a person with emotional problems who tends to be violent, they didn't have a good relationship with their parents. It's hard to honor your father and mother when they really suck. How can you honor them if they didn't teach honor? How can you honor them if they didn't set honorable examples? But as I said earlier, it's about living a life that brings your father and mother honor. If you have heard the commandment to honor your father and mother, then that means you can hear the rest of what God says in His Word to learn how to be an honorable person even though your father and mother may not have taught you. There's no excuse. You may not be able to have a relationship with your Father and Mother. You may just not be able to communicate with them. That's not the issue. People should observe you to have such good character that they should assume that you had the best parents ever! That Honors your father and mother, even if they don't deserve it! That's an example of grace. That's the light of the Lord.

Notice it says father first. Why? Because fathers are usually the first to bail on their kids. God is saying fathers first because they need to hear it first! Be a man worthy of honor! Be an honorable husband! Be an honorable father! Set the example for your family! Honor God to be worthy of honor from your wife, and honor your wife! Be the first to set the example of honor for your children to look up to with your wife! Too many males haven't been stepping up as husbands and demonstrating honor, and too many females haven't been stepping up as wives and demonstrating honor. And It's rendering generations of kids growing up not caring about being honorable. They think being honorable is accusing others of not being honorable, while they idolize dishonorable people. It's not that this is new, it's just that it keeps happening when we should have learned better long before now, but instead, another generation comes up, pridefully wanting to do better, but they're just better at making the same mistakes.

Violation of the said commandment renders a screwed up society that invites oppression and murder while blaming others for it.

God is very strict when it comes to honoring the father and mother because a kid who doesn't is most likely going to become a menace to society; like a drunkard, thief, rapist, or a murderer, perhaps.

If a son or daughter willfully chooses to dishonor their parents, this includes, cursing and striking their parents, then they are to be put to death. Why? Because if they're violent with their parents they most likely won't think twice about doing violence to others.

"He who strikes his father or his mother shall surely be put to death. - Exodus 21:15 NASB

"Anyone who curses their father or mother is to be put to death. Because they have cursed their father or mother, their blood will be on their own head. - Leviticus 20:9 NIV

For God said: 'Honor your father and mother' and 'Anyone who curses his father or mother must be put to death.' - Matthew 15:4 NIV

For Moses said, 'Honor your Father and your mother,' and, 'Whoever curses his father or mother must be put to death.' -Mark 7:10 BSB

"Anyone who curses their father or mother is to be put to death. - Exodus 21:17 NIV

"'Cursed be anyone who dishonors his father or his mother.' And all the people shall say, 'Amen.' -Deuteronomy 27:16 ESV

Whoso curseth his father or his mother, his lamp shall be put out in obscure darkness. - Proverbs 20:20 KJB

"They shall say to the elders of his city, 'This son of ours is stubborn and rebellious, he will not obey us, he is a glutton and a drunkard.' "Then all the men of his city shall stone him to death; so you shall remove the evil from your midst, and all Israel will hear of it and fear. - Deuteronomy 21:20-21 NASB

Obviously, this is important to God, and it results in capital punishment. Why? Because there's no excuse for it.

If a son or daughter, old enough to know better, behaves this way while God Himself is present giving instructions and the son or daughter still disregards the instructions and continues with such behavior, then the penalty is death. They don't need therapy or an intervention program. God is right there! He is the cure! But the son or daughter rejected God in His presence. There's no excuse for that. Satan and a third of the angels rejected God in the presence of God. There's no excuse for it. Such pride and obstinacy results in horrors being brought to others.

Godless liberals try to judge God for saying, "Have a willfully evil son or daughter put to death," but Liberals demand the right to have a pre-born that has performed no evil put to death.

Which brings us to the clause to not murder. That includes abortion. Liberals say the Bible doesn't say anything about abortion. That's funny. Like Liberals would stop being pro-abortion even if the Bible did say, in explicit terms, "Do not have an abortion"

That's like a person saying they don't believe in the Bible because it doesn't mention dinosaurs. Like a dinosaur is going to make them obey God!

The law to not commit murder, is quite enough to prohibit abortion, but in case ya need another to show that God views the unborn as human life and that depriving them of life doesn't sit well with Him, then please observe Exodus 21:22-23 NASB

"If men struggle with each other and strike a woman with child so that she gives birth prematurely, yet there is no injury, he shall surely be fined as the woman's husband may demand of him, and he shall pay as the judges decide. "But if there is any further injury, then you shall appoint as a penalty life for life,

If that woman is made to miscarry, the man who struck her is to forfeit his life for the life he cost.

Murder is the eventual result of breaking the commandments. Having other god's before God results in murder. The murderer has no respect for man being made in the image of God.

Making graven images or idols results in murder. Since a murderer has no respect for man being made in the image of God, the murder has shaped his own images of a gods. From Molech to Money. And for this idol, they'll sacrifice another. Money isn't evil. Loving it is. Idolizing it is. It results in murder.

Taking the Lord's name in vain results in murder; using God to assume justification for destroying another person. *"The Lord says I can enslave others or wage genocide against a group"*. Hitler said "I am doing the Lord's work" That would be taking the Lord's name in vain.

They will put you out of the synagogue; in fact, the time is coming when anyone who kills you will think they are offering a service to God. - John 16:2 NIV

Or, you shall not Misuse His name. Do not invoke the name of the Lord to justify sinning, sinning against others, and God. It results in murder.

Don't forget the Sabbath. Remember who God is. Keep His commandments. Not doing so results in murder. Work, and earn income. People who won't work tend to feel entitled to other people's stuff, ultimately feeling desperately entitled enough to their life, thus resulting in murder.

If there is no God, then ultimately there is no reason to not murder or sin against others. According to what is murder wrong, besides God? What else is there to have proven to be the thing we're ultimately accountable to? Jesus came back from the dead to prove that He is ultimately the One we're accountable to. He proved that there is life after death, in heaven or hell. And He can either save a person from hell or save heaven from sucking by preventing the nonbeliever from being there.

Not honoring fathers and mothers results in murder. Chances are if you have no respect for them, you'll be short on respect for others.

Murdering people definitely doesn't honor fathers and mothers. Be the kind of person a decent father and mother should be honored by even if your parents sucked. Living a resentful life of the father and mother can lead to taking that resentment out on others which can lead to murder.

Do not commit adultery. I don't think I need to explain how that leads to murder. But I will add that adultery tends to result in pregnancy, which the adulterers tend to resolve with abortion. That's Another way adultery leads to murder. Do not commit adultery.

Jesus says don't even think about having sex with anybody else but your spouse!

You have heard that it was said, 'Do not commit adultery.' But I tell you that anyone who looks at a woman to lust after her has already committed adultery with her in his heart. - Matthew 5:28 BSB

This does not mean single people can't be sexually attracted to another. That's like kinda how people end up getting married. You were sexually attracted to your spouse before y'all got married, right? I hope ya still are. Sexual attraction is probably why y'all wanted to meet, and then ya found yourselves even more attracted to what makes each other tick. Y'all might have even thought about having sex with each other before ya got married! OOOOOH! I'm telling Jesus! Y'all, it's anybody [married] looking upon another lustfully is what's adultery.

The reason why it focuses on men doing it isn't because it doesn't apply to women too, but because it's us men who constantly have our minds on women and women on our mind. Our brain lives in the bottom of a woman's draws' and in their bras. And women who are promiscuous usually justify their behavior as being equal to men. *If men can behave this way, why can't women behave like men?* That's why Jesus focuses on the men concerning adultery, because we set the example. *Why does Jesus lay this on us? Why is it adulterous to just think about it? Isn't that a little extreme to call that adultery? Besides, what goes on in my mind is my own business, and it's not like it's hurting anybody.* That's what the selfish think. The reason why Jesus

276

doesn't want married people looking at other's lustfully is because what you think about is what you tend to come about. Eventually, your imagination won't satisfy you. You will try to make it real. It's natural for these thoughts to pop into our heads, but they're not to be entertained. Jesus does not want those thoughts weakening you.

But the main reason why this is adultery is simply this. Would you want your spouse fantasizing about someone else? Do you think it would please your spouse that you're fantasizing about someone else? I found myself weakening; letting my mind go where it wanted. Before I knew it I'm having conversations with women I shouldn't have. It wasn't my wife's fault. She's amazing! It was just me being a greedy male. I'm not going to act like I'm clean as a whistle, and be like "I am a stone when it comes to the temptation of women!" That would make me either a liar or gay. I got convicted and had to confess to my woman that my attraction for other women is about to have me do something really stupid. She was devastated. It didn't matter that I was just thinking about it or even having flirtatious conversations. It wounded her deeply. She didn't deserve that. This is why Jesus says don't even think about. It will hurt your spouse deeply. You wouldn't want them thinking of someone else sexually instead of you.

If you love your spouse don't justify even thinking about another sexually. It's difficult!!! But God and the spouse He blesses you with are worth the effort. This is why The devil is also called Beelzebub; lord of the flies. Because he is like a fly that relentlessly buzzes around your head. He will not leave you alone, and flies always try to get in your eyes and ears. The Beelzebub wants to lay maggots in what you see and hear. Lustful and Lying Larvae. You have to swat this fly away all day every day. The Lord of the flies sometimes brings a swarm, and it feels like all you can think about is sex with another person. You have to keep that Can of Christ with ya at all times to spray, spray, spray, to keep the flies away. They're immortal so they don't die. All you can do is keep using the repellent on them and not let them consume you. The struggle is real!

So no highlight reels folks. Keep your mind on your spouse. It's not easy. It's just in our instinct, but we have to master it through Christ. The Lord is worthy of obedience and the spouse He blessed you with deserves your loyalty. Remember, adultery leads to murder, and even thinking about another person can cause a spouse to bust your skull open and drag that Sancho or Sancha you've got in your head out and murder them too. Or in some cases people murder their spouse to pursue another they lusted after. Indeed, Jesus knows how far adultery in the heart can go, and warns us. For the record, this ain't no, "The devil made me do it" type of cop-out crap. We have a responsibility to call for Biblical backup!

Do not steal. It results in murder. Murder itself is stealing another person's life. Rape is also stealing, so rape is a no-no too. Forced slavery is also the stealing of liberty. Slavery is a no-no. A person who steals and really doesn't want to go to jail might murder a person who can get in the way of getting away, or the thing they want to steal may be more valuable to them than the life of the person they want to steal the item(s) from. Taxing income is also stealing. And states have committed genocide against citizens who could no longer stand their government crippling them with income taxes.

Do not bear false witness against your neighbor. Folks need to understand the commandment isn't, "Do not lie." You can lie and help somebody. A lie can save someone's life. "Are you hiding any Jews here?" "Uhhhh Nope." And Viola! A lie just saved a basement full of Jews from Nazis.

"You hiding any slaves or know anything about the underground railroad?" "Uhhhh Nope."

And Shazam! A lie saved a shack full of slaves from slave traders.

"Does this dress make my butt look big?" "Uhhhh Nope." And "Ahhh Laahhh Peanut Butter sandwiches!" A lie helped you to still get to go out for the evening in peace, and your wife will keep that nice plump booty instead of trying to work it off! As Sir Mix-a-Lot says "…You can do side bends or sit-ups, but baby don't cha lose that butt!"

Lying is not the sin. The commandment is to not slander. The aforementioned would be more like lying *for* your neighbor, as in to help them. The commandment is to not lie AGAINST you neighbor as in to destroy them. The worst thing you can do to a person without touching them is falsely accuse them. The Devil destroyed the human race with an accusation, without laying a finger on Adam or Eve. That's proven by the fact that snakes don't have fingers. (You know that was funny.) Satan the accuser, the slanderer, falsely accused God of withholding power from them. This caused distrust, and ultimately death. Slandering people kills relationships, businesses, and of course, people. A false accusation results in people being murdered. God hates a deceitful tongue. God hates deceit for personal gain at the expense of others. Or they may not even care about gain, but just the satisfaction of destroying someone they don't like.

Do not covet peoples stuff. Remember, what you think about is what you tend to come about. Covetousness results in theft, adultery, rape, and murder. Don't entertain the thought that you're entitled to someone else's stuff. That's how we get higher taxes. *That person makes too much money. It's not fair, and I'm entitled to some of it.* And up go Income taxes, mandated wage increases, and of course the cost of living, and we're back to square one with covetous people demanding more. Out of covetousness, the state ends up committing genocide against people who are a liability to the state; Non-conformists. If they resist the agenda of the state which covets and requires the fruits of serf's labor they are to be terminated. Coveting another person's spouse can lead to murdering them to get them out of the way. Coveting a woman leads to rape and maybe murder to keep her quiet. Or lead to her murdering the child she was impregnated with.

Don't be coveting another man's donkey n' stuff. You can end up getting smoked trying to make off with it if you decide to act on your covetousness.

If we were to stick to those commandments the world would be a far better place! And Jesus has prepared that better place for us, because He will write the Law on our hearts. This means we will abide by the commandments out of love not out of fear of punishment. We live in a republic where we are free to report of the King who establishes this place for us! I want to do my part to make the best an most of it. I don't want us to end up like a country where proclaiming the gospel gets you killed and that's the law of the land.

This can happen in America. It can become a law to kill Christians. It can be made law to kill groups of people. It happens. It can be made law to persecute and deprive people of rights. It happens. It can happen in our God-given republic. A blessed land like this can become overrun with chaos. The paradisiacal garden of Eden was on the continent of Africa. It's overrun with chaos now. God dwelt with people there, Jesus walked around there. These places were blessed big time, and got screwed up. God blessed us with this republic and it's getting it screwed up too. If we don't start sticking and moving with the gospel we're going to get knocked out for the count. The more America gets away from God the more caustic it becomes. I don't care how patriotic you are, or how conservative you are, or how republican you are or how smart you are, none of that will preserve the republic, and will in fact speed its rot by not making The Lord the capital of all you do. Treat this republic as an annexation of the Kingdom. The whole World is the Lord's, but let this republic resonate with revival and inspire the world to seek the Kingdom, and know the One true Gate! Don't cheapen this republic by just assuming it's a free country for you to be free to satisfy your own interest. We have the opportunity and the freedom to send people the invitation to eternal paradisiacal freedom! That's making really good use of this republic! Don't let that freedom get taken away from us. Hold the line long enough to point others to the Kingdom to come.

CPSIA information can be obtained
at www.ICGtesting.com
Printed in the USA
BVHW040043050720
582969BV00005B/1047

9 781632 638748